MOTORCYCLE ENGINEERING

by

P. E. IRVING

M.I.Mech.E., M.S.A.E.

Published by

CLYMER PUBLICATIONS

222 North Virgil Avenue, Los Angeles, CA 90004, U.S.A.

FOR DISTRIBUTION BY

SPEEDSPORT MOTOBOOKS
51 YORK ROAD, BRENTFORD, MIDDLESEX, ENGLAND
ISBN 0-85113-075-5

P. E. IRVING, M.I.Mech.E., M.S.A.E.

Motorcycle Engineering

Written by an eminent designer with an international reputation, *Motorcycle Engineering* sets out, for the first time, all those problems—technical, commercial and aesthetic—upon whose solution the success of any new motorcycle design must depend. It describes present-day constructional methods, contrasting them with some practices of the past and, avoiding unnecessary discussion of basic theories, clearly shows their practical application in solving the special problems of size, weight and stability inherent in the design of a single-track vehicle.

Every component part of the machine is thoroughly dealt with; ignition, timing, carburation, and steering geometry are discussed, and there are accounts of manufacturing methods and materials. A notable feature of the book is the large number of illustrations, in both line and half-tone, which clarify the text and depict features of motorcycle design from the earliest days up to the present time.

This is a book for which there has long been a need. It will be welcomed by all students of motorcycle design and, to quote the distinguished author of the Foreword, "will be read with equal interest by the youngest apprentice and by the 'Gaffer' himself", wherever motorcycles and their engines are designed or built.

"Phil" Irving—motorcycle designer, engineer, rider, and, as "Slide Rule," one of the best-known technical writers on motorcycling—was born in Melbourne, Australia, in 1903. Having established his reputation as a successful rider of competition and racing machines he came to England in 1930 and after drawing office experience in the Velocette factory, joined the Vincent–H.R.D. Company as Chief Designer. Here he contributed to the Vincent range such varied models as the water-cooled J.A.P. and Villiers-engined model "W", the "Meteor" and "Comet" high-camshaft "singles" and the Series A "Rapide" twin.

Returning to the Velocette factory in 1937, he designed the adjustable rear-suspension system and stressed-steel frame which are still used on Velocettes today, and remained with them until 1942, being subsequently engaged on war production. A short period with A.J.S., assisting the late Joe Craig in designing the "Porcupine" racing twin, was followed by a Government posting back to the Vincent factory to develop a special engine for airborne lifeboats. After the war, as Vincent's Chief Engineer, he designed and developed the Series B "Rapide", with its renowned variants, the "Black Lightning" and the "Black Shadow".

Now resident again in Australia, but a regular visitor to the T.T. Races, he has designed a six-litre diesel engine for an Australian tractor and is at present engaged in the development of racing cars and high-performance equipment.

Fifth Printing September, 1973

For Distribution By

SPEEDSPORT MOTOBOOKS

51 York Road, Brentford, Middlesex, England

ISBN 0-85113-075-5

Printed in U.S.A.

Foreword

by R. C. CROSS, M.I.Mech.E., A.F.R.Ae.S., M.S.A.E.

Past Chairman, Automobile Division of the Institution of Mechanical Engineers

THERE has long been a need for such a book as this and I know of few people better qualified than Phil Irving to have written it.

An engineer who combines first-class technical knowledge with sound common sense, he has had a long and distinguished association with the motorcycle industry and as Chief Designer and later Chief Engineer of the Vincent-H.R.D. Company was responsible for the design and production of a number of outstanding models including the renowned Series "A" and Series "B" Rapides and their equally famous variants, the "Black Lightning" and "Black Shadow".

Not only is Phil Irving capable of saying what he means firmly and believing with all his heart in what he says but he can also write with equal lucidity and conviction—an attribute all too rarely possessed by experts who seek to impart their knowledge in writing.

The result is a book of unquestionably high merit and value. Essentially practical in approach, its scope embraces every component part of a motorcycle and it should find a place in every office where motorcycles or engines are designed or built. Moreover, and this is the true measure of its quality, it is a book which will be read with equal interest by the youngest apprentice and by the "Gaffer" himself and both will benefit as much from its accumulated wisdom as from the author's stimulating approach to his subject.

Contents

CONTENTS

Introduction

THE motorcycle industry has been in existence for little over sixty years and, at the start of its life, the line of demarcation between it and the automobile industry was not very clearly drawn. However, while the conception of a "horseless carriage" was quickly abandoned in favour of a superior idea in which engine and chassis were considered as being an entity designed as such, it was possible, and remained practicable for many years, to manufacture a motorcycle merely by adding an engine to an existing, even if slightly modified, pedal-cycle. A somewhat similar chain of circumstances affected the technical literature produced on the two subjects. Many eminent engineers, of whom perhaps the name of Dr. Lanchester springs most quickly to the mind, devoted themselves to mathematical and practical investigations of the host of new problems posed by ever-increasing demands for more speed, better handling and greater comfort on four wheels. The two-wheeled brigade were not so fortunate, and, to a large extent, had to rely on "cut-and-try" methods which were easier to apply to their less-complicated machine. Again, though most users of motorcycles were, and still are, much more interested in the construction of their machines than the owners of cars (after all, nobody ever possessed a chauffeur-driven motorcycle) comparatively little has been written on the subject of motorcycle engineering, except in the form of articles appearing in the motorcycling journals and a limited number of papers read to the Institution of Automobile Engineers, a body which commenced life as the Institution of Cycle Engineers and later became the Automobile Division of the Institution of Mechanical Engineers.

Such information, by its very nature, is scattered and not readily available, and this volume endeavours to fill at least some of the gap by setting out the precise problems which the motorcycle designer must solve—commercially and aesthetically as well as technically—and at least some of the methods adopted in the past as well as in the present. It is, of course, impossible to compress sixty years of progress (or even thirty years of personal participation) into one book; much more has to be left out than can be put in, and for that reason most of the basic theory and mathematics concerned with engine design in general have been omitted. To "leaven the lump" to some extent, historical examples have been chosen usually for their aptness and not necessarily because they were unique or even the best of their class; some, indeed, are merely representative of practices which are best avoided.

The greater part of the contents of this book first appeared in serial form in *Motor Cycling*, but much new material has since been added, corrections have been made and some ambiguities resolved. In case of argument, it may be taken that the present version is correct (with present knowledge) and it is the author's hope that it will be of some help to motorcycle engineers of the future and of some interest to those whose active designing days are ended.

P. E. IRVING

CHAPTER 1

An Outline of the Problem

THE title of this book may seem a trifle grandiose to those who are accustomed to view the single-tracker as little more than a toy in the engineering sense; but in fact the modern motorcycle is an engineering feat of no inconsiderable magnitude, on which a great amount of technical skill and manufacturing "know-how" has to be lavished in order to maintain any make in a highly competitive market, composed for the most part of customers who are selective and knowledgeable and not to be easily swayed by a copy-writer's catch-phrase, unless it is backed up by public performances of indisputable authenticity and merit.

There are two outstanding factors which go to make motorcycle design a somewhat specialized art: one is that, in the ordinary run of events, the crew sit *on* the machine, and not *in* it; and the other is that, by its very nature, a single-tracker is in unstable equilibrium, i.e., it cannot, when stationary, stand up by itself.

The first of these factors automatically sets limits to both the height and the width, and, if reasonable proportions are to be maintained, to the length as well. An exception may be made of the all-enclosed record-breaker in which the rider lies either prone or supine, but for the moment it is only the more conventional type of mount which is under discussion; the others may come in later.

The second factor entails designing the machine in such a way that its condition of unstable equilibrium, when stationary, is converted into a condition of auto-stability when on the move—and, moreover, achieving this in such a way that stability can still be maintained, either automatically or by the rider's efforts, under such widely differing conditions as going downhill at three-figure speeds or climbing a rocky hillside track at little more than a walking pace. Rarely, of course, is there any need to combine in one model of motorcycle a superb ability to meet both these extreme cases; but the closer the approach which can be made, the safer the model will be under all the conditions likely to be encountered in normal use.

Let us deal first with the question of proportion and size. What the

1

limitations described amount to in practice is that the space available for the engine and gearbox between the wheels is, at a maximum, 24 in. long after allowing for the necessary clearance between tyres, mudguards and frame members, and about 14 in. wide, except for local protuberances or projecting cylinders. In height, 24 in. is again about the usable maximum, though for reasons of balance and, for ease of moving the machine by hand with a dead engine, the lower the height can be kept the better, especially with regard to heavy components which naturally raise the centre of gravity of the power unit if located towards the upper limit of height.

In this space, then, of 24 × 24 × 14 in., has to be housed an engine of whatever size is deemed necessary, a clutch, a gearbox, usually with four but possibly with anything from three to six ratios, some method of starting and all the electrical gear; whilst somewhere in the vicinity must be placed a tank holding anything up to four or five gallons of petrol and storage for several pints of oil, either within the engine itself or in a separate tank.

Nor must appearance be forgotten, for an eye-taking design, even of mediocre performance, is almost certain to sell more freely, in the first few months at least, than one of far better performance but lacking in good looks, whatever the virtues of the sounder machine may do subsequently to redress the balance. Strictly speaking, this is more the province of the stylist than of the engineer, but motorcycle design is one field where the stylist must not be allowed to wield undue influence at the cost possibly of propounding a machine which is unsuitable, or even dangerous, in some respect. The stylist's real function in this special field is to produce a design which will be pleasing to the eyes of next season's buyers and will remain so for two or three years, without in any way embodying something useless or non-functional just for the sake of being strikingly different. In this connection, of course, fashions change; total enclosure, for instance, is quite acceptable today, whereas attempts to introduce it 20 years ago met with failure.

Before one can face a clean sheet of paper and a draughting machine and start work with confidence, it is a first essential to know just what sort of motorcycle you wish to design. A man free from the trammels of commercial life might set out with preconceived notions to design a "dream-machine" which suited his own ideas exactly but would be quite an impossible proposition to produce at a competitive price; usually, however, the practising designer is informed by the sales or the competition department of the general overall specification that is required. This may vary from the cheapest thing which can be made on two wheels up to something in the 100 m.p.h. class with every conceivable aid to comfortable travel: or it may be of the strictly functional variety, such as a road-racer or a scrambler, in which appearance and cost are secondary to performance and handling.

In this connection, it is always better to aim in one direction first. Experience, both with motorcycles and with other forms of transport, has shown quite clearly that if you make a machine to do one thing superlatively well it can subsequently be adapted to perform related, but different, functions equally well. But if you endeavour to make a model which can do everything, it usually ends up by not being able

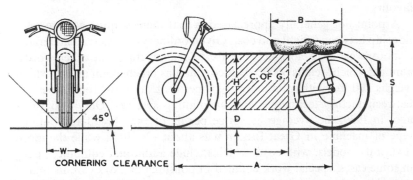

FIG. 1.1. Designer's strait-jacket: the limiting dimensions within which the motorcycle must be built. They are the wheelbase A; ground clearance D; seat height S and length B; height H, width W and length L of the "engine room"; and the minimum permissible cornering clearance. Also indicated is the position of the centre of gravity.

to do anything; consequently, it gains no real friends and will have but a short commercial span of life, though its loss of esteem may remain and give rise to considerable sales resistance to subsequent products of the same marque for many years.

Weight is another matter which calls for great consideration. From the point of view of ease of handling, the lighter the machine the better. But lightness must on no account be gained at the price of flimsiness, especially with regard to the running gear, or to parts which might readily fail under the battering administered by, for example, Belgian *pavé* or the corrugations traversed for mile after unending mile on dirt or gravel roads in Australia, South Africa and similar territories where smooth tarmac is by no means the rule.

Weight, like appearance, can also be a matter of fashion. In the U.S.A., for instance, some of the population were so conditioned by high-power advertising into the belief that mere size was a measure of desirability and excellence that the two best-selling home-grown makes became heavier and heavier until some models scaled over 550 lb.— and even then they were on occasion so bedecked with extra lights, flags, false radio aerials and such-like bric-à-brac that the total must have come to 600 lb. or more. Development along these lines must, of course, either reach its own limit or be halted by some other circumstance—which, in this particular instance, was the realization that the much lighter imported motorcycles gave as good, or even better, performance with less likelihood of crushing the rider to pulp in the event of a fall. Today 450 lb. is about the upper limit of weight which any market will accept, but lighter models are coming into more general favour.

A point not generally appreciated is that there is quite a close relationship between weight and cost. Given ordinary commercial materials, a motorcycle costs so much per lb. to manufacture—in other words, a model which weighs 300 lb. will cost half as much again as one which weighs 200 lb., within limits of ±10 per cent. to allow for differences between factory techniques and accounting systems. Only two years ago, in 1959, the average list price per lb. of the "bread-and-butter" type of machine in Great Britain was about 12s. 10d., while the more luxurious models, with costs which include additional equipment and, in some cases, special work entailed in polishing or extra care in engine assembly, sold at something in the region of 15s. 1d. With these figures in mind, and knowing the ceiling price which the sales department have set on a new model, the designer can determine the maximum permissible weight within a few lb. either way.

That there *is* any close relation at all between cost and weight comes as a surprise to many people—in fact, it is sometimes hotly disputed. At first sight it may seem that an assembly made up of a large number of small parts, bolted or fixed together by any other means, will be more costly than a single casting or forging—but it does not work out that way. Roughly speaking, small parts are made quickly in large numbers on inexpensive automatic machinery, while big parts are more cumbersome to handle and are machined either one at a time by hand or automatically on large and very expensive machine tools. Then, again, aluminium is lighter than steel, but its much higher price just about evens the score.

What the total weight proves to be is less important, so far as handling is concerned, than its distribution. By "distribution" is meant the proportion which is carried by each wheel; assuming that the frame will be rear-sprung, reasonable handling should be attained with

50 per cent. of the weight on each tyre. This is, of necessity, only a first approximation, and work with the experimental models will undoubtedly have to be carried out to settle the best proportion, which in any case is dependent to some extent on the suspension characteristics at front and rear. Test reports upon handling can vary with personal tastes; for that reason, it is always wise to obtain a variety of opinions.

Consideration must also be given to the state in which the model is most likely to be used. A "straight" solo racer never has more than one rider on board and can be tailored accordingly, whereas a 500 or 650 c.c. road-going mount may do most of its work with a crew of two and is frequently burdened with luggage as well. In this condition it should be as safe as—or, better still, even safer than—with only one up, and though this ideal is difficult to attain in practice it should be aimed at in theory. Anything above the lightweight class is also likely to have a sidecar attached to it; this places additional and quite different stresses on the frame and forks and is another matter which must be borne in mind when designing for strength in relation to weight and rigidity.

All the foregoing remarks are by way of being a general introduction to the subject—a broad outline of the limits within which the designer must work. Only a passing reference has been made to the power-unit which, though usually given pride of place, is in a sense a secondary consideration at this stage, except insofar as it is the heaviest single component and may or may not act as a frame member. It will, however, come in for its fair share of attention later in this book, which will deal with every portion of the machine. However, it is manifestly impossible in a volume of this size to go very deeply into the fundamentals of engine design and related problems; neither is it necessary, since most of that information can be obtained from standard textbooks, some of which are mentioned, while a further list of helpful volumes is given on page 321. The real purpose here is to outline some of the special aspects, peculiar to the design of motorcycles, which are rarely mentioned. Practical examples, some only of historical interest, have been freely used, but it must be emphasized that many of the designs or ideas described may be the subject of patents and cannot necessarily be employed commercially unless arrangements are made to do so.

CHAPTER 2

Steering Geometry

A MOTORCYCLE in solo form is unable to keep itself upright because it is supported only at two points in the central plane and the whole of its weight is above these points. Consequently the slightest deviation from the vertical, or the application of a side-force, as from a gust of wind, will cause it to fall. Given only a modicum of forward speed, however, it can be maintained upright by the skill of the rider, and above a certain minimum velocity it will balance itself if correctly designed. Moreover, a good example will proceed in a straight line even on irregular surfaces with no guidance at all, thus achieving a condition known as "auto-stability".

To some extent, a child's hoop behaves in the same way. It will travel in a straight line above a certain speed, but below that speed will incline to one side or the other and proceed to run in ever-decreasing circles until it falls flat. An interesting point is that it can only be prevented from circling by a correcting touch at the *top*. It cannot be steered back into line by applying the stick to the outer side at the rear of the hoop; in fact, this will only hasten the fall.

GYROSCOPIC EFFECT

The hoop runs straight because it is, in effect, a gyroscope rotating round an invisible axle. When it starts to fall, say, to the left and thus runs to that side, it acquires an anticlockwise angular velocity, viewed from above. This immediately creates an effect known as "gyroscopic precession", which sets up a force—or, more correctly, a couple—tending to return the hoop to the vertical position (see Fig. 2.1).

Moreover, the displaced hoop becomes subject to centrifugal force acting radially outward. This force also tends to restore the hoop to the vertical, whereupon it again runs straight and the centrifugal force vanishes.

As the forces are proportional to the weight of the hoop they are just sufficient to maintain equilibrium above a certain minimum speed. And as the corrections are applied automatically and instantaneously the hoop always runs straight unless violently deflected, in which event

6

it may follow a sinuous path until stability is again reached.

In a single-tracker with a steerable front wheel, somewhat the same processes take place, but conditions are very different because the weight to be kept upright is many times greater than the weight of the rims and tyres, which supply most of the gyroscopic forces. The rear wheel being fixed in relation to the frame, can only play a part so small as to be insignificant—though, as we will see later, it can become the villain of the piece and really upset the steering if it is capable of being deflected from its true position.

Though it is possible to maintain balance on a two-wheeler which has the front fork and steering column in a line drawn vertically through the axle, as in the old velocipedes, the thing would be very difficult to handle on any but a dead-smooth surface, because if the wheel struck a bump the point of contact would necessarily be forward of the steering axis and, unless forcibly held, the wheel would be knocked round to full lock. This condition is overcome, and the steering tends to maintain a straight-ahead position naturally, if the wheel is given some "trail", i.e. if its axle is moved in relation to the column axis so that the theoretical point of tyre contact lies some distance to the rear, so providing a castor action (see Fig. 2.2).

Provision of "Rake"

If trail is applied while still retaining a vertical column, the wheel is likely to develop a wobble, for reasons which are a little too complicated

Fig. 2.2.

Fig. 2.1. The principle of gyroscopic precession: a bicycle wheel is spun clockwise (viewed from the operator's right). When he swivels the wheel about its vertical axis anticlockwise (viewed from above), it will tilt to the right.

7

to delve into here. However, if the axis of the column is laid backwards at a considerable angle, or "raked", and the position of the axle then readjusted to furnish the required amount of trail, one arrives at a steering system which can be very good indeed—if it is exactly proportioned to the rest of the model. If it is not, then one may get something which is heavy on corners, or becomes uncomfortably light and tends to wander at speed, or develops front-wheel wobble.

Endeavours have been made to derive a formula by which wobble-free steering may be designed into a machine, but there are so many factors involved, some of which can only be assumptions at best or wild guesses at worst, that empirical methods, based on known data, are probably the safest in the original design stage. It may well be, in fact it is practically certain, that some adjustments will be required later.

It is not always appreciated by motorcyclists that a pneumatic tyre has an inbuilt tendency to run straight; it possesses a self-centring action, due in the main to the reaction between the road surface and the resilient tread, which tends to turn the wheel in the direction of any side-force applied to it. Thus, if the wheel happens to be turned while in the air after negotiating a severe bump, so that the tyre lands at an angle, the self-aligning force generated will move the wheel back into line, so fast, perhaps, that it overshoots and turns in the opposite direction.

Meanwhile, this oscillation of the wheel about the column axis sets up gyroscopic precessional forces (as in the case of the hoop) which tend to make the whole wheel and fork oscillate from side to side, and if the two sets of forces act in harmony the action will build up until a full-lock wobble is in progress. That is one reason why a machine which steers well with one size of tyre may be inclined to "shake its head" with another size, even though the diameters (and thus the rake and trail also) are identical; the geometry is the same, but the gyroscopic mass and the self-aligning force of the tyre have been altered.

Pendulum Effect

Other things come into it, of course. One is the "pendulum effect" of the whole front assembly, which tends to resist rapid turning of the bars or conversely wants to maintain a turn once it has started. Another is the rigidity or otherwise of the rest of the main frame; if this can bend or twist, it must deflect the rear wheel out of line and thus cause it to steer the rear end. This may only cause the tail to wag, but it may equally well accentuate any defects at the front should resonance occur between the disturbances at both ends, and the steering system may be blamed for faults which really lie elsewhere.

One effect of rake is to lower the whole front of the machine when the wheel is turned to either side. This can be appreciated by visualizing a system brought to an extreme, with the head so far back that it is almost horizontal: obviously, if the bars are turned the wheel will lean over and the axle will drop in relation to the ground. The same thing occurs with a normal amount of rake (though, of course, to a smaller extent) and its effect in practice is to cause the steering to turn in the direction in which the machine is trying to fall, provided there is some trail as well. It can be demonstrated merely by tilting a stationary bicycle to one side, whereupon the front wheel will promptly turn in the same direction; if the machine were moving, it would immediately run to that side and centrifugal force would bring it upright again.

This is the main factor in achieving stability at low speeds when the gyroscopic effects of the wheel are small. A nice balance between the head angle and the trail must be achieved if good steering at low speeds is the primary aim; too much rake in particular causes the model to fall inwards too far, and reverse correction may have to be applied to the bars.

The effect of trail is to move the contact-point of the tyre off the centre line and away from the direction of turn. Should the wheel be deflected whilst the machine is vertical and travelling straight ahead, the rolling resistance of the tyre, combined with the fact that it is now at a slight angle to the mean line of travel, will try to pull the wheel back into line in just the same way as the castor-wheels of an armchair move round until they lie straight behind the pivots.

The effect of trail, then, is to make the machine run straight whilst it is vertical—but conversely, when it is banked over, trail tends to turn the wheel into the direction of lean and operates as a corrective influence in conjunction with rake.

Trail, however, is really a theoretical conception of the distance between the tyre contact point and the column axis at ground level, assuming a rigid tyre of zero width. In practice, the tyre has a finite area of contact, not merely a point, and it also has a cross-section which is approximately circular. The effect of flattening the tread at ground contact is to shorten the effective trail (hence the need to maintain tyres at their correct inflation pressures) and the effect of the circular section is to reduce the distance by which the theoretical point of contact moves out of line when the machine is in a banked turn. That is because the tyre acts, as it were, as a roller between rim and road, and the amount of displacement is reduced, as shown in Fig. 2.3.

If instead of being circular the tyre had a section with a flat tread, as employed on cars, the virtual point of contact might actually move to the inside of the curve, and would attempt to turn the wheel still farther inwards, i.e., in the wrong direction. This variety of tyre usually possesses a large self-aligning force, which would then take charge and pull the wheel back into line, possibly so quickly that it would swing through to the other side and commence to oscillate. This, incidentally, is a problem encountered in tricycle-type aeroplane landing gear, in which on at least one occasion the "shimmying" so initiated ended in the total destruction of the aircraft. Another disadvantage of very-big-section tyres is that when an object such as a large stone is struck a glancing blow the disturbing effect on the wheel is much greater than with a narrow tyre, hence the use of small-section front covers on trials models.

Of course, this movement of the contact-point out of the centre plane occurs on the rear wheel also and to some extent cancels out the

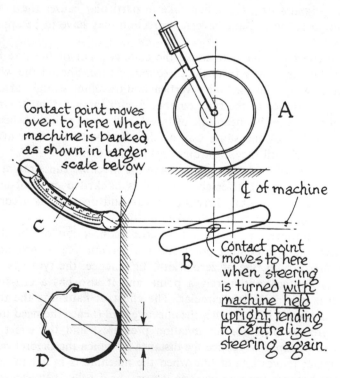

FIG. 2.3. The effects of trail and tyre section: *A* is the side elevation of a steering system, *B* its plan view when the handlebars are turned but the machine remains upright, *C* and *D* are sections through the tyre when banked.

effects at the front. In fact, the relation between the two tyre sizes is quite important, and explains why some machines handle better if front and rear tyres are "odd" than if they are of similar section.

At speed, the conditions are the same when travelling upright in a straight line, except that gyroscopic forces become much more important since they increase with the square of the velocity of the rim. At very high speeds they may even become an embarrassment—when, for instance, traversing a series of right and left bends. It is in these circumstances that lightweight tyres and aluminium rims pay a dividend in increased ease of banking the model from one side to the other very quickly.

CORNERING FORCES

When rounding a curve at a steady speed, the model is banked inwards to an angle such that the centrifugal force, acting outwards through the centre of gravity of the whole equipage, is exactly balanced by the tendency to fall inwards. When this condition is reached—which is, of course, slightly later than the transitional period of change from straight travelling to cornering—a condition of equilibrium is again established.

The resultant of the two forces now acts substantially in the plane of the frame, as shown in Fig. 2.4, and conditions are roughly similar

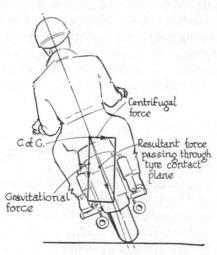

FIG. 2.4. Showing how the centrifugal force and gravitational force (weight) of the complete machine can be combined into one larger force passing through the points of contact with the road.

11

to straight travelling, except that the ground contact-points have moved round the tyres by an amount depending upon the angle of bank and the tyre sections. The resultant force must lie in the plane containing these two points and the centre of gravity to maintain equilibrium.

Apart from this small deviation, the resultant force, although greater than the gravitational force by as much as 40 per cent. at maximum bank, has little effect except to increase all the loadings by the same percentage. If, however, either wheel passes over a bump, the machine is subjected to an impulsive force which is substantially vertical and thus at an angle to the centre-plane. One effect of this is a tendency to turn the front wheel farther into the corner, which has to be resisted by the rider through the medium of the handlebars. It will also bend or twist the whole machine to an extent which depends upon the rigidity of its construction and the disposition of the major components. The second point must be mentioned in any discussion on steering, because, whatever geometry is employed on paper, its virtue can be entirely destroyed by secondary causes of this nature.

To get down to some solid figures, the experience of years has shown that a rake of between 25° and 30° from the vertical will give good results combined with a trail in the region of 3 in. Some authorities claim that the precise angle is not very important, others state very emphatically that it is critical to within half a degree.

Such differences of opinion are hard to explain but may be accounted for, at least in part, by fundamental constructional differences in the various types of machines tested. However, rake is a thing which is difficult to vary during production and it certainly pays to experiment with differing angles at the experimental stage, using if possible a variety of test personnel, to establish the figure which gives the nicest handling under the conditions for which the particular model is intended.

FORK TRAIL

Trail does appear to be of somewhat less importance. It can be varied quite widely without any very serious ill-effects, but any alteration is bound to make a difference to the "feel" of the machine. Generally speaking, a trail of 3 to 4 in. will give very good high-speed steering, with some heaviness on corners, while a figure around $2\frac{1}{2}$ in. will give lighter cornering but less feeling of solidity at high speeds.

So far, we have been talking only about conditions as they exist in normal riding—that is to say at moderate speeds in calm atmospheres and on good surfaces—and it is quite certain that if the handling is bad then it will be even worse under less favourable circumstances. If, for instance, a machine is pushed to its limit on a corner, which may be done deliberately under racing conditions and inadvertently (one hopes) in touring, questions of roadholding and tyre adhesion may take precedence over the accuracy of the steering.

Roadholding in this context means the closeness or otherwise with which the tyres remain in continuous contact with the road. Should either wheel aviate for any appreciable period, only the gyroscopic ıorces are available and they can, in fact, operate to the rider's disadvantage. If, during a long jump over a humpbacked bridge, the bars are turned to the left in anticipation of a turn which immediately follows, gyroscopic precession of the front wheel will cause the model to lean over to the *right*, so that when it lands it is banked the wrong way and the only method the rider has of saving his skin is to alter course, then straighten up and bank over for the left turn—always supposing there is room to execute this tricky operation.

The lighter the wheel is in relation to the total weight, the less this effect will be, but it is always present to some extent and the only way to avoid it is never to turn the bars when the front wheel is off the ground.

In the days of rigid frames, now almost extinct except on speedway machines, it was very difficult to maintain rear tyre contact on anything but a billiard-table surface, and the back end was always liable to "step out" on a corner and might even slide right round. Even with a well-sprung rear wheel this can still happen, partly because no suspension ever devised could possibly absorb every bump completely, and partly because the sprung motion, which takes place in the plane of the frame, cannot absorb any of the *vertical* components of the road shocks received when the machine is inclined.

When, in consequence of this, the tyre is bumped clear of the surface, centrifugal force carries the rear wheel outwards (Fig. 2.5). If the rider grimly maintains the bars in a fixed position the whole machine, including the front wheel, will be at a slight angle to its correct line of travel and will try to head in towards the inner side of the corner; but if he relaxes sufficiently to allow the front wheel to steer itself, that wheel will maintain its true path, although almost immediately afterwards correction may have to be applied to bring the model as a whole back on course.

Tyre adhesion is a different matter from roadholding. It is a measure of the amount of grip existing between the tread and the road, and depends upon the type, character and dryness of the road surface, the composition of the rubber in the tread and, to some degree, the tread pattern. This is far too long a subject to deal with here; it is sufficient to say that as soon as the force available from adhesion becomes insufficient for steering purposes on *either* wheel, maintaining balance becomes a matter purely of riding skill.

For racing under good conditions, where long sweeping curves must be taken at full speed, it is desirable to distribute the weight and select tyre sizes and patterns so that both wheels will start to slide at the same time, which is the reason why modern racing machines have their power units placed well forward. The main snag of this arrangement is that, if the road surface suddenly changes its character—for instance, through an unexpected patch of oil or gravel on a bend—the model may go down flat on its side before the rider can do anything about it, whereas on a mount which handled less well the cornering speed would be slower and the front wheel might have just enough adhesion left to permit the necessary correction to be applied as the rear wheel slid outwards.

It is worth noting at this juncture that a tyre loses its adhesion and commences to slide sideways or slip circumferentially whenever the vector sum of *all* the forces acting parallel to the road surface exceeds the frictional grip of the tread. By "vector sum" is meant the resultant of the circumferential and lateral forces, determined graphically by representing each force as a line in the direction of the force and proportional in length to its value, as is done in Fig. 2.6, to show the resultant of centrifugal and gravitational forces.

As soon as the tyre commences to slide in any one direction, it will lose its directional stability in *all* directions and incidentally entirely loses its self-aligning property. Thus, if a corner is being taken near the limit of safe speed, quite a light application of the rear brake will cause the tyre to lose adhesion and once it starts to slide it will go anywhere. In a sense, a similar thing happens at the front too, but owing to a phenomenon known as "weight transference", the initiation of a slide by braking on a corner is more likely to happen at the rear than at the front. Rear "break-away" can also be caused by applying too much power on a corner, particularly when accelerating from a low speed with the model banked hard over, but its onset can be controlled to some extent by correct design of the tread. Some years ago racing tyres had a fairly narrow band of studs, with several continuous side-ribs extending well up the walls and under the conditions described only some of these ribs and not the studs were in proper contact with the ground and the tyre would consequently spin relatively easily when

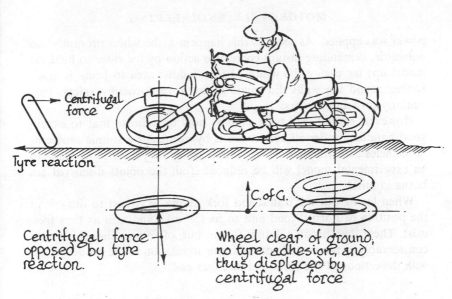

Centrifugal force

Tyre reaction

Centrifugal force opposed by tyre reaction.

C. of G.

Wheel clear of ground, no tyre adhesion, and thus displaced by centrifugal force

Fig. 2.5. When cornering on a rough surface, the rear wheel is likely to "step out" after being thrown clear by a bump.

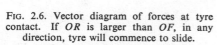

Fig. 2.6. Vector diagram of forces at tyre contact. If OR is larger than OF, in any direction, tyre will commence to slide.

OC = Centrifugal force (smaller than OF);
OB = Braking force (also smaller than OF);
OR = Resultant of OC and OB;
OF = Frictional force of tread.

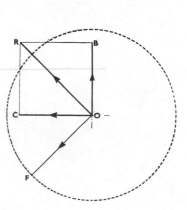

power was applied. As soon as this happened, the wheel promptly slid outwards, demanding instant corrective action by the rider to hold the model up; increasing the width of the studded area to bring it much farther round the walls did much to improve cornering safety, particularly on acute corners.

However, enough has been said by now to indicate that to obtain good handling under all conditions is by no means a simple problem; nevertheless, the number of corrections which may have to be made to an experimental model will be reduced if all the points discussed are borne in mind.

When laying-out the frame and fork design, it is best to draw it in the position of normal load and to fix the rake and trail as they then exist. These then become datum figures but, of course, they must alter considerably as the attitude of the frame in relation to the ground alters with deflections of the springing at either end.

CHAPTER 3

Front Suspension in Practice

FROM the very earliest days of the motorcycle, front fork design has been in a fluid state. Apart from the plain, unsprung variety, which was inherited from the velocipedes of the period, almost all the types which are in use today were tried, even in the crudest possible way, about 50 years ago—as anyone who visits the Montagu Motor Museum can verify for himself.

However, at no time did any particular design-style attain universal adoption, in the way that the beam-axle did on four-wheelers, though there were periods when a single type was predominant, largely as a result of its success in racing. Thus for a number of years the so-called "girder" or "parallel-link" fork in various guises held the field, though there were many who did not think it was the best form. The situation changed very rapidly after the telescopic fork commenced to win races regularly, and in a few years this almost completely ousted the girder type on English machines, while even American designers who for long had remained faithful to the bottom-link variety—leading in the Harley-Davidson example, trailing in the Indian—were shaken in their allegiance and changed to other types.

The same state of flux exists both in England and on the Continent today. It is not unusual to find one factory using dissimilar designs on its various models, while experimental machines, utilizing yet other

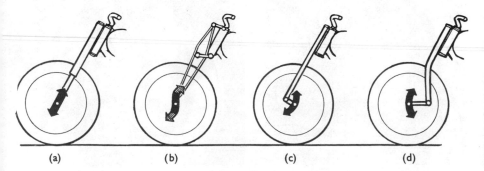

(a)   (b)   (c)   (d)

FIG. 3.1. Four basic types of front fork.

17

FIG. 3.2. A pioneer combination of telescopic and leading link design—the 1909 NSU.

FIG. 3.3. Typical American practice—the Harley-Davidson bottom-link type, also on certain British Brough Superior models.

FIG. 3.4. The Webb girder fork, used by Velocettes for both racing and touring models with great success.

FIG. 3.5. AMC "Teledraulic" fork. The first of its type to be standardized on British touring machines.

designs, are continually making their appearance. It may be instructive to examine the pros and cons of the known variants to see why all this chopping and changing has taken place.

In general, all fork designs now used fall into one of four groups: on page 17 (Fig. 3.1) is a diagram showing each of these four types, (a) telescopic, (b) girder, (c) trailing link, and (d) leading link, the path of each axle being indicated by the heavy lines and arrows. The angle and shape of these paths affects the suspension in ways which will be described later. There are two variations of group (d); the long-link commonly referred to as the Earles type, and the short-link, the main difference being that in the former the links are united by a cross-member behind the wheel which contains a pivot bearing and in the latter they are usually separate.

SIDECAR STEERING

The principles underlying the way in which a solo machine is endowed with auto-stability have already been described and the importance of correctly apportioning the rake of the head and the trail of the front wheel outlined. When a sidecar is fitted the whole vehicle possesses a two-dimensional wheelbase, and auto-stability is no longer required, in fact a steering geometry which is best for two wheels is by no means ideal for three. There is bound to be a certain amount of side-drag from the third wheel and air-resistance from the body both of which try to swing the machine around to the sidecar side, which, for the purposes of this exercise, we will assume to be always on the left. This drag is resisted by the front tyre, but as the point of tyre contact lies behind the steering axis, the wheel will turn to the left and the outfit will run round in a circle unless it is held on a straight course; the greater the trail, the more pronounced the effect will be. Likewise, extreme rake is a disadvantage, because as soon as the wheel is turned the front of the frame drops and quite a lot of effort is required to centralize the wheel again, as naturally a portion of the sidecar weight has to be raised as well as that of the machine. Rigging the outfit with a considerable "lean-out" of the frame cancels out the effect of trail to an extent which will enable the outfit to run straight on a flat road, but it will still want to run down the slope of a cambered road, either towards or away from the chair if the trail is excessive. For that reason, forks for dual-purpose models should have some means of altering the trail quickly and easily, and those designed especially for sidecar use, which would probably only be pure racing machines, should have the head angle much steeper than usual; somewhere about 15°, with the trail reduced to 1 in. or less, will give effortless steering on smooth surfaces. On rough surfaces, or if sand or mud is being negotiated, the actual point of contact with rocks or the wall of soil ahead of the tyre may be so far forward of the column axis that the trail, if only slightly positive, will become, in effect, considerably negative and a lot of work may then be required to hold the wheel on a straight course; so for adverse conditions it does not pay to reduce the trail too much.

In any case, sidecar or solo, the rake and trail must both vary continuously when the machine is traversing bumps. To quote an example, if the forks on a 52 in. wheelbase frame are compressed 3 in., the head angle steepens in relation to the ground by about 4°—and if at the same time the rear wheel is off the ground, or is at the limit of its rebound travel on the rear springs, the head will steepen by another 4°. Conversely, if the front forks are extended and the rear suspension compressed, the head will lie back by a total of 8°—so that it may, under extreme conditions, vary from its designed static position by plus or minus 8°, though only rarely will it alter by more than plus or minus 5°.

Fig. 3.6. An early pattern of telescopic fork standardized on production machines —the B.M.W.

Fig. 3.7. For many years Indians fitted this quarter-elliptic leaf-spring type of trailing-link fork to their big-twin machines.

Under similar conditions, the trail is bound to decrease or increase according to the fall or rise of the rear end of the frame, though this effect is not very marked; a much more important factor is the alteration in trail and wheelbase introduced by the mechanism of the front suspension. With telescopic forks lying parallel to the steering-head the trail will remain approximately constant, though the wheelbase will alter; but if the axle is controlled by some form of linkage, so that it moves vertically, the trail will become less as it rises, though the wheelbase will then remain substantially constant. With yet other forms the axle may move in a circular or an S-shaped path, and both trail and wheelbase may alter (Fig. 3.1).

Which principle is the best is hard to say. For many years the KTT Velocette, which was justly famed for its accurate steering, possessed girder forks with the linkage very carefully designed to give the wheel a straight-line vertical motion—that is to say, on the "constant wheelbase" principle. The difficulty with girder forks is that straight-line axle motion can only be achieved by making the top and bottom links of differing lengths and with the spindle centres in the girders farther apart than those on the head assembly. Also the straight-line motion exists only for about 3 in. or so of travel; the axle will move sharply backwards at the extreme upper limit, and sharply forwards at the extreme down position, and an undesirably great alteration of the steering geometry will result unless the total movement is restricted to keep out of these disturbed regions, shown shaded in Fig. 3.1 (b).

No such limitation applies to telescopic forks, in which the axle motion is purely "straight line" (Fig. 3.1 (a)) usually, though not necessarily, parallel to the steering column. This rearward inclination of the line of action provides the argument often, and quite correctly, advanced in their favour that when the wheel passes over a bump it lags behind a little as it rises, and thus "rides" the obstruction more easily than if it could rise only vertically.

The axle motion of either leading-link or trailing-link forks is bound to follow a circular path, but the general direction of this arc can be varied by altering the position of the pivot in relation to the axle. Trailing links, in particular, can be made to exhibit the lagging effect on bumps by placing the pivot point well above the axle, which used to be a feature of the original Indian design and is to be found in the modern Ariel "Leader".

Whatever one does must be in the nature of a compromise; but that the compromise can be successful is beyond dispute, for at one time or another specific examples of all the various forms have given good

21

results. The failure of other designs to do so is most likely attributable to mechanical features which have not been able to cope with the stresses involved in steering on rough surfaces or under heavy braking.

Torsional Stiffness

Even on an apparently smooth surface, some effort is involved in holding a straight course or in turning a corner, and to withstand this there must be as much torsional rigidity as possible between the handle-bars and the wheel. If there is any mechanical slackness the wheel can be deflected out of the true path even if the bars are held steady; but if there is a general lack of stiffness, due to twisting of the components, accurate steering control may be impossible, especially when the machine has to be taken quickly through a swervy section with successive bends to right and left.

One can get an idea of the torsional strength of any fork by grasping the wheel between the knees and then trying to turn the bars. A well-designed girder fork will be almost immovable; the very best of the telescopics will be almost as good, though the poorest examples will not only twist several degrees but may even stay twisted when the bars are released! Bottom-link forks can be quite good in this respect, especially if the fork-tubes are of large diameter and very firmly fixed to the top cross-members, as they are, for instance, in the experimental Reynolds design (Fig. 3.11); but equivalent stiffness is not so easy to obtain with the Earles type without an excessive weight penalty, because of the more complicated and longer path along which the forces are transmitted (Fig. 3.11).

Undesirable deflection will also occur if there is any deficiency in lateral rigidity. If the tyre receives a sideways blow (and even an oblique blow has a sideways component) it will then be deflected out of its true position, and front and back wheels will momentarily be out of track. The back wheel may either try to swing back into line, by which time the front wheel has sprung back again, or it may try to come round still farther. In either event, the rider is not, for the moment, in 100 per cent. control, and he may be in severe trouble on a succession of bumps, as when crossing a set of tram-lines at an angle.

Improving Lateral Rigidity

Girder forks can be very bad offenders in this respect, especially if the links and spindles are of small section and poorly attached to each other. Being so high up, any flexure of the rectangles formed by the two pairs of links and their spindles is greatly magnified at ground level, although this movement can be reduced almost to nothing by using integral forged links, as on the Rudge and Vincent "Girdraulic" designs.

Telescopic forks are intrinsically poor also, because one slider can move up while the other moves down, not only permitting the tyre to go out of track but allowing considerable tilt to the wheel as well. This action is resisted only by the rigidity of the axle and its attachment to the sliders, and again it can be seen that in the more successful designs this point has received attention. Greatly increased rigidity could be obtained by a stiff bridge connecting the sliders at their upper ends, though this is rarely done; it is surprising, however, that wider use is not made of large-diameter, hollow spindles rather like the one which Eric Oliver fitted on his Norton sidecar outfit.

The Earles type can be very rigid laterally because, despite the length of the side tubes, they can be joined by a short tube of large diameter without serious increase in unsprung weight; the wheel-guiding mechanism can, in fact, be almost a replica of the forks used at the rear end. But short trailing links, without resorting to a cumbersome arrangement, are of necessity independent.

Fig. 3.9. The long-trailing-link 1949 F.N. fork is complicated but very effective on Belgian *pavé*.

Fig. 3.8. (Left) The trail and effective spring strength can be altered simultaneously on Vincent "Girdraulic" forks, for solo or sidecar use.

SHORT LEADING LINKS

Short leading links are usually also independent, and in both cases the pair of links plus the axle constitute, in effect, a single-throw crank which can twist or bend if the axle is weak or the links are not virtually in one piece with it. The right way to secure adequate rigidity would be by splining or keying a large-diameter axle to which the mating links would be held tightly by pinch-bolts; but the more usual system is merely to rely on friction, which is probably sufficient for solo work if the attachment is really firm.

A good, but long-discarded form of construction is to join both links by a secondary fork, roughly parallel to the main blades and, if desired, with the springs or only a single spring located at the top of this fork. This was the basis of the Harley-Davidson design and many others, but it involves extra load-carrying bearings, and, by increasing the unsprung weight, partly nullifies the bottom-link type's chief virtue, minimum unsprung weight.

Another method—used, for example, on the Greeves and racing Honda forks—is to join the links by a loop-tube passing round the rear of the tyre; but, while acceptable on a competition model, this oscillating member is somewhat of an embarrassment when a touring mudguard is used.

The action of the fork under heavy front braking is most important. Adverse disturbances can be set up, partly by the transference of weight to the front end which then occurs, and partly by local forces and deflections within the fork mechanism. If the line of action of the axle is rearwardly inclined, as with telescopics or sloping trailing links, the fork springs will compress considerably, and the machine will also "throw back" immediately it comes to rest. Girder forks can be designed to remain substantially level; though, should the layout of the links be incorrect, a fearful vertical shudder can develop if the front brake happens to be applied when the forks are almost fully extended.

With leading links, the forks tend to depress under the increased load; but if the brake torque-reaction is resisted simply by bolting the brake-plate to one link, the upward reaction may be greater than the downward load on the link and the model may try to stand on tip-toe, so to speak. This undesirable state of affairs can be minimized by lengthening the links, and it hardly exists at all in the Earles type. But a better method is to float the brake-plate on the axle and resist the torque by another pin-jointed link; by correctly laying-out the various angles and lengths, an absolutely level ride can be obtained. Even then, the local forces involved may be in the region of 400 or 500 lb. and deflections may be caused by these very high loads which will tend to make the model veer to one side—an effect which is best obviated by using dual brakes, whatever type of fork is employed. It is noticeable that this symmetrical system has gained a lot of ground recently amongst racing machines.

THE WEIGHT FACTOR

Given equal attention to detail design and choice of materials, there is not a lot of difference in total weight between any of the types for equivalent strength; but all the bottom-link varieties score over the girder and telescopic forms in *unsprung* weight. Under deflection, the main fork of a girder or the sliders of "teles" move at wheel speed,

FIG. 3.10. Torsional rigidity for the short leading-link can be provided by a "hoop" passing round the rear of the wheel. On the Greeves roadster (top left) it lies inside the mudguard; on the T.T. Honda (above) outside it. But individual links are sufficiently rigid for the NSU "Quickly" (left).

whereas with links, only the active ends move at wheel speed. Further, if the springs are attached at about the mid-points of a pair of short links, even their weight and that of the hydraulic damper mechanism is virtually 50 per cent. sprung, so the short-link varieties are potentially the best of all in this very important aspect. The Earles type is good also, but the springs move almost at wheel speed, and this type loses on the score of "pendulum effect"—that is to say, a big proportion of its weight is located behind the wheel and thus at a long distance from the steering column axis, whereas it is desirable to keep all the mass as close as possible to this axis for nicety of control.

In a sidecar machine this is of less importance, and further it is easy to provide alternative pivot points in the Earles links to give a long trail for solo use and a short trail for sidecar work. Similar provision is also made in the Vincent "Girdraulic" fork by mounting the lower links on eccentric spindles which are turned through 180° to alter the trail, this action simultaneously moving the upper spring anchorages,

FIG. 3.11. (Left) Low in weight, both sprung and unsprung, are the leading-link Reynolds forks on Geoff Duke's Junior Norton. (Right) Earles-type forks are fitted to all 1959 B.M.W. roadsters with alternative pivot positions for varying trail only.

so that in the "sidecar" position the springs are more nearly vertical and thus in a more favourable position to handle the extra weight imposed on them (Fig. 3.8).

Trail adjustment can also be carried out on telescopic forks by using reversible sliders with the axle attachments offset to their centre-lines, as on Royal Enfield and Panther forks, although of course this method makes no provision for the extra weight and the wheel must be removed to perform the trail adjustment.

In the B.M.W. (Fig. 3.11) two positions are provided for the fork pivot spindle to vary the trail, but without much alteration to the effective spring strength.

Telescopics come out top of the class on the score of neatness and a deceptive air of simplicity, while the trailing-link is probably the least tidy, although, by cunning use of pressings of tasteful design even this variety can be made quite attractive—as, for instance, on the Ariel "Leader". Taking all things into consideration, lateral rigidity of the wheel in the forks, torsional rigidity of the whole assembly, minimum unsprung weight, absence of "nose-diving" during braking, and neatness, the short-leading link type with floating brake-plates and springs enclosed in the main tubes is probably the best form though there still remains some difficulty with trail adjustment. The ideal solution here would be to construct the head in such a way that the column axis could be varied at will, and thereby alter the rake and the trail simultaneously to switch from solo to sidecar trim.

Little mention has been made in this chapter about the springing and damping methods, reference to which will be found in Chapter 6.

CHAPTER 4

Rigid Frames

THE frame of a motorcycle has two main functions. It acts as a beam supported by the wheels to carry the weight of the propelling machinery and the rider, and it provides for free steering movement of the front wheel while maintaining the rear wheel continuously and accurately in the centre-plane of the machine.

If the second requirement is not fully met, the rear end will do some uncontrolled steering of its own accord, with adverse effects on the handling. Besides road shocks which, as described in previous chapters, have a tendency to deflect the rear wheel and, in effect, to twist it in relation to the frame, very powerful forces may be generated by power-transmission from engine to rear wheel and by braking on either wheel. The frame must be strong enough, both generally and locally at points of major stress, to withstand these forces without undue deflection.

These statements might appear to be self-evident and are certainly well appreciated today, but many years went by in the formative period of the industry before their full import was realized by designers generally, with the result that machines went into production which did not handle well, or suffered from frame breakages in service or, in extreme cases, combined both defects.

EARLY DESIGNS

The earliest popular designs were, understandably, merely powered versions of the pedal cycles of the period. The frame of such a machine consisted essentially of a diamond-shaped structure made with steel tubes brazed into lugs, and with a simple front fork mounted in bearings in the tube or lug which formed the steering-head (Fig. 4.1 (a)). The engine, while it was still only of small capacity, was clipped or bolted to any part of the frame where a good home could be found for it. In the total absence of clutches or gearboxes and the relative absence of power, pedals were retained and, in fact, were often indispensable to forward progress on hills.

To permit effective operation of the pedals the saddle had to be kept high and the bars had to be at a corresponding level for reasons

28

of comfort, so the whole machine was inclined to be ungainly, especially when engines of larger size came into use and were fitted vertically in the centre of the frame. Nevertheless, this form of motorcycle is still built today under the title of motor-assisted bicycle or, more succinctly, "mo-ped". In principle, modern examples differ very little from their ancestors, although, of course, the standard of workmanship and the method used to obtain good performance and a minimum of weight without sacrifice of reliability are vastly improved.

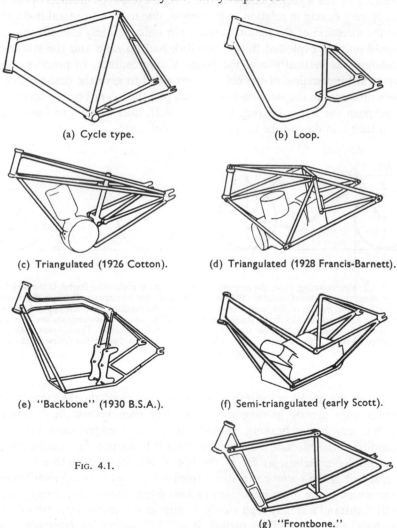

(a) Cycle type.

(b) Loop.

(c) Triangulated (1926 Cotton).

(d) Triangulated (1928 Francis-Barnett).

(e) "Backbone" (1930 B.S.A.).

(f) Semi-triangulated (early Scott).

Fig. 4.1.

(g) "Frontbone."

When clutches and variable-speed transmissions made their appearance, the necessity for pedals ceased and with it the need to provide clearance for a pair of revolving feet and enough saddle height to permit freedom of leg-action. This cleared the decks considerably and gave any designer with an unfettered mind the opportunity to devise something original—if perhaps of doubtful merit.

Considered as a beam supported by the rear wheel and the lower bearing of the steering column, the classic cycle-type frame is potentially very strong in relation to its weight, due to its considerable depth in the direction of the major stresses, but unfortunately this advantage could only be exploited fully if the fork had no rake and the steering column was vertically over the point of tyre-contact. In practice, the rearward inclination of the column, provided to give the desired rake, sets up forces in the steering-head which pull the lower bearing forward and push the upper bearing back (Fig. 4.2), thus tending to bend the top tube and down-tube into the shapes indicated.

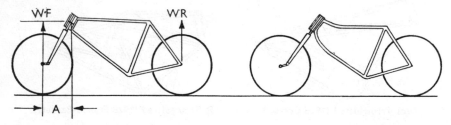

Fig. 4.2. Forces acting upon the steering head of a simple cycle-type frame. If the weight supported by the front spindle (*WF*) is 150 lb. and the horizontal distance from the spindle to the middle of the head stem (*A*) is 10 in., the bending moment applied to the steering head will be 125 lb./ft. Radial loads of 250 lb. will act forwards on the bottom bearing and backwards on the top one under static conditions. These loads may be multiplied from 3 to 10 times under impact. They tend to distort the frame as shown on the right.

When the model is moving and subjected to road shocks these local forces vary greatly in magnitude and may even reverse in direction under very heavy braking, though, fortunately under most braking conditions the effect of the retarding force is to reduce the local bending action. Nevertheless, as far as the life of the frame structure is concerned, it is the *variation* in stress from a high value to a much lower one which is the most important factor. While almost any component will withstand a steady load nearly as high as the tensile strength of the material for an indefinite period, it will fail sooner or later under a varying or alternating stress unless the maximum value is very much less than the ultimate stress or, more correctly, the yield stress of the material.

FATIGUE FAILURE

Failure of this nature is termed "fatigue failure". It is most likely to occur at places where there are concentrations of stress, or where different sorts of stress—i.e., tension plus bending, torsion (twisting) plus bending, or more complex combinations—act on a component simultaneously. Any rapid change in section, such as at the point where a tube leaves a lug, acts as a "stress-raiser", and if the tube is locally reduced in thickness by careless filing-up after brazing two bad effects are introduced simultaneously—the stress-raising effect due to change in section is intensified, and there is less metal left to withstand it anyway (Fig. 4.3).

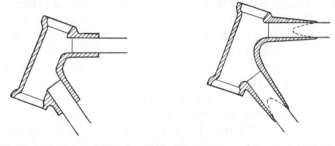

FIG. 4.3. Short, thick lugs (left) cause tube failure through stress concentration and lack of flexibility. Long lugs tapered to thin edges transfer stresses gradually for no greater weight. They are better still if fish-tailed.

The front down-tube is subjected to tension (from the weight of the engine) as well as bending, while the top tube is subjected to compression and bending; but as compression in the normal course of events does not cause fatigue failure, the down-tube is the most likely to fracture and in the old days frequently did so, always with embarrassing and sometimes with fatal consequences.

Adding a horizontal tube from the base of the head lug to the saddle down-tube will absorb most of the bending forces, and in fact if both the top tube and this additional tube (sometimes called the tank rail because it was used to carry the tank) are straight and their centre-lines intersect at or close to the saddle lug, the head lug forms one side of a triangle which is extremely rigid in the vertical plane. Even if the tubes are not absolutely straight, but are bent to accommodate a tank, the structure is still very stiff, though some makers made the error of joining the tank rail to the down-tube with an additional lug and leaving a short section of tube exposed between it and the head-lug, instead of combining the two. As there was then a tube of relatively small section joining two much more massive lugs, fatigue failure in this area was almost inevitable, especially under the additional lateral bending stresses set up by sidecar work.

Carrying the idea still further, it is quite possible to design the frame in such a way that it is completely triangulated, in which event bolted-up joints are all that is required. Francis-Barnett did produce such a frame in the 'thirties and, as Fig. 4.1 (d) shows, the triangulation was carried out in the transverse as well as the vertical plane by duplicating all tubes. To be effective all the tubes in such a frame need to be straight as indeed they were, otherwise they will alter in length under the action of end-loading and the value of triangulation will be lost. However, this requirement places serious limitations on the size and shape of the power unit, tanks and so forth which have to be accommodated, and in practice the idea is not so attractive as in theory, though it might well stand resuscitation for the design of a "space-frame" (to employ a car-builders' term) on which full enclosure is to be carried as a standard fitting.

Another fully triangulated design was the Cotton, though in this instance the small-diameter tubes were brazed into lugs in the conventional fashion (Fig. 4.1 (c)). The ingenious frame originally designed by A. A. Scott, which is frequently referred to as "fully triangulated", was not so in fact because, seen in side elevation, the head lug, the front down-tubes, the top tube and the crankcase form a four-sided structure in which fore-and-aft head stresses are resisted solely by the strength of the lug and tubes as in a cycle-type frame; otherwise, with engine installed, this frame is triangulated at the rear end (Fig. 4.1 (f)).

Staying the head-lug by a tank-rail often involved difficulty with the installation or maintenance of a tall engine, and was undesirable on that account. Furthermore, while a limited amount of fore-and-aft flexibility of the head is not greatly detrimental to handling, twisting of the head out of the centre-plane is most decidedly so, because its effect in moving the tyre contact point off-centre can be considerable due to the distance between the head and the ground.

PROPERTIES OF THE TUBE

The properties of the tube also affect this issue. While the weight of a thin-walled tube increases almost in direct proportion to its diameter, its torsional strength increases as the *cube* of the diameter and its deflection (for any given twisting moment applied to it) decreases as the *fourth power*. Therefore, a single 2 in. tube weighs the same as two 1 in. tubes, but is four times as strong and will twist through only one-eighth the angle for the same load. Put in another way, a single $1\frac{1}{4}$ in. tube is almost as strong as two 1 in. tubes, deflects slightly less for the same twisting moment, but is only five-eighths the weight.

It is, then, clearly more economical in material, machining and labour to use a single tube, taking care of the local head stresses by careful design of the lug or by using a butted tube, which means one that is increased in wall thickness at one end, usually by two gauge sizes. Thus a 12-gauge tube may be butted to 10-gauge for, say, 3 in. at one end, with a tapered portion of 2 or 3 in. to give a smooth change of section. On occasion, double-butted tubes—i.e., with a thicker gauge at both ends—have been employed for top tubes to give a slightly greater margin of strength at the saddle-lug end.

When there are only two tubes attached to the head, another factor, that of the *relative* flexibility of the tubes, must be considered. It was occasionally found that an attempt to eliminate down-tube failure by increasing the gauge of this component was not successful until the thickness had been increased to a disproportionate amount, whereas the original thickness was quite satisfactory if the top tube—i.e., the one which was not giving trouble—was stiffened by butting.

FIG. 4.4. High strength/weight ratio of the large-diameter top tube in a racing frame, made for Arthur Wheeler's Guzzi "special" by Reynolds. The tube acts as an oil tank.

This apparent paradox can be explained by envisaging the lug and tubes in a distorted state, as shown in Fig. 4.2. If the down-tube is increased in thickness, it becomes less flexible than the top tube. It will then attempt to do more than its fair share of the work, and will continue to break until it has been thickened so much that it can do all the work by itself, with the top tube acting more or less as a strut. On the other hand, if the top tube is strengthened it becomes stiffer and consequently takes a greater share of the work, with a corresponding reduction of stress in the down-tube and less chance of failure.

It is, of course, quite possible to design the frame in such a manner that almost the whole duty of supporting the head lug is performed by a rigid downward extension, a form of construction introduced by Francis-Barnetts many years ago and still retained (Fig. 4.1 (g)). Originally the head-lug had an H-section extension (since altered to a lighter and stronger tube) reaching down to crankcase level and maintained in the correct fore-and-aft position by bolted-on duplex tubes on which the tank rested. In the Greeves, a similar structure is used but the main member is a casting of high-strength light alloy with a single top tube running back from the upper end to the saddle; this tube is of steel and is welded to a steel head insert cast in position.

A variant of this scheme is to make the head and tank rail integral, and resembling one half of the beam-axle now almost extinct on cars. This method (once used on small P. & M., B.S.A. and Vincent machines) simplifies the tank design; but if the weight is to be kept down the long horizontal portion must be of H-section, which is deficient in torsional stiffness (Fig. 4.1 (e)).

An interesting recent development of the idea is found on Triumph frames, in which a single top tube running horizontally just above the engine is curved upwards at the front to fit into the angle between the tube forming the head lug and the front down-tube. Increased resistance to fore-and-aft loads is provided by a single gusset in the space between the top and down tubes, which helps to distribute the bending loads between these two components.

FRAME-BUILDING PROBLEMS

Multi-tubular brazed or welded frames are neither easy nor cheap to manufacture; a lot of machining is required on the lugs and very frequently the frames warp during fabrication and subsequently have to be pulled into alignment by the application of heat and brute force. Also, it is not uncommon to find that there are very severe stresses

FIG. 4.5. Modern example of the "frontbone" is the massive H-section light-alloy member of the Greeves.

FIG. 4.6. Interesting treatment of the junction between head lug and tubes is seen in Triumph frames; shown is that of the "Twenty-one"

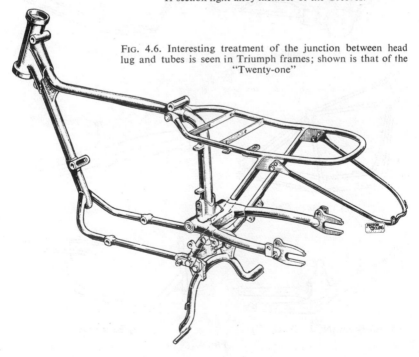

locked up in the completed structure which are bad in two respects: first, a permanent high stress is placed in the tubes affected, to which any dynamic loads occurring in service will be added; secondly, the frame when subjected to transverse loads may bend easily in one direction, but be very stiff in the other, according to which way the locked-up stress itself is tending to deform the structure.

These internal stresses arise through one part of the frame, which is heated during fabrication, contracting as it cools, thereby putting itself in tension and some other component in compression. They may be detected if a suspected frame is sawn through at some point. It will often be found that the saw-cut will either open out or close onto the saw, according to whether the tube is in tension or compression; or, if the cut is made in a transverse lug, the two sides may move out of alignment.

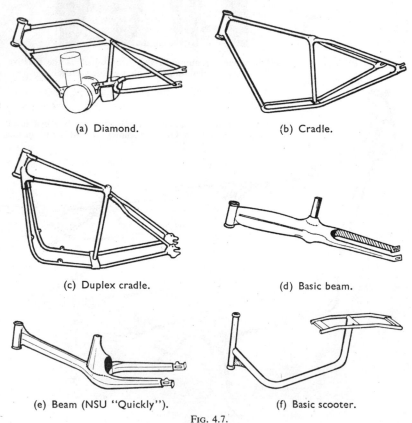

(a) Diamond.

(b) Cradle.

(c) Duplex cradle.

(d) Basic beam.

(e) Beam (NSU "Quickly").

(f) Basic scooter.

Fig. 4.7.

Avoiding Pre-stressing

Usually a welding or brazing sequence can be evolved which will obviate such undesirable stressing by ensuring that thermal contractions are equalized, but some makers prefer to have at least one or two joints bolted-up instead of thermally united, so that the final closure does not involve the application of heat. If the holes do come out of line, the adjacent components can easily be set or the bolt-holes reamed so that no residual locked-up stresses are brought into being.

The simplest of the many structures developed in the days when frames without rear springing were in general use was the "diamond" type (Fig. 4.7 (a)), in which the engine formed one of the members. Despite its lack of triangulation, this could be made to give good handling for a very low weight if due attention were given to maintaining strength at the corners.

A variant of this was the "loop" type (Fig. 4.1 (b)), with the down-tube continued in one sweep under the crankcase and up to the saddle; the gearbox, if used, was usually mounted abaft this tube on a lug to which the chain-stays were attached, and the frame was inclined to be narrow and weak in the region of this lug. Additional strength was sometimes gained by adding a second pair of tubes, called torque stays, running from the rear fork-ends to the lowest point of the crankcase, and these did have the effect of steadying the engine against its own torque reaction as well as tending to prevent the frame from bowing under the influence of transmission stresses.

Fig. 4.8. The large-diameter tube-cum-oil-tank allied to duplex tubes: a special Reynolds frame to accommodate a 250 c.c. NSU engine.

Looked at in plan view, both primary and secondary chains are offset by several inches from the frame centre-line and thus lie well outside the plane of greatest stiffness; consequently there is a strong tendency to bend the frame when power is being transmitted (Fig. 4.9).

Assuming a single-cylinder engine developing, say, 20 b.h.p., and a mean torque of 24 lb./ft., the average pull in the front chain with a normal-sized sprocket would be 112 lb.; but allowing for cyclic irregularity due to the widely spaced power impulses, the *maximum* pull would be around 450 lb., acting at a distance of, say, 4 in. from the centre line. If the distance between engine and clutch shaft is 10 in., the lateral force tending to bend the frame between these points is four-tenths of 450, or 180 lb.

This by-no-means-negligible figure may be nearly equalled by that resulting from the rear chain pull, because in bottom gear, with a box reduction-ratio of, say, 3 to 1, the mean rear chain pull is increased to 336 lb. (assuming that the engine and final-drive sprockets are the same pitch diameter), but the maximum pull might well be several times this figure during a violent clutch start when the energy of the rotating parts is being absorbed. A figure of around 500 lb. in this instance might be taken as reasonable for calculation purposes. With a chain-line distance of $2\frac{3}{4}$ in. and 18 in. from clutch to wheel centre, the bowing force works out at 78 lb., so that the total lateral force comes to nearly 260 lb. even with an engine of quite modest power development.

Under stresses of this order, a weak frame must bend to some extent, and as the loads are not steady, but fluctuate in unison with the firing impulses, there is a possibility that they may come into resonance with the natural period of vibration of some component, either of the frame itself or attached to it, in which event vibration of an unpleasant sort may occur. If, however, the frame is made in such a way that it is wider than the chain-lines, the bending effect will be reduced considerably, and this was accomplished to a degree by the addition of the torque-stays mentioned.

A more satisfactory solution was to bring the chain stays themselves below the gearbox, and continue them forward on each side of the engine (thus enabling it to be positioned low down without sacrificing ground clearance) and forming what was termed the "cradle" frame, a design which won many races and competitions (Fig. 4.7 (b)). It was introduced in the U.S.A. many years before it became popular in England.

A logical development of this design is to continue the tubes upward to the head-lug to form the "duplex cradle" type (Fig. 4.7 (c)). This pattern appears to be immensely strong when inspected sitting on the cradle-tubes on the ground, but it is not necessarily any stronger in torsion than one with a single down-tube, and possibly less strong fore-and-aft unless large-diameter tubes are used or the head-lug is extended downwards by several inches. It is, however, an excellent form of construction for sidecar machines, being triangulated laterally, especially if the top connection is made integrally with the head-lug. B.M.W. have developed a very neat though expensive solution by using duplex tubes which are tapered and also change from circular to oval section as they approach the head-lug to which they are welded.

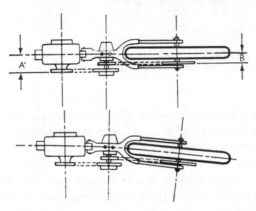

Fig. 4.9. How transmission load tends to distort a narrow frame; *A* and *B* indicate the offset from the centre line of the two chains.

The transverse-twin ABC of the early 'twenties used a logical development of the duplex frame with the tubes spaced so widely apart that they protected the engine in the event of a fall and also formed footboard supports. This construction might well be used again now that partial enclosure has become acceptable, but in its original form it possessed a weakness in that the two tubes were joined to the base of the head with a wide included angle between them. Under fore-and-aft loads these tubes become subjected to bending *and* twisting, in addition to tension from the weight of the powerplant, and in rough conditions would fail in fatigue—a point which would have to be rectified in any future similar design.

There is, of course, an alternative approach to the whole problem, which is to do away with all forms of lattice-girder or triangulated structure and make the frame as a simple beam (Fig. 4.7. (d)) similar,

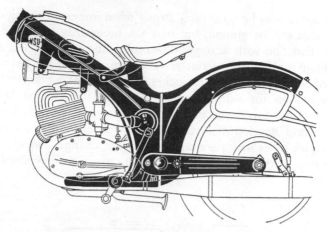

Fig. 4.10. The backbone of the NSU "Max" has great depth and strength at the centre. In neither this case nor the Ariel "Leader" (Fig. 4.11) does the engine act as a frame member.

in fact, to the original velocipede. The essence of the idea is simply to take a large-diameter tube, provided with steering-head bearings at the front and bifurcated to embrace the rear wheel. This results in a simple structure which, with modern facilities, can be made very easily from two light pressings, welded together, though the rear fork-legs should also be made into closed sections by welding-in another strip to form two box-sections.

Open channel sections are extremely weak in torsion and not much better under cross-breaking loads, which cause the flanges to crumple. A good idea of the relative torsional strengths of open and closed

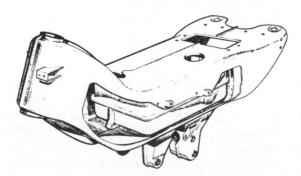

Fig. 4.11. The built-up beam frame in modern practice: the box girder of the Ariel "Leader" contains a separate, unstressed fuel tank.

FIG. 4.12. The engine as "down-tube" on a Panther 120 (left) and on the T.T. Honda (the continuation of the "spine" is shown in dotted lines).

sections can be gained by twisting a rectangular tobacco-tin in the fingers, first with the lid open and then with it closed.

A simple beam frame of the type described is enormously strong in torsion and strong enough vertically to carry moderate loads, so it is an acceptable proposition for mo-peds and pedal-assisted bicycles, the power unit simply being bolted to downward extensions of the tube or backbone and the saddle supported on a pillar, which can be made telescopic to provide both height adjustment and springing. Obviously, local stresses are produced at the base of the pillar which can be allowed for by blending it into the backbone with generous fillet radii, and the backbone may be curved downwards in the centre, partly to keep the engine weight low and partly to provide the "open frame" feature desired by ladies who ride in normal attire (Fig. 4.7 (e)).

There are innumerable possible variants of this basic conception. For instance, a single tube can slope down to the engine and then up to the saddle, with either rigid or sprung rear forks attached to the rising portion; or the tube can run almost vertically downwards, then horizontally and upwards, this being the underlying construction of the majority of scooters built today (Fig. 4.7 (f)). Obviously the greater the length of unsupported tube the more flexible the structure will be, particularly in bending; but on most scooters the idea is acceptable because most of the weight of crew and power-plant is concentrated

Fig. 4.13. On the post-war Vincent twin front and rear cylinder heads were attached to a welded backbone-oil-tank, bolted at the front to the head-lug and providing attachment points for the spring units of the suspension at the rear.

over the rear wheel. One or two models, however, are so lacking in rigidity that if the bars are pushed forward with the front brake hard on, the steering-column can be observed to alter its angle.

The NSU pressed-steel frame is an excellent example of the backbone type, the pressings extending down behind the power unit and rearward to provide attachments for the rear springs, thus providing great depth and strength in the centre. The power-unit, though firmly attached at the rear, is merely suspended by a tension link at the front and does little or nothing to stiffen the structure (Fig. 4.10).

Once one has gone to the trouble of making a frame from pressings, it seems reasonable to go a little further and utilize the frame as a tank for either petrol, oil or both. Attractive though this is, it is not always as simple as it looks and is not necessarily economical in material, because a tank can be made in a much lighter gauge of metal than is desirable for a stressed structural member, unless a lot of care is taken to weld in gussets or local reinforcement where necessary.

On the Ariel "Leader", for instance, it has been deemed wiser to fit a simple rectangular tank inside the box-section main frame member, to which the power-unit is attached by downward-extending lugs. In this way the tank can easily be constructed from two pressings with simple welds which are easy to make petrol-tight, and it is unlikely to be damaged even in the most spectacular of crashes. The backbone itself is immensely strong both in bending and torsion, although weakened in the latter respect by the cutaways provided for access to the interior (Fig. 4.11).

It is, however, quite feasible to use a welded backbone as an oil-tank holding about half a gallon without waste of material. This form of construction was adopted on the Vincent twin, the backbone being attached to the front and rear cylinder heads so that in effect the power unit was held up by its ears. This was done for two reasons—first to eliminate the front down-tube and so shorten the wheelbase, and secondly because during overhaul it is easier to lift a light frame off a heavy power unit than it is to juggle the unit out of the frame if only one pair of hands is available (Fig. 4.13).

It is interesting to note that the pre-war Vincent single-top-tube brazed frame weighed $12\frac{1}{2}$ lb., and the backbone, of much greater strength in all directions, weighed the same. The experimental design of this backbone had the head-tube welded-in, but if warpage occurred during welding it was almost impossible to eradicate the twist, so a separate component, with the head-lug jig-drilled and bolted in position, was adopted.

This idea was really an extension of the principle introduced on the early P. and M. and continued in current Panther "big singles" whereby the long-stroke, inclined cylinder engine was bolted to the head-lug and therefore acted as a down-tube. The tensile stresses were carried by four long bolts extending from the bracket on the head right through to the bottom of the crankcase, so that as far as frame stresses were concerned the cast-iron barrel simply acted as a distance-piece. In the racing Honda, the head-lug, formed in this instance from welded tube and sheet-steel pressings, is attached to the cylinder head with transverse bolts, the single top tube curving down behind the unit to form what has come to be termed a "spine" frame; the power-unit is, however, an integral part of this assembly, and the frame is incomplete without it.

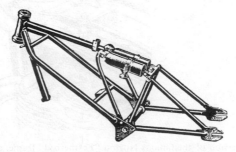

Fig. 4.14. The Vincent-H.R.D. spring frame of 1928, a predecessor of the Vincent twin (Fig. 4.13); it was triangulated in side elevation.

In the main, the foregoing has been concerned with the front section of the frame, omitting reference to the rear forks. In an unsprung tubular frame, each side of the fork is usually formed of two, or possibly three, tubes forming a triangle with the rear axle lug as the

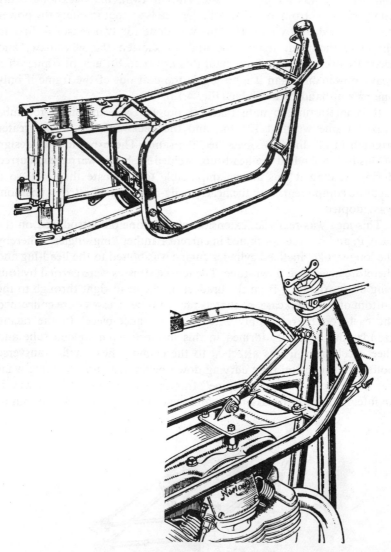

FIG. 4.15. Racing version of the famous Norton "Featherbed" frame, as it appeared at the T.T. of 1950. Close-up of the head shows the supplementary bracing tube to the engine-head steady.

apex. This structure automatically stiffens the front section and prevents it from "lozenging" under the action of horizontal forces, which may be applied by chain tension or by road shocks. Also, the whole structure, consisting of two triangles attached to a common tube, is extremely rigid in torsion and it is very difficult to twist the axle out of true.

If, however, the triangulation is partially destroyed by cutting off the rear fork-ends in order to attach some form of plunger-springing system, or removed entirely to utilize a swinging-fork design, this stiffening action is largely lost and the main frame should then have to be strong enough in its own right to resist deformation, although many are able to do so only through the additional rigidity supplied by the presence of a bolted-in power unit.

Since the general type and detail design of any rear springing adopted has a bearing on the frame design, this is the logical place to initiate a discussion on rear suspension systems and this follows in Chapter 5.

CHAPTER 5

Rear Springing

THE desirability of rear springing was recognized 50 years ago and a number of makers experimented with it or even went into limited production. Many of these pioneer designs showed a disregard of essential principles and some merely took the form of additional mechanism attached to the fork-ends of existing unsprung frames—an expedient which has also been followed in more recent times.

Anyone who cares to delve into history will find that almost every type of springing system was tried in these early years (even to the use of air-sprung units), but the poor handling which many springers exhibited led to the whole conception of rear springing falling into disrepute, then to be almost abandoned for quite a while, despite sporadic attempts to reintroduce it.

This is a good example of a pattern of events noted in the introduction to this volume—it is in effect a mechanical translation of the adage about "giving a dog a bad name". However, the picture has changed completely since then. Nowadays a motorcycle without rear springing would be almost as hard to sell as an unsprung motorcar, and the benefits in the way of better roadholding and braking are just as well appreciated as the more obvious improvement in bodily comfort.

To perform satisfactorily, a rear springing system must provide 3 in. of wheel movement (and preferably even more) and must ensure that the wheel remains strictly in the centre-plane of the frame at all times and under all stresses generated either by road-shocks or transmission forces. Further, it must not impair the transmission's efficiency or reliability and must be able to cope with wide variations of load—which may comprise one light rider or two heavy-weights plus luggage. The effect of these requirements upon the detail design of the rear suspension system will come under review later; at this stage, it is desirable to concentrate on the structural problems involved in building a rear-sprung frame which will be mechanically rigid laterally and in torsion, without detrimental effects in other ways.

Basic Types

Broadly speaking there are three basic layouts: (a) the "plunger" system, with the axle carried by sliders moving inside housings attached to the fork ends; (b) the "short-link" system, with the axle attached to the ends of links pivoted at or near the fork ends; and (c) the "swinging fork" system, with the axle carried in a fork, pivoted on an axis lying between the tyre and the rear of the power unit. (See Fig. 5.2.)

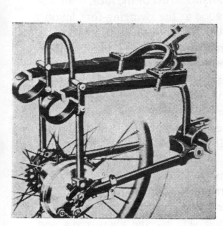 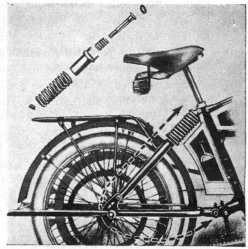

Fig. 5.1. Early swinging forks: leaf springs on a 1915 Indian (left) and a modern-looking coil spring unit on an NSU of 1911.

Any conventional rigid frame can be adapted fairly easily to systems (a) or (b) without introducing a host of minor problems such as mudguard, silencer and rear stand attachments. Consequently they had considerable attraction in the days when alternative rigid and sprung models were listed.

System (b), however, has little to recommend it, because if chain drive is used the variation in distance between gearbox-mainshaft and rear wheel centres is excessive, leading to a great variation in chain tension. Further it is difficult to maintain torsional stiffness because the link-axle-link combination forms, in effect, a single crank, just as in the case of a bottom-link front fork, and this will twist easily unless the three components are so firmly attached that they form virtually a unit—a difficult requirement when the axle has to be made movable for chain adjustment.

An interesting marriage of the short-link and plunger systems was used for some time by Ariels, the linkage being so arranged that the axle moved in a curved path virtually centred on the gearbox mainshaft, thus obtaining almost constant chain tension at the expense of extra complication.

System (a) had a very good run for a number of years, largely because of its successful adoption on Norton racing machines. This public demonstration of the fact that a rear-sprung model *could* be made to handle did much to dispel popular distrust of the idea, although the system used is not, in principle, as good as the swinging-fork layout, represented at that time by a few British and Continental makes.

The main trouble with any system involving parallel sliding members joined by a relatively flexible cross-member (the axle) is that under the action of loads applied more or less transversely to the tyre, the axle will bend into an S-shape and one slider will move farther up than the other, thus permitting the wheel to deflect from the centre-plane (Fig. 5.2 (a)). Any running clearance provided to permit free sliding movement will accentuate this bad effect. So will any lack of rigidity of the fixed portions in a vertical plane, and it is difficult to make these rigid because they are merely attached to the ends of tubes which are overhung several inches from the centre-section of the frame.

An additional source of weakness in some plunger systems was that the triangle previously formed on each side by the chain-stays and seat-stays was converted into a quadrilateral, dependent for vertical strength upon the strength of the tubes rather than upon the geometrical shape. Consequently fatigue failure of the tubes was not unknown, though its onset was largely a matter of how hard and over what surfaces the model was driven.

Plunger springing is the worst of the lot with regard to variation in chain tension, because the chain tightens at the *extremes* of travel and so must be adjusted to be slack in the mean position. It therefore spends most of its time running slack and is liable to jump the sprockets, even if the chain-guard is arranged to act as a retaining device—a somewhat barbarous expedient which has been resorted to at times.

On the other hand, if a swinging fork could be arranged to pivot about the centre line of the final drive, the chain tension would remain constant over the whole sprung movement. While it is not impossible to attain this result, in practice it is unnecessary, because if the pivot is placed fairly close to the gearbox the variation in tension over the permissible range of movement is so slight that it can be tolerated—especially as matters can be so arranged that the tension is correct in

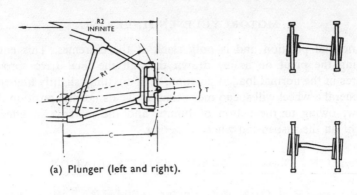

(a) Plunger (left and right).

(b) Short link (below).
(c) Swinging fork (right).

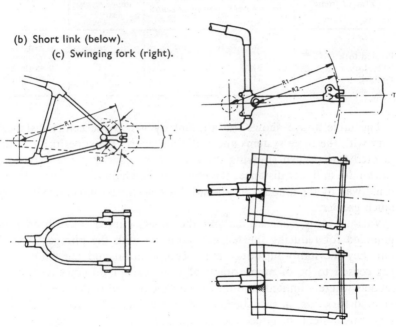

FIG. 5.2. The three principal systems of rear springing.

In all sketches, R_1 = distance between centres of gearbox shaft and axle, R_2 = radius of axle movement (in the plunger, movement is straight-line), and T = travel.

(a) In the plunger system, axle and gearbox centres diverge with movement away from the mean position, therefore chain must be run slack. End elevations on right show how lateral loads tend to twist the axle and how play in the sliders will permit axle movement.

(b) Weakness of the short-link system is the large divergence between R_1 and R_2 at extremes of movement. The "single crank" assembly, shown in plan view, is also weak in resistance to torsion.

(c) With the swinging fork, the difference between R_1 and R_2 remains small. Plan views show how poor designs may bend due to weakness of pivot mounting or be displaced laterally due to weakness in the fork itself.

the normal position and is only slack at the extremes. This entails placing the pivot on a line drawn through the final-drive sprocket centres in the normal loaded position, or if anything slightly higher, as in general a wheel will spend more time above its normal position than below, owing to the action of bumps and the increase in effective weight on the suspension when cornering.

TABLE 5.1. CHAIN CENTRE VARIATION

Type of frame	Gearbox shaft to rear axle	Gearbox shaft to pivot centre	Rise of wheel above mean position	Centre variation
	in.	in.	in.	in.
Pivoted fork	21	4·5	3	0·07 slack
Short-link	21	13	3	0·35 slack
Plunger	21	∞	2	0·40 tight

The table above shows the amount by which the centre-distances vary with the three systems and indicates clearly the superiority of the pivoted fork. When studying the table, remember that the variations shown are in linear distance; the effect on the chain as measured in the usual way by the amount of up-and-down slackness introduced is very much greater.

Various ideas, such as making the sliders curved, have been propounded for reducing the tension variation with the plunger system, but they inevitably introduce extra complication and the whole idea has ceased to be of much practical value except on some very light models where a limited amount of movement is all that is needed. The pivoted fork has, in fact, become almost universally adopted, though even this system introduces some complications which must be given close attention if a successful design is to be the outcome.

A criticism sometimes levelled at the combination of a pivoted fork and a chain is that there is an epicyclic effect created by fork movement if, as is usual, the sprockets are of different sizes. This criticism is valid, and the chain has an erratic variation in velocity imposed on it which is not by any means helpful. However, there is another factor which complicates the situation, whatever the form of suspension or even if the forks are rigid. When a wheel traverses a bump, it must accelerate in r.p.m. at the start of the slope, because the length of surface traversed, measured along the slope, is greater than the horizontal distance through which the machine moves. The wheel must then decelerate back to average speed at the crest, accelerate again down the far slope and again drop back to average r.p.m. on reaching level ground again. What happens to the actual tension in the chain under the combined effects of this condition and the epicyclic action of the sprockets depends upon whether the model is under power or rolling freely; at times the two effects act in unison, at others they cancel each other out. An efficient shock-absorber of the Enfield hub pattern could help materially in taking some of the snatch out of the drive, and it would also be helpful, though difficult and complicated, to make the sprockets of equal size and mount the front one co-axially with the pivot.

Fork Bearing Attachment

As the only positive connection between the fork and the frame is the pivot-bearing, it follows automatically that the duty of resisting dynamic and transmission loads devolves solely upon this component and its attachment to the main frame. Any inadequacy in stiffness of mounting, or looseness in the bearing, will permit the wheel to move out of line, irrespective of whether or not the fork itself is sufficiently robust.

Consequently the bearing—or rather bearings, as there is usually one at each side—should be as far apart as possible. But this is not sufficient in itself; if for instance, a wide lug carrying the bearing is brazed in the middle of a long, slender down-tube, this tube will be subjected to severe bending and torsional stresses and in time will fail by fatigue unless of adequate diameter.

The directions of the loads imposed depend upon the layout of the springing adopted. If, for instance, leaf springs extending backwards from the frame were fitted and connected to the fork ends by shackles —a layout which was used on several ancient models and one or two more recent experimental jobs—the weight is carried almost directly by the springs and the bearing has to withstand only transmission loads and those due to transverse forces on the wheel. This obsolete method, however, places very high local stresses on the spring anchorages.

Almost universal nowadays is the use of coil-spring units, usually inclined forwards at the top to some extent and thereby generating a horizontal component of the gravitational force, which tends to pull the bearing backwards by an amount depending upon the angle of the springs and their disposition with regard to the rear axle (Fig. 5.3). This force acts in the opposite direction to the pull of the rear chain, therefore if any slackness or flexibility is present in the bearing or its mounting the rear fork will not remain in a central position but will swing to one side or the other according to whether power is on or off.

An indication of whether a suspension system is lacking in lateral rigidity can be obtained by squeezing the top and bottom runs of the chain together with the fingers. If there is any flexibility, it will be possible to observe movement of the fork-ends in relation to the frame; it may also be possible to detect just where the flexure is occurring and, with this guidance, to reduce or even eliminate it entirely by adopting an appropriate course of action.

However effective the bearing itself, the result will not be good unless its mounting is sufficiently substantial; further, the more direct the path which transmission loads must follow, the better. The ideal is to mount the bearing actually on the engine-gearbox unit (big M.V.s and Ariel "Leader") or by short, straight, widely spaced engine plates in direct compression. Satisfactory results, however, will be obtained from a frame with a single saddle down-tube provided this is of large diameter and the lug forming the pivot bearing attachment is bolted to the power unit with plates preferably spaced several inches apart.

The pivoted fork appears to be particularly suitable for shaft-drive machines because the propeller shaft can be concealed within one leg and only one universal joint will be required, whereas there must be two if a plunger system is employed. Further, the angular deflection is low enough to permit the use of an ordinary Hookes-type universal (that is, of the Hardy-Spicer pattern) though a constant-velocity joint would be preferable if the fork is very short and has a large range of movement.

Torque Reactions

The effects of power and brake reactions are, however, quite different in the cases of chain-drive and shaft-drive, and this alters the picture considerably. With a chain, there is no direct torque reaction, except the tendency under power to lift the front wheel and rotate the whole machine around the back axle—an effect which transfers some or all of the weight on the front wheel to the back, thus causing the rear springs to compress beyond their normal position and the pivot-bearing to sink. This action is augmented or diminished according to the height of the pivot bearing in relation to the rear axle; if the pivot is the lower of the two, a downward vertical component of the compression-load in the forks will be introduced tending to depress the pivot still further, whilst if it is the higher the reverse is the case. Usually both are at about the same level and the effect in practice is never very considerable.

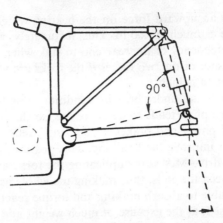

FIG. 5.3. How inclination of the spring unit in a swinging-fork assembly produces a rearward-acting horizontal component of the reaction to the weight.

With shaft drive (Fig. 5.4) the conditions are altered by the presence of strong torque reactions, one of which (*A*) tends to rotate the bevel-box backwards in relation to the wheel, and the other (*B*) tends to rotate the bevel-box in the same direction as the propeller shaft.

These effects can be easily envisaged. First, consider the crown wheel to be locked in position; the pinion will then try to "climb up" the crown-wheel teeth and attempt to take the casing with it. Next, if the pinion and crown-wheel are envisaged as locked together, the whole assembly will try to rotate around the propeller shaft. If the bevel-box is bolted to one of a pair of plungers, reaction (*A*) is resisted locally by that plunger; but if the forks are pivoted they tend to rotate back-

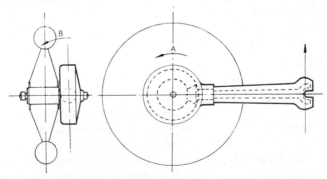

FIG. 5.4. Torque reactions upon a shaft drive with power "on". In a pivoting fork system force *A* places an upward load upon the pivot bearing. Force *B* tends to twist the assembly about the longitudinal axis of the machine.

53

wards, putting an upward force on the bearing which, on a powerful model, may be as much as 400 lb. This, fortunately, acts in opposition to the general tendency of the rear end to sink when accelerating, but may be the greater of the two forces if the forks are very short and the torque transmitted is high.

On the other hand, under braking conditions this torque reaction is reversed and the pivot tends to be depressed, so that under alternating applications of power and brakes a "bucking" action can be initiated which does not improve the handling. This possibility was avoided in the early shaft-drive M.V.s by duplicating the forks and mounting the bevel-box between the ends, thus making the whole assembly a jointed parallelogram able to absorb braking and torque reactions in a vertical plane within itself, at the expense of much weight and complication.

The transverse torque-reaction (B), tending to twist the axle out of the horizontal plane, would have still worse effects on steering if not guarded against by sufficient torsional stiffness of the forks, but if they are stiff enough to cope with normal road shocks they should be able to handle this reaction without a detrimental degree of deflection. The reaction as measured in foot-pounds varies with the gear ratio and engine power, but in round figures may be taken as 150 lb./ft. per litre of engine capacity in bottom gear. It can reach much higher momentary values when rapid down-changes are being made against the inertia of the engine. The reversal of torque may then cause the rear end to kick sideways as the rear fork momentarily twists.

Resistance to lateral loads is a major factor in the design of any suspension system. Since many bumps are struck obliquely, alternating lateral forces are continually applied to the tyre, and if the suspension mechanism contains any slackness the wheel will oscillate from side to side even if the impulses are small. Heavier forces may cause elastic deformation or even a permanent set in the structure, as when cornering at extreme angles the lateral impulsive load on a 400-lb. machine may exceed 600 lb.

To resist forces of this order without detrimental effects, the stiffness of the wheel relative to the centre-section of the frame should be such that a load of 250 lb. applied sideways to the tyre near its contact point will not twist the wheel more than $1°$ (or a little less than $\frac{1}{4}$ in. by direct measurement), nor displace the whole wheel by more than $\frac{1}{8}$ in. It is of course essential that on removal of the load the wheel should return to its original position, which may not occur if the fork is built up from several components in such a manner that it relies for its rigidity on frictional grip rather than on precise mechanical location.

When cornering with a sidecar the lateral forces may be very much higher, but in this instance flexing of the structure will not have such serious effects as on a solo, provided that there is sufficient strength to prevent the structure taking a permanent set.

It will be appreciated, therefore, that the design of a frame with pivoted rear springing introduces many problems which do not exist in the rigid frame and obviously this has a profound effect on the whole layout. Provision has to be made for a crew of two, with the passenger's weight overhung a long distance from the main frame, and means must be found for attaching silencers, stands and other items which can

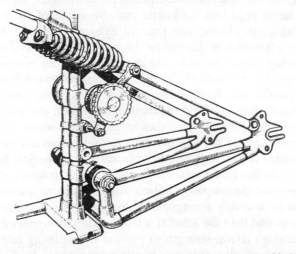

FIG. 5.5. The Bentley and Draper rear springing system, incorporating friction damping. The two pivot bearings were independent (see Fig. 5.10).

simply be bolted to convenient places on a rigid or plunger-sprung design. The fitting of a sidecar also must be borne in mind.

In discussing the general effect upon frame design of swinging-fork suspension, the first part of this chapter stressed the importance of eliminating flexure in the region of the bearing-mounting. It is clear that the best way of doing so is to design the centre section with this primary object in view, rather than to utilize a composite structure which depends on several components bolted together; at the same time, provision can be made for carrying the overhung weight of the crew.

In many of the early designs, such as the Bentley and Draper type (Fig. 5.5), the rear springs were mounted under the saddle in a nearly horizontal position, which is quite a good arrangement in one way because the forward thrust from the springs is acting in opposition to the rearward thrust in the top tube created by the rake of the forks, so that the tendency towards "lozenging" of the centre section is reduced, at least under static conditions.

One of the first significant examples of a frame conceived from the beginning as a rear-sprung structure, instead of being merely a rigid frame with springing added, was the one designed in 1928 by P. C. Vincent, which incorporated a patented triangulated rear fork of great strength. It was illustrated in Chapter 4, Fig. 4.14.

In side elevation, this frame comprised three triangles, the front and rear ones being rigid and the centre one, by virtue of the pivot and springs, elastic. It will be seen that all dynamic loads on the pivot bearing were transmitted directly to the main frame tubes and, as the whole structure was 11 in. wide, the chain pull was not overhung from the bearings. At the front the design was not so sound because, as originally made, the front down-tube supplied more fore-and-aft rigidity than the top tube and the duplex side tubes, due partly to the closeness of these three higher tubes at the points where they joined the head and partly to the way in which the side tubes left the head at a wide included angle. As a result the front tube broke just below the weld; but since the frame was still complete as a structure even with this tube broken, the simplest solution was to make an artificial break in the tube by inserting a tongue-and-slot joint with a horizontal pin through it, so that the tube acted as a tension stay to support the power unit with enough lateral strength to prevent it oscillating laterally.

A still better solution that was finally adopted was to discard this frame altogether in favour of a simple tubular edition (Fig. 5.6), with the bearing contained in a robust casting surrounding the gearbox and

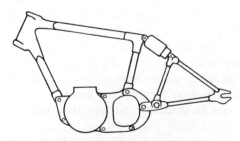

Fig. 5.6. In the Vincent "springer" of 1932, the swinging fork pivot was housed in a stout casting surrounding the gearbox.

bolted to engine plates of such vertical height that the whole unit was very rigid in itself, as well as being lighter than the earlier design.

Carrying a Passenger

The difficulty with any design which has the springs located under the saddle nose is that of accommodating a pillion passenger (or a rider in the accepted racing attitude) other than by seating the passenger on a violently oscillating mudguard. There are only two alternatives—to build a structure which is cantilevered out from the centre section and may or may not incorporate the mudguard, or to design a seat-frame hinged at the front and supported at the rear by stays from the forks.

The first solution is the cleaner mechanically, but has two disadvantages. First, the overhung length is unavoidably great due to the far-forward location of the spring abutments, which in turn entails a liability for the tail-section to oscillate laterally. Secondly, the effect of the passenger's overhung weight on the springs is very great, causing them to compress much more than normally and leaving less available movement before the limit of travel is met. To realize how serious this effect may be, it should be appreciated that the weight on the rear end of a 380-lb. machine with an eight-stone rider is 250 lb. in round figures, whereas with a crew of two 14-stoners the weight increases to 500 lb.

This variation, of course, is bound to occur whatever sort of springing is used and necessitates some action to meet it—such as using springs of variable length or strength, or altering the mechanical leverage of the springing system—and successful solutions along these lines are found on many machines built recently.

The Hinged Pillion Seat

The method of using a hinged pillion seat is interesting more as an exercise in mechanics than for its practical application, since it is no longer used. The scheme (illustrated in Fig. 5.7) is to pin-joint a seat-base to the saddle-lug and support its rear end by jointed stays rising from the fork tubes, the whole arrangement forming a pin-jointed quadrilateral. If the stays were pivoted near the rear axle, the end of the seat would rise at wheel speed and thus be virtually unsprung, but by placing the stay-pivots nearer to the line *PB* the movement is reduced, although clearance must then be provided between the seat and the guard. If, as a compromise, the movement at the top of the stays is arranged to be $1\frac{1}{2}$ in. when the wheel rises 3 in., the rear end will be semi-sprung without being raised too high, yet at the same time the increase in weight on the springs will be only about 30 per cent. of what it would be if the seat were attached directly to the centre-section. Therefore the effect of the additional weight can be borne by the same set of springs without much more liability to bottoming, although the comfort provided is not of such a high order as if the seat were fully sprung.

Swinging forks produced about 30 years ago were, in the main, built to resemble the rear stays which they replaced, but lacked rigidity because the triangles at each side were not interconnected with sufficient care. In one design, used by several makes, each fork-leg was composed of a shallow triangle joined by a cross-member which did not surround the bearing, but lay several inches below, the two corners in which the bearing bushes were housed being, in effect, free (Fig. 5.10). When a twisting moment was applied to the rear axle, the cross-member was placed in bending as well as in torsion, instead of in pure torsion as it would have been if it had surrounded the pivot. Transverse loads also tended to distort the whole structure, and it was in consequence not very successful. The stays which transmitted loads to the springs added a little strength, but with a degree of complication not commensurate with their effectiveness.

A less complicated and more effective method is to join the two side-triangles rigidly together at the upper and lower front corners, making one of the connections the housing for the pivot-bearing. Ideally, excluding this short cross-member there should be six tubes forming a

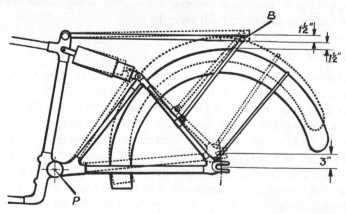

Fig. 5.7. The principle of the hinged pillion seat. By locating the lower seat-stay pivots nearer to the line *PB* than to the wheel axle, seat movement is reduced as compared with axle movement—in this case, by two to one. There is $1\frac{1}{2}$ in. of clearance between seat and guard at normal load.

FIG. 5.8. A large cross-tube close behind the 3½-in. down-tube gives great torsional rigidity to the swinging fork of this Reynolds frame.

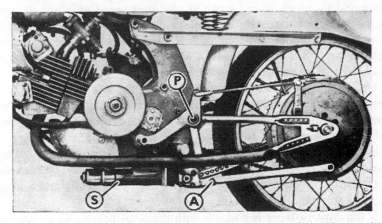

FIG. 5.9. Sprung rear end of the 1947 250 c.c. Guzzi twin. A swinging fork with triangulated side members, joined at *P* and *A*, and pivoting at *P*, was controlled by a horizontal spring unit *S* below the engine.

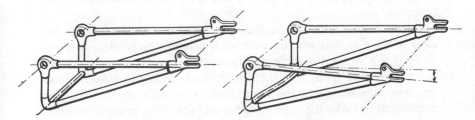

FIG. 5.10. How the cross-member of a built-up swinging fork will bend as well as twist if located at some distance from a pair of independent bearings.

pyramid of immense rigidity, but the substitution of a well-designed lug at the apex, although it has to be wide enough to clear the mud-guard, gives results which are almost as good. "Apex" in this context means the corner not occupied by the pivot; it could be located either above the pivot or below it, as in some Guzzi designs. The Guzzi arrangement permitted the springs to be mounted horizontally below the power unit, keeping the weight low and leaving more free space for the oil tank. However it is laid out in detail, the essence of this scheme is to provide rigid junctions at both front corners of the two triangles as shown in Fig. 4.14 (page 43).

LIGHTNESS WITH STRENGTH

It is axiomatic that in any suspension system the unsprung weight should be kept to the minimum. Although the triangulated rear fork is not too bad in this respect, because the heavy parts are close to the pivot and therefore do not move at any great speed, it is not so good as the plain fork consisting of two legs and a cross-member, which has now become almost universal. When the springs are attached to the axle-lugs, the fork legs are relieved of weight-carrying stresses and their major duty is to maintain wheel alignment.

Under both transverse and twisting loads, the side-tubes of the fork are subjected to almost pure bending stresses, which increase in intensity towards the bearing. Ideally, therefore, they should be tapered tubes, though parallel tubes are often employed. The difference in weight is only a matter of ounces, while the raw material cost of the parallel tube is very much less; also it becomes possible to do away with cast or forged axle-lugs by flattening the tubes locally and slotting them to accommodate the axle.

If the cross-member is co-axial with the pivot-bearing—i.e., consists either of a tube surrounding it or a solid spindle passing through the centre—twisting moments on the rear axle subject it to pure torsion, while lateral loads subject it to bending stresses which are most intense at the junction-points; the shorter the fork, the less do these loads become.

In the case of shaft-drive, the cross-member can be located just clear of the tyre, but with chain drive it may not be possible to get as close as this without making the distance between the gearbox centre and the pivot so great that undesirable chain-tension variations are set up. Also, the design of the main frame may be such that it is not convenient to make the cross-member and the pivot co-axial, in which event the former has to be moved towards the wheel and thereby becomes subject to bending as well as torsion under the influence of axle-twisting loads. It must therefore be stronger for the same degree of stiffness as that furnished by the co-axial design—a point which evidently is not always appreciated. A very good example of the way it should be done is the Reynolds frame illustrated, which has a large cross-tube located behind the $3\frac{1}{2}$-in. down-tube, affording a structure of great strength and simplicity (Fig. 5.8).

Another method, used on the racing Velocettes which first demonstrated the value of a well-engineered plain fork, is to clamp two separate fork-blades to a solid spindle, splined at each end to provide a positive mechanical resistance to movement. This entails some very accurate machining, as the slightest error in angular location of the splines on the shaft or in the lugs would have a magnified effect at the fork-ends.

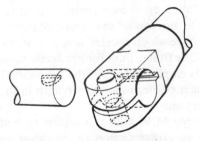

FIG. 5.11. Arm of a swinging fork keyed to the spindle.

An easier scheme (Fig. 5.11) is to cut two Woodruff keyways dead in line in the spindle and mill each lug with a slot which cuts into the metal on the far side of the bore, thus forming a keyway and, in the same machining operation, providing a gap to permit the lug to be clamped to the spindle. Of course, each keyway must also be very accurately located in relation to its opposite number and the keys *must* be a tight fit in the keyways. This form of construction lends itself to adoption if the frame has a single down-tube, as the spindle, which should be case-hardened, can then oscillate in bronze bushes housed in a wide, substantial lug and assembly becomes a simple matter.

This is, however, still rather an expensive solution and is heavier than a welded-up fork with a cross-tube surrounding the bearing. The latter layout fits in very well with a full duplex frame, because the inner member of the bearing can be mounted directly on the two vertical tubes below the saddle, as exemplified in the "Featherbed" Norton frame (Fig. 5.13). These tubes are very widely spaced, so they afford good support to the fork-bearing, but as the loads are applied approximately midway along the tubes they are locally stiffened by gusset-plates, to provide a good depth of section in the plane of major stress.

This frame, which has been eminently successful ever since its introduction in 1950, deserves special mention. In its original form (see Chapter 4, Fig. 4.15, page 44) it was constructed from two tubes, each bent to a four-sided shape and with the forward ends crossed just before they arrived at the head-lug. As the corner bends were of several inches radius there was not much likelihood of undesirable stress concentrations, but looked at in side elevation it did not appear to be unduly strong at the point where the tubes crossed along a common horizontal axis. The engine, which fitted between the tubes both above and below, was stayed to a cross-member joining the tank-rails just behind the main tubes' cross-over point, and there was another stay running upwards to the top of the steering-head; in effect these two stays formed a triangle which resisted fore-and-aft loads in the column. In later editions of the frame, built for production models, an additional sheet-steel gusset is employed to join the head-tube to the down-tubes, thus providing much greater inherent strength in this region. Fig. 5.13 shows the 1960 version.

The half-litre racing M.V. utilizes a similar type of frame. Reference has been made in an earlier section to the clever way in which transmission stresses have been absorbed in this model by passing the pivot

Fig. 5.12. Shaft drive of the Velocette "Valiant" is housed in the nearside arm of the swinging fork, which is a one-piece alloy casting.

spindle through a lug cast on the rear of the power-unit and also through the rear down-tubes. The primary transmission stresses are, of course, all internal to the unit and have no effect on the frame, but the large block bulk of the engine poses a problem in assembling and dismantling. This has been solved by making the duplex tubes detachable, with long spigots at each end, but it is doubtful whether such an

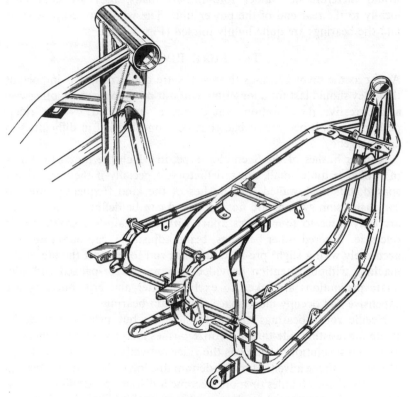

Fig. 5.13. The 1960 version of the Norton "Featherbed" frame has "waisted" rails; The top drawing shows the gusset plate uniting down-tubes and steering head.

arrangement would have provided sufficient rigidity had the pivot-bearing design been less effective. In the 350 c.c. model, although the power-unit is the same size, the loop tubes are integral but the single top tube is removable. Great care has been taken with the end-attachments of this vital member; additional branch-tubes enable it to be attached with three close-fitting bolts at each end.

On the small shaft-driven Velocette machines, which have duplex tubes below the saddle, an interesting rear fork is employed. This takes the form of a one-piece casting made of strong aluminium alloy with the propeller shaft and universal joint enclosed in one leg; the section uniting the sides is co-axial with the pivot-bearings, which are spaced very widely apart and attached to the duplex down-tubes. As, for other reasons, these tubes are bowed outwards to a considerable extent and would therefore flex under fore-and-aft loads, they are connected locally to the rear end of the power unit. The whole structure is rigid and the bearings are quite lightly loaded (Fig. 5.12).

THE FORK PIVOT

As far as the pivot bearings themselves are concerned, it is important that they should last for a long time without developing wear, otherwise a progressive deterioration would occur, unnoticed by the rider, perhaps, until it became so bad that he found himself in difficulties in an emergency.

Rubber bushes of the Silentbloc type, in which the radial thickness of rubber is quite small, are satisfactory, especially if they are widely spaced, but thick-walled, soft bushes of the kind frequently fitted to car suspension systems are not good and can be definitely bad if they are only three to four inches apart with the chain-line overhung on one side. Tapered roller bearings, being adjustable, can be set up very accurately with a slight pre-load and will run for almost the life of the machine without attention provided they are grease-packed and adequate precautions are taken to exclude water and grit, but they are expensive and occupy more space than plain bearings.

Needle roller bearings are quite suitable, but provision must be made for resisting side-thrust. Bronze bushes are probably the cheapest and lightest solution, so long as the rider remembers to lubricate them, although with the advent of molybdenum disulphide lubricants, greasing intervals of 10,000 miles or more become a distinct possibility. Porous-bronze, oil-impregnated bushes are also suitable, provided that they are not too heavily loaded; but even with these, provision should be made for periodic lubrication and, of course, great care should be taken to exclude dust and water by the provision of adequate seals.

THE TAIL SECTION

In the design sense it is not possible to separate the tail section from the main frame, as the two finally form a single assembly, but there are a number of minor points and one or two major problems which it is convenient to group under the general heading of "rear end".

It has already been noted that the tail structure must be able to carry 300 or 400 lb. weight on a touring model, and all this is overhung or cantilevered out from the centre section.

Lateral movement in relation to the main frame, although it does not affect wheel-alignment, is detrimental to good handling because of the jelly-like sensation it engenders. Even if such major oscillations do not occur, any overhung structure, especially if it is approximately of an inverted U section, is likely to vibrate in resonance with the engine at some speed, as demonstrated by the persistence and rapidity with which some mudguards have cracked under racing conditions.

The leverage exerted by the tail structure on the centre section can be reduced to a very small amount, when using a plain swinging fork, by running the spring-units almost straight up. It is advisable, however, to lean the top ends of the units forward so that their centre-lines shall be more nearly square to the radius drawn through the fork pivot to the mean centre of the units. This reduces the movement of the heavily loaded bearings and indirectly improves the life of the units, because there is then less side-loading applied to the small-diameter sliding spindles which keep the units in line and operate the hydraulic damping mechanism.

Since the units should take absolutely no part in maintaining wheel-alignment, soft rubber bushes are quite satisfactory. In any event it is desirable for both the upper and lower bearings to be of a type which are self-aligning in all directions without strain on the units, as there is bound to be a certain amount of malalignment existing at times between the extremities of the springs.

Once the location of the springs has been decided, the design of the supporting structure can be tackled. The most straightforward idea is to attach a tubular frame to the seat lug, extending back to the end of the dual seat, and brace it by means of a diagonal stay on each side, running from a point close to the top spring anchorage to another point adjacent to the pivot bearing.

When this form is adopted on a wide duplex frame, such as the Norton "Featherbed", the structure is reasonably rigid laterally, though much of the stiffness in the "Featherbed" case is derived from the fact that all four tube-ends are welded to the main structure. If the attachments are closer together, or composed only of bolts passing through flattened and drilled tube-ends, lateral rigidity may well be insufficient unless some additional cross-bracing is supplied to the tube forming the top run of the structure, such as by the addition of a built-in toolbox or by firmly uniting the mudguard and the tube.

65

A logical development of the duplex cradle frame is to bend the two lower tubes upwards below the power unit and run them from there to meet rearward extensions of the top tube close to the upper spring mounting points. The fork-bearing can then be carried in a substantial lug at the lower end of the saddle down-tube.

A modification of this plan is seen in the 1960 A.J.S. and Matchless heavyweight touring frame (Fig. 5.14). Here, the duplex main frame is

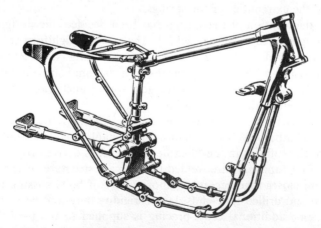

FIG. 5.14. A.J.S. frame treatment in two fields. The 7R racer (above) has a simple form of duplex cradle. A sturdy separate sub-frame is employed in the 1960 heavyweight touring frame (below); a massive lug carries the fork bearing.

Fig. 5.15. B.M.W. contrast. The main frame members of the R69 tourer (top), extending farther back than those of the racer (bottom), provide attachment points for pillion footrests and silencers.

matched by a sub-frame formed of a single tube on each side, a "lazy V" in elevation, with the fabricated upper anchorage lug of the spring unit welded to the apex. The two tubes are united by a cross-brace below the seat.

In the racing versions of the A.J.S., however, the down-tube is omitted and the pivot is carried directly on the cradle-tubes. This layout involves rather an extensive length of top-tube, and as the engine is steadied against torque reaction by a bracket which hangs below the tube approximately half-way along it, there is a distinct possibility

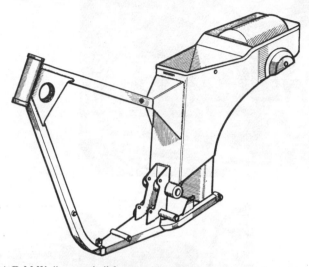

FIG. 5.16. A D.M.W. "composite" frame, with squared tubes married to a central pressed "box" which neatly accommodates various auxiliaries.

FIG. 5.17. On some M.V. "fours", welded-up cantilever brackets carry the upper suspension pivots. Note the three-rate spring.

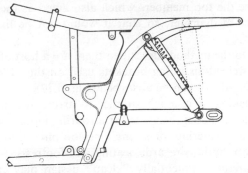

Fig. 5.18. The "seat tubes" themselves are produced to form a cantilever support for seat and suspension pivots in this modern Guzzi lightweight frame; they are actually pressings.

that this member might be set into resonant vibration at some point in the engine speed range. Even at the expense of a couple of pounds extra weight, additional stays between the top tube and the pivot-bearing brackets might well improve this frame, as indeed some experiments have already indicated.

It is interesting to note that many years ago the Nimbus, of Danish origin, employed a frame which was basically similar in essentials, but

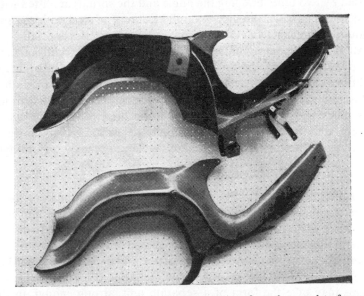

Fig. 5.19. The simplest treatment of all—two pressings form the complete frame and "rear end" of the Dutch Magneet moped.

in this instance the top member, which also acted as the petrol tank, was five inches in diameter, so that it would not be likely to suffer from vibration.

In addition to the methods described there are a host of others, such as the simple welded-up spring brackets used on the M.V. "four", by which the spring-thrust can be absorbed (Fig. 5.17).

Broadly speaking, it is much simpler to arrive at a neat, effective design for a racing model than it is for a touring mount because in the former case one is catering for a single person only, instead of having to allow for two, both as regards seating and footrests. In fact, unless one is very careful, a potentially "clean" design may end up as an unsightly collection of bent tubes and brackets by the time that mountings for extra footrests, two silencers and the rear stand have been provided, as well as places for attaching a sidecar.

The racing and touring versions of the B.M.W. illustrate the way in which the matter can be approached from two directions. The racer has a duplex cradle frame with near-vertical down-tubes and a bolted-on seat frame and practically nothing else extending rearward behind the pivot-bearing. In the road model, however, the duplex tubes run back past the tyre, curve upwards just ahead of the axle and finally meet the end of the top tube near the saddle-nose. The pivot bearing is carried by two tubes bridging the angle and the springs are fitted within fixed housings which provide enough clearance to deal with the small amount of angular swing of the units as the wheel rises and falls.

All the additional mounting points are fixed to the bottom run of the tubes, which are braced by a gusset to a cross-member to give additional lateral rigidity. A sidecar mounting ball is provided on the right-hand side only. The extreme rearward location of this ball-joint must place very great bending loads on the tube, despite the bracing gussets, and from this aspect it would be preferable to move the mounting farther forward and design the sidecar chassis accordingly.

MUDGUARD TREATMENT

When the mudguard is fully sprung, it is desirable to make it deeply valanced, partly for cleanliness and partly to obviate the unpleasing gap which would otherwise exist between guard and wheel when the model is unladen. It is then but a short step from a framework supporting the guard to a sheet-steel structure which forms the guard and a platform on which the seating accommodation can be placed.

This may take the form of a separate unit, strong enough in itself to be fixed directly to the main frame, or may be more in the nature of full enclosure applied over the top of a framework. In this way, it is possible to clean up the whole appearance of the rear end, with little additional weight, especially as toolboxes, battery-compartments or even the air cleaner can be let into recesses in the sheet-metal work and smoothly covered with flush-fitting lids or by a hinge-up seat cushion.

This is one of the fields where the stylist can be allowed a certain amount of scope. It is necessary to achieve smoothly flowing lines without a bulky appearance, as bulk to many people implies heaviness as well; also, it is all too easy to finish up with a model consisting of two utterly contrasting styles, with the front end looking about 10 years out of date compared with the rear.

Ease of wheel removal presents a problem. The best course is to make the rear end of the mudguard portion either hinged or completely detachable—preferably the former, because there is then no need to detach the wire running to the tail-light. Whichever method is preferred, it is not too easy to provide a joint which will remain rattle-proof and watertight indefinitely, and nothing looks much worse than streaks of mud sullying an otherwise clean surface.

Further, the presence of the joint weakens the structure to a considerable degree, and if this is in fact a stress-bearing member and not just an added enclosure it is necessary to reinforce the section locally with a welded-in pressing to prevent the sides of the U from spreading under load, which in turn would allow the tail section to vibrate vertically, especially if its mass were increased by a number-plate and tail-lamp.

Provided that the stand has enough lift to permit the wheel to drop to the full extent of its travel, the wheel may possibly be removed from the side without much juggling if the valance is not too deep, but if the valance is very deep the rider may have to lean the machine to one side and hold it there with one hand whilst extracting the wheel with the other—a feat which may well be beyond the capabilities of some individuals.

Since tyre trouble, though rare, almost invariably occurs at the most inconvenient moments, it is in the rider's interests to go to some pains to make wheel removal as easy as possible under all circumstances, which might include the presence of heavy pannier bags. All in all, the hinged guard is probably the most convenient system, though the Norton idea of providing a slot closed by the number-plate is quite good.

When a pressed-steel frame of the backbone or spine type is used, making the end of the guard separate is a natural thing to do, because

71

it reduces the length of the main pressings and enables them to be blanked out of sheets of more economical size and with less waste of material. Also the press-tools are much smaller, and since their cost goes up roughly as the square of the general dimensions of the part being manufactured the tooling cost is lessened considerably. Admittedly, additional tools are required for the tail-piece but this can be made from a single pressing of relatively small size, and possibly of lighter-gauge material.

However, opinions differ on this point and some makers, especially in Italy, prefer to use two complete half-pressings, welded together, particularly for the lightweight class of machine where every ounce of extra weight makes a difference.

How Much Movement?

A subject which must be given consideration at the design stage is the amount of sprung movement which the rear wheel is to have. For various reasons, the movement has perforce to be reduced below that necessary to absorb the largest bumps in full—partly because, if this were done, the increase in head angle and trail which would result when the rear springs were fully compressed and the front ones fully extended might adversely affect the steering at a critical moment, especially on short-wheel-base models. Also, as the clearance of the crankcase or the lower frame members above ground, and that of the mudguard above the tyre, must both be fixed in relation to the "full-bump" position, a large spring-range is inclined to give rise to an unduly high and ungainly appearance when no rider is on board, and unfortunately it is in this state that the lines of a model are usually judged.

The point is of no importance for trials and scrambles models, where functionalism is more important than good looks and a high ground clearance is better than a hole in the crankcase. Quite apart from pure appearance, however, a high unloaded seat position makes it difficult for small persons to support the model with both feet on the ground when stationary, though of course the wheel diameter exerts an influence in determining the final seat height.

The question of how high the seat should be is one which has been debated for years. At one time there was a craze for ultra-low seats, achieved by frames which ran almost straight from the head to the rear axle, and even after it had been proved that such lowness was not only uncomfortable but undesirable the phrase "very low saddle position" reappeared annually in publicity material.

72

Trials riders go to the opposite extreme using heights which enable them to stand upright on the footrests easily. Raising the centre of gravity of the rider also helps in another way, which is analogous to the actions of a juggler balancing a plate on top of a stick. This is easier to do with a long stick than with a short one, because the plate, being so far away from the juggler's hand, remains almost stationary in space, while the lower end of the stick is moved about to maintain the edifice in equilibrium. Similarly, when a rider is poised high the wheels can veer from side to side when forced to deviate from the straight by gutters or stones, without much tendency to move the rider's centre of gravity.

In normal use, some consideration has to be given to comfort and convenience, especially in view of the fact that human beings vary not only in height, but in their proportions. This can be accommodated to some extent by adjustable footrests, but there is a limit to how far these can be moved without introducing the serious hazard of grounding on corners. As previously noted, the outer ends of the rests must not protrude beyond two planes drawn at 45° to the maximum upward wheel positions if this possibility is to be avoided.

Present F.I.M. regulations governing road-racing models stipulate that the minimum angle of lean before *any part* touches the ground shall be 50° from the vertical measured with the machine *unladen*.

Generally speaking, a saddle height of 30 to 31 inches is a reasonable compromise which seems to meet most conditions, both as regards stability and the stature of the rider. The modern trend towards fixed dual seats has almost eliminated one of the virtues of the old-pattern saddle—adjustability for height; although there is no reason why even a dual-seat top could not be made with a possible variation of one or two inches.

CHAPTER 6

Springing and Damping Methods

ANY suspension system for a road vehicle must possess two basic properties—elasticity to absorb bumps, and damping to prevent the build-up of undesirable oscillations. The necessity for the first-named is evident, but the second needs a little explanation.

Briefly, if a body suspended by a spring in such a way that there is no friction present, is displaced and then released, it will oscillate or vibrate for a considerable time. The amplitude or total length of movement at the commencement will be just twice that of the original displacement, but will eventually die away to zero, partly because of air-friction and partly through energy-loss in the spring material. Acting together, these damp out the vibration and dissipate the stored energy in the form of heat.

In practice a vehicle with undamped springing will bounce up and down several times after striking a single bump, and if it traverses a succession of bumps at a speed corresponding to the natural frequency of vibration of the main mass of the vehicle on the springs, the oscillations will build up until they become dangerously violent. If, however, some means of absorbing energy is incorporated—such as by friction-pads or by forcing oil through small orifices—free vibrations will be damped out rapidly and forced vibrations will be kept within tolerable bounds.

Damping also works to prevent "overthrow" of the wheels over bumps. When a bump is struck at high speed, the wheel attains a considerable upward velocity and may leave the ground at (or even before) the crest of the bump because the momentum of the wheel over-compresses the spring. An additional damping force will reduce this overthrowing tendency by absorbing some energy which would otherwise be applied to the spring.

If a model "takes off" over a bridge or meets a sudden drop in height of the surface, the suspension will momentarily have little or no weight on it, so that on landing the springs are partly or fully extended. As the weight comes down hard, the springs will be compressed beyond their normal-load position and immediately afterwards will throw back

74

violently unless damping can be provided on the rebound stroke. Some makers, in fact, consider that rebound damping is all that is necessary, and that any damping on the bump stroke only results in a harder ride. Whilst that view is true to some extent, it is possible to meet conditions—on corrugations, for instance—where the wheel is repeatedly jolted upwards and does not have time to recover from one bump against the rebound damping before the next bump pushes it up still farther, so the springs become over-compressed and the ride remains uncomfortable as long as the conditions continue.

However, this is a point which will be discussed later (see pages 80–84). The salient fact is that no suspension system can function satisfactorily without some form of damping, which may or may not be inherent in the springs themselves.

Types of Spring

As to these components, there are three main materials employed in the manufacture of elastic devices for suspension systems in general. These are steel, rubber and air. All have been tried in one way or another for both the front and the rear springing of motorcycles. Steel is by far the most popular, but as the two non-ferrous materials possess qualities which are peculiar to themselves, it may be worth while to examine them first before turning attention to the more usual material.

Air

Air can operate as a spring only when compressed in an airtight container of variable volume. The variation may be achieved by a cylinder-and-piston arrangement, in which the piston is either a plunger or a rising column of oil. Alternatively, the air-chamber may be closed by a flexible diaphragm which is itself acted upon by oil under pressure transmitted from the suspension mechanism, on the lines of the system used in Citroën cars.

In whatever way it is compressed, air has the property of providing a progressive spring-rate, this being one of its outstanding properties. The term "rate" as applied to a spring means the amount of load, measured in pounds, which is required to compress the spring one inch—or, in the case of air, to compress the device in which the air is contained.

A normal parallel-wound helical coil spring has a constant rate; that is to say, if it takes 100 lb. to compress it one inch, another 100 lb. will compress it a further inch, and so on until it becomes coil-bound. However, with air (taking as an example a simple piston-and-cylinder arrangement) the rate rises continuously from the start of compression until it reaches an infinitely high value at the end of the stroke. Furthermore, as air cannot be compressed into no space at all, mechanical bottoming is impossible, though the final pressures generated might be hundreds of pounds to the square inch.

Maintaining a perfect air-seal indefinitely with a reciprocating piston would be virtually impossible, but if the air is compressed by a rising column of oil, as in the Dowty oleo-pneumatic strut utilized on Velocette racing models, or the Dowty fork, direct leakage of air is prevented and hydraulic damping can be provided at the same time by making the oil pass through controllable orifices on its way to and from the air-chamber. Sealing glands are still necessary to retain the oil, and entirely eliminating leakage past these, though not impossible, is a difficult problem, partly because of the inevitably gritty environment and partly because the pressures developed can reach very high values.

Consequently oleo-pneumatic struts are both expensive and heavy and are not at present employed on motorcycles. The fact remains that they provide suspension characteristics which cannot be exactly duplicated by any coil-spring system. Moreover, they are easily adjusted to sustain various loads, or to alter the quality of the suspension to suit different road conditions, merely by the application of a tyre-pump.

On the other hand, when air is compressed it becomes hot and some of the heat of compression generated on each bump stroke is transmitted to the cylinder, so that under continuous working the whole unit rises in temperature and consequently in pressure, thereby jacking up the rear end a little (in the case of rear suspension) and increasing the hardness of the ride. This effect can be quite noticeable and was, in fact, a matter which had to be allowed for in setting the air-pressure when oleo-pneumatic legs were employed for racing.

Despite its disadvantages, however, air-springing might well merit further attention today, especially on machines with an overhung rear axle carried, scooter-style, on a single arm. As only one unit would be required, the additional cost would not be excessive and the problem of obtaining equal pressures in a pair of units without an undesirable balance pipe would be non-existent.

Historically-minded students of design may recollect that a single air-spring was fitted to both the front and the rear suspension of the A.S.L., *circa* 1910. The air was retained by an ingenious rolling sleeve which, however, precluded full use of the progressive-rate feature, as, being made of soft rubber devoid of reinforcement, it would have been unable to withstand the high peak pressures developed at full bump.

Rubber

Rubber has several properties which make it an attractive springing medium. It can be used in tension or compression. It can be moulded into almost any shape. It can be bonded to metal parts so firmly that the rubber will fail before the bond gives way. Finally, by suitably varying the "mix" or by the addition of fillers it can be endowed with a great amount of inherent damping capacity through the absorption of energy by hysteresis ("internal friction"). This action generates heat right in the heart of the rubber, and if too much inherent damping is provided, extremely severe conditions may cause softening or even destruction of the material; on that account some additional form of damping is usually necessary.

One disadvantage of rubber is that the working range is rather small and therefore it is necessary to multiply the deflection by some system of leverage. A simple way of achieving this is to use a pair of blocks, one above and one below the pivot-bearing of a swinging fork, and compress them between abutments on the frame and the forks; but this introduces heavy local loads which do not exist when the springs are arranged in a direct line between the axle and the weight to be supported. A rather interesting construction, using conical rubbers in torsion mounted co-axially with the pivot, was developed some years ago by Spencer-Moulton, but here again heavy local loads were generated and, owing to the low rate of the torsion-rubbers, additional rubber stops were necessary to limit the travel in both directions.

Rubber has been used on front forks, in a very simple way, merely by hooking a number of rubber bands over bobbins, a progressive rate being obtained by making some of the bands slack in the normal position so that they only came into action towards the end of the bump stroke.

In the Greeves front fork, bonded rubber bushes are used at the pivots of the leading-link forks to act both as oscillating bearings and as springs, the rubber in this instance being in shear, not torsion. As the links are joined by a loop-tube as well as by the axle, the assembly is stiff enough laterally to provide excellent steering for solo work. Hydraulic dampers concealed within the main fork tubes are required, because the small amount of rubber employed does not provide enough inherent damping for the arduous conditions in which these models usually perform (Fig. 3.10).

Three Ways with Steel

Steel can be utilized in three forms—laminated or leaf springs, torsion

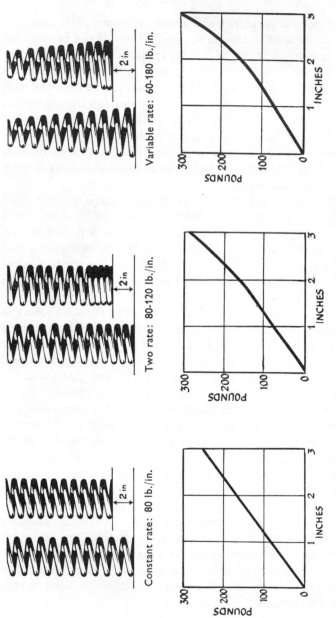

FIG. 6.1. What happens when, three types of spring are compressed. Change of rate is indicated in the graph below each example. The spring of equal pitch has no change of rate. The rate of the two-rate spring increases when its close-pitch coils have become "solid". Closure of the coils in the variable-rate spring, beginning with those of the greatest diameter, gives a progressive increase of rate.

bars or coil springs. All have been used at one time or another, either for front or rear suspension.

Leaf springs are not very suitable for motorcycles because the only shape convenient to install is the quarter-elliptic, which, being over-hung, creates heavy local loads in the mounting brackets with conse-quent liability to fatigue-failure. In any case, the leaf spring is much heavier than an equivalent coil giving the same suspension rate. Inter-leaf friction supplies a degree of inbuilt damping which is bene-ficial, but difficult to control—in fact, at times leaf springs may become almost solid if allowed to become rusty.

Torsion bars are entirely the reverse. They possess virtually no self-damping, but are difficult to employ because to avoid over-stressing the material the bars must be of considerable length, a fact which precludes their being mounted transversely. Instead, they must be installed parallel to the frame and then connected to the moving components by a link-and-lever system, all of which introduces extra weight and complication. The inboard anchorages are again a long way from the point of application of the major loads, and about the only thing that can be said in their favour for motorcycle work is that adjustment for height (though not for rate) can easily be made by turning the anchor-ages a few degrees in the desired direction.

The simplest, lightest and most convenient form is undoubtedly the coil spring, which can provide enough travel to enable suspension units to be mounted almost in line with the rear axle and then take the most direct route towards the supported weight. The ordinary spring, with coils of constant diameter and pitch, has a constant rate, but by the simple expedient of winding the coils with two or even three pitches, two-rate or triple-rate springs can be obtained.

A multi-pitch spring has a low initial rate during which *all* the coils are closing up until those with the closest pitch commence to touch or "come solid". After that point there are fewer active coils to absorb further motion and the rate becomes higher because for any given outside diameter and gauge of wire the rate is directly proportional to the number of active coils. The change in strength of a triple-rate spring occurs twice and this type begins to furnish an approximation to the characteristics of an air-spring (Fig. 5.17).

Another way to obtain a variable rate is to wind the spring to conical or barrel shape. In either form, the coils with the largest diameter are deflected farther for the same load than are the smaller ones; conse-quently they close up first, leaving fewer coils of progressively smaller diameter (and therefore greater stiffness) to take up the remainder of the travel. Barrel springs were almost universal in girder forks. This was due partly to the lack of sufficient space at the upper end to employ a parallel spring of equal overall stiffness, but in view of the short available movement a variable rate was almost essential in order to obtain a comfortable ride without undue bottoming.

This is, in fact, the prime advantage of a variable rate. The suspension is relatively soft over the initial part of its movement, thus giving good "cobblestoning", or comfort on short, small irregularities, whereas the increasing resistance at larger travel tends to prevent bottoming over severe bumps. It also has an additional advantage, when compensation for varying loads is being provided, but the additional cost of manufacture is not always considered to be justified.

Damping

Damping is an essential feature of any but the simplest type of lightweight suspension system. If the springing medium itself has no (or insufficient) internal friction, some damping device must be incorporated.

Dampers were originally termed "shock-absorbers" because their addition to an undamped system prevented bottoming, partly through

Fig. 6.2. "Full bump", Derek Powell tests the rear suspension of his Matchless to the limit as he lands at Ballaugh in the Senior T.T. of 1957.

artificially increasing the resistance to bump deflection and partly because they checked the build-up of rebound oscillations. Although the term is still in general use it is misleading, because it attributes a quality to these devices which they do not in fact possess. Their real function is to dissipate the energy stored in the spring through compression from some external source by converting it into heat, not necessarily in one stroke but in a succession of strokes in which the amplitude becomes progressively less.

Frictional Devices

Damping can be applied externally to the springs by either frictional or hydraulic methods. The former is intrinsically the less expensive,

FIG. 6.3. Friction damping with hand adjustment, as employed on rubber-in-torsion Greeves front forks up to 1956.

especially if existing components can be utilized or modified to accommodate friction-discs or pads. This method was adopted in the first girder forks to be made with in-built dampers and was later applied to the B. and D. rear suspension (see Fig. 5.5, page 55). An alternative is to fit a multi-plate damper of the Hartford pattern, as in some Guzzi designs. Contracting bands were used on the telescopic tubes enclosing the spring on some models of the Druid fork.

In all of these schemes, the amount of damping force supplied, which quantitatively is about 10 per cent. of the load on the spring, can be quickly and easily altered by turning a hand-wheel or by remote control through a Bowden cable. The damping effect is not seriously altered by temperature changes, but it is liable to be very much reduced by the presence of water or oil.

A more serious shortcoming of friction-damping is the "stiction" which is present at the break-away point when movement is commencing, or is reversing in direction at the end of each stroke. This causes the resistance to be momentarily higher than it is when the movement has been established—which is just the reverse of what is needed under "cobblestoning" conditions.

To some extent, this bad effect can be reduced by restraining the fixed plates in a manner which allows a little flexibility—for example, by the use of soft rubber bushes surrounding the reaction pins—so that a small angular movement can take place before the discs commence to slide; but this is more of a palliative than a cure. Contrary to what one might expect, the effect is made worse by the presence of a lubricant; this is so because the difference between the coefficients of static and of sliding friction is more when the surfaces are oily than when they are dry.

Another feature of friction damping as normally applied is that it is equal in intensity in both directions, so that bump damping is equal to rebound damping. This is sometimes considered to be undesirable, but a great difference of opinion exists amongst suspension engineers as to the most suitable relationship between the two. Too much bump damping leads to a hard ride, while too much on rebound may result in lack of tyre-contact following a severe shock. It is also worth noting that it is not possible to compensate for insufficient spring strength by over-damping; this merely results in a state where the spring is over-compressed and less than the normal amount of wheel movement is available.

Hydraulic Damping

Hydraulic damping is achieved by forcing oil through restrictions. These may take the form of small holes, tapered slots or annular gaps, or may be valves containing balls or discs and closed by springs. By a suitable choice of these methods, hydraulic dampers may be made to give an almost infinite variety of resistance-patterns, with practically no damping in the centre of travel and stiffening up at each end, with different resistances on the bump and rebound strokes, or any other combination required. It is also possible to make them "velocity-conscious", with the damping automatically increasing according to the rate of vertical rise of the wheel, if this is considered to be desirable.

Another excellent feature is that it is possible to provide hydraulic stops at one or both ends of the travel, by trapping a small quantity of oil in spaces from which the avenue of escape diminishes to zero in a distance of, say, half an inch or so. This brings all relative motion of the moving parts to a stop, but introduces a time-factor into the operation that greatly reduces impact-loads in a manner which is absolutely silent and moreover does not give rise to the "throw-back" which may occur with rubber stops (Fig. 6.4).

"Low-rate" Factor

When employed as a travel-limiting device on the rebound stroke, as in most telescopic forks, hydraulic stopping permits the use of low-rate springs which are partly compressed even when the forks are fully extended. This feature was in fact one of the main reasons for the superior characteristics of the telescopic fork as compared to the typical girder forks. In the latter, it was usual to anchor the springs at both ends, so that under full rebound the stress changed from compression to tension, in order to limit the fork travel—a practice automatically entailing the use of springs with a very high rate, giving a short, choppy action which was not nearly so comfortable as the long, soft movement obtainable from telescopics. Nevertheless, the "low-rate" characteristic of telescopics can be, and on occasion has been, over-emphasized to a point where the front end progresses with a slow pitching motion almost bad enough to make the rider "sea-sick" on a long journey.

Hydraulic Troubles

Hydraulic dampers are not without their troubles. One is the difficulty of retaining the oil indefinitely, a mechanical problem which has largely been solved by the use of synthetic rubber seals and polished hard-chrome-plated spindles. Another bother is frothing or aeration of the oil, which makes the damper feel "spongy" and reduces the damping effect, because the aerated oil can pass more readily through the restrictions or valves.

A third difficulty is the change in oil viscosity with rising temperature. This rise may be due simply to a change in atmospheric temperature, but it is also brought about by the heating experienced by the oil as it is forced through the restrictions. If ordinary engine oil with a low viscosity index (i.e., one which becomes noticeably thinner when warmed) is used as damper fluid, the suspension may be over-damped on a frosty morning so much that it will scarcely move, and in the resulting absence of internally generated heat, the ride will remain hard until the ambient air-temperature rise, combined with a corresponding increase in movement of the suspension, thins out the oil sufficiently to reduce the damping effect until it is back to normal.

Proprietary dampers are therefore filled with a special grade of thin oil which has a high viscosity index. Air-bubbles entrained in such oil can "separate out" more freely than from thick oil, but in any case a trace of silicone anti-foaming agent will almost entirely suppress trouble with aeration or frothing.

Coil springs which are long in relation to their diameter must be provided with some form of guide, otherwise when compressed they will suddenly buckle into a boomerang shape. The simplest method is to fit the spring over a telescopic damper which maintains the whole unit in alignment, with additional external shroud-tubes to exclude grit and improve the appearance.

Rebound Check

The spring may be attached at each end coil by some form of claw, so that under extreme rebound it acts in tension as a travel-limiter, but it is easier and cheaper to locate the spring between collars on the damper mechanism and design the latter so that it cannot extend beyond a certain distance. Mechanically this is much the simpler method of restraining the wheel from dropping too far when unloaded.

If desired, the damper can also form the bump-stop. However, the design of its internal parts may preclude this. In that case, either the spring can be permitted to close up solid or a rubber bump-stop can be incorporated, but care should be taken to avoid the occurrence of direct metal-to-metal contact on full-bump, otherwise destructive impact loads may be imposed. Even the provision of thick rubber bushes at top and bottom of the spring units will diminish the hammer-blow effect very markedly.

Whatever provision is made for limiting the travel—which, as already noted, should be in the region of $2\frac{1}{2}$ to 3 in. above the normal load or mean position—the springs will last almost indefinitely if designed so that the maximum stress does not exceed 90,000 lb./sq. in. in the most heavily stressed coils.

COMPENSATION FOR VARYING LOADS

The rear suspension of a two-wheeler suffers more than any other suspension system, except perhaps that of a motor truck, from variation in the load carried, and this is a particularly serious matter in view of the limited amount of travel permissible. If no compensation can be

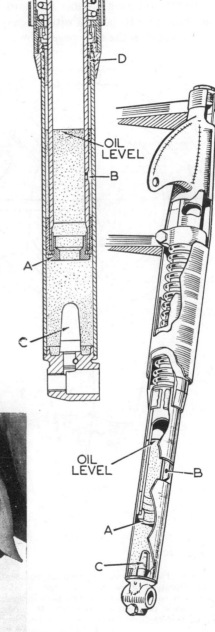

FIG. 6.4. The action of a hydraulically damped (and stopped) front fork—a B.S.A. telescopic of 1946. On compression, oil is forced through the centre of gland nut A into the upper sliding member and through hole B into the increasing annular space between the two tubes. On "full bump", tapered plug C enters A, leaving a decreasing escape route for the oil. On full rebound, maximum damping is secured when B is covered by bush D.

FIG. 6.5. (Below) Simple rubber-intension springing on the forks of a Motobécane scooter.

made the springing is either too hard for a light solo rider or too soft, and too liable to bottom with a heavy crew of two.

The table on the next page shows the effects of load variation upon

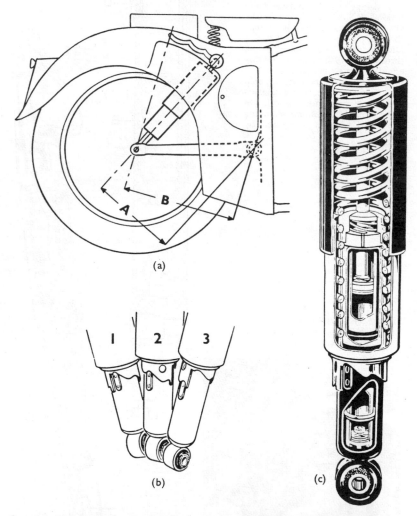

(a)

(b)   (c)

Fig. 6.6. Two methods of providing compensation for varying loads, (a) The early 1940s prototype of the modern Velocette system. Backward movement of the upper spring-unit anchorages along their slots increases the length of the lever-arm from *A* to *B*, increasing the effective spring-rate. (b) (above) Adjustment by notched cams, as used on the modern Girling unit shown in (c) on the right, varies the initial spring setting from soft (1) to medium (2) or hard (3).

travel and error in attitude (i.e., the amount by which the model is down or up at the stern from the designed mean position). The example used is a 385 lb. machine with different crews, allocating the weights carried on the rear suspension in the proportions of 66 per cent. for the rider and 100 per cent. for the passenger. Figures are given for two sets of springs, rated at 225 lb./in. and 350 lb./in. respectively, measured *at the axle*.

It will be seen that with the maximum load and the lighter springs the machine is badly down at the rear and there is only 2 in. of bump-travel available. Under the same conditions, with the heavy springs, the attitude of the model and the travel available are virtually normal, so the head angle remains unaffected and the general "feel" of the rear suspension would be the same as with the single 12-stone load and the lighter springs. With the 8-stone rider and the heavier springs, however, the ride would be very hard and the rear end elevated nearly $\frac{3}{4}$ in. above normal. This illustration makes the necessity for load compensation quite clear.

A method of achieving partial compensation by relieving the frame of most of the additional passenger weight was described in the previous chapter, but a better solution, developed and used by Velocettes, is to alter the position of the springs in relation to the axle by making the locations of the upper anchorages, adjustable; see Fig. 6.6 (a).

As the top ends are moved backward along the slots, the length of the effective lever-arm A is increased to B and the spring-rate *measured at the axle* is increased in the same proportion. The mounting points

TABLE 6.1. EFFECT OF VARIOUS LOADS

State of machine and crew	Load on rear springs	225 lb./in. 4·25 in. total compression			350 lb./in. 4·4 in. total compression		
		Deflection	Available movement	Error in height	Deflection	Available movement	Error in height
	lb.	in.	in.	in.	in.	in.	in.
Solo, unladen	170	0·75	3·5	+0·5	0·49	3·91	+0·91
Solo, 8-stone rider	250	1·1	3·15	+0·15	0·71	3·69	+0·69
Solo, 12-stone rider	280	1·25	3·0	nil	0·8	3·6	+0·6
Solo, 14-stone rider and 14-stone pillion passenger	500	2·22	2·08	−1·17	1·43	2·97	−0·03

Spring loadings, ratings and total compressions quoted are as measured at the rear axle, after allowing for any possible mechanical advantage conferred by the installation.

87

FIG. 6.7. Flash-back. This J.A.P.-engined A.S.L. (Air Springs Limited) of 1910 had pneumatic suspension at front and rear.

are not placed at a fixed radius from the axle-centre, but are arranged to be progressively lower towards the front in such fashion that the height of the saddle will remain almost constant when unloaded, irrespective of the spring setting. A rather similar scheme is used on a recent Guzzi road model, but in this case without rapid adjustability (Fig. 5.18, page 69).

The second and more common solution is to use a hydraulically damped spring-unit of a fixed maximum length which controls the full-rebound position, and to provide a moveable abutment for the lower end of the spring, so that its initial compression can be varied merely by twisting the abutment, which has graduated stops bearing on fixed pins (Fig. 6.6 (b)). If the springs are of constant rate, this expedient corrects the attitude of the machine and leaves the full amount of travel available, but does not alter the rate, so that the suspension is still liable to bottom under heavy loads. Also the periodicity or frequency of vibration is reduced and the "feel" of the suspension is different.

If, however, double- or triple-rate springs are used, the effect will be to utilize all the coils and therefore bring the low rate into action at the light-load settings, but to push the close-wound coils up solid and thus increase the spring-rate in the heavy-load setting, thereby providing a very neat and relatively inexpensive solution to a problem that did much to reduce the value of rear springing in its early days.

CHAPTER 7

Manufacturing Methods and Materials

WE have now surveyed many of the design features which theory and experience have shown to be necessary or desirable in the forks, frame and suspension system. This appears to be a good stage at which to consider the practical task of putting these features into metallic shape, which includes the choice of the most suitable materials and methods for uniting the various components embodied in the construction.

BRAZING

The classic (or, some might say, archaic) method of frame-building is by brazing steel tubes into lugs made from malleable cast-iron or steel, and this time-honoured procedure is still used in many factories today.

Most of the machining on the lugs consists of simple drilling or milling operations, with no extreme degree of accuracy in size or surface finish required. The lugs can be designed to accommodate any angles or changes in direction of the tubes, so that usually these can be either straight or contain, perhaps, one simple bend, while concentrations of stress can be taken care of by suitably ribbing the lugs or locally enlarging their cross-sectional area.

Brazing is a simple and cheap method of making joints. The process is to coat the parts with a flux in paste form after removing all grease and scale, assemble them in a frame-jig, drill one or perhaps two small holes in each joint to be brazed and drive in steel pegs to retain the parts in position while they are brought to a red heat on a hearth with the aid of a torch burning coal-gas and fed with compressed air. Brazing-brass, in the form of rod, is then applied to the joint at one end, and when molten it will penetrate right to the other end, provided the joint is at the correct temperature all through.

In the absence of a gas-torch, brazing can be done by home constructors using only a large paraffin blow-lamp on a hearth liberally heaped with coke as a backing around the joint. If no proprietary flux is available, either borax or boracic acid mixed with water can be used; in fact, boracic acid, though expensive, is the cleanest flux of all and the residual scale is easily removed.

Fig. 7.1. Assembling an A.M.C. duplex frame in its jig before brazing. Locating pegs are inserted by hand pressure only; the operator's hammer may be used to tap the frame. Flux, on the left, has been applied before jigging.

If possible the brass should always be applied to the *lowest* part of the joint, whereupon it will flow *upwards* by capillary action, pushing the lighter flux ahead of it; if it is applied at the top, it has to flow downwards in the opposite direction to the natural flow of the flux and the result may be a joint which is incompletely brazed although the brass may have appeared to run right through. For a similar reason the brass should be fed in only at one end; if it is fed at both ends, flux will be trapped in the centre of the joint.

With fork-ends or other lugs which have blind holes, it is common practice to load each hole with a mixture of flux and granulated brass called "spelter"; the joint is then heated until brass is seen to exude from the end of the lug. In order to facilitate handling and to prevent the lightly pinned joints from moving, it is usual to braze such small lugs to their mating tubes as individual sub-assemblies before finally assembling the lot in the frame-jig; this also enables a batch of components to be brazed at one time.

Reference has been made in Chapter 4 to the liability of brazed or welded frames to finish up either distorted or with internal stresses in the tubes through unequal expansion during final jointing. This must be guarded against in duplex frames by arranging the heating sequence so that the tubes are always at the same temperature at both sides of the central plane, which they will not be if the joints along one side are completed while those on the other are not.

Jigging

For pinning preparatory to brazing, frames and forks are assembled in jigs, with the lugs accurately located by hardened bars or pins fitting into hardened bushes. These jigs are sometimes built up on heavy cast-iron tables with the frame lying horizontal. Alternatively, they may be constructed to hold the frame vertical which, though a more costly form of jig to make, is preferable because there is less liability for the frame to sag when being pinned.

Brazing is also accomplished with oxy-acetylene torches, using one of the easy-flowing copper alloys specially developed for this purpose. Torch-brazing can be facilitated by the use of roll-over jigs which can be turned as the job proceeds to give better access to the joints.

All brazed frames must be checked for alignment and trued-up if necessary after cooling, this process demanding a tolerable degree of "know-how" if it is to be done quickly and accurately. The important points to check are the positions relative to the centre-line of the steering-head and pivot-bearing brackets, and the squareness of the latter to the centre plane in all directions. The smallest error in the second particular will result in a machine which has an inherent tendency to run to one side; the same point applies, of course, to the rear forks.

One trouble with brass as a jointing material is that it has the extraordinary property of penetrating into the steel itself with such rapidity that if a tube is heated and then bent when coated with molten brass it will break clean through. This is the reason why, when a damaged tube is being unbrazed from a lug, it often breaks off and leaves a piece inside if handled at all roughly. Therefore when a frame is being "set" the heat must always be kept well away from any areas covered with brass or bronze, otherwise an incipient but quite un-suspected crack may occur with the probability of subsequent complete failure due to stress-concentration in the weakened area.

Filing Up

However carefully it is made, a brazed joint always requires to be cleaned-up by shot-blasting and filing to remove scale and any excess brass, especially if the frame is to be rust-proofed before enamelling, as rust-proofing by Bonderizing or similar processes does not "take" on yellow metals and consequently the bond between such metals and the primary coat of enamel will not be the same as it is on the surface of the steel.

Frames can be either ruined or improved by filing, according to the skill or carelessness of the operator and the time spent. Sometimes, in a misguided endeavour to remove every vestige of visible brass, the tube is severely "necked" at its most vulnerable spot, just where it leaves the lug, whereas it is preferable to leave a small fillet at this point (Fig. 7.2). In fact any scratches or deep file marks are focal points from which fatigue failure can start.

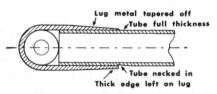

FIG. 7.2. Good filing practice is shown above the centre line—bad, causing a sharp change of section, below it.

Conversely, tapering the lug metal down to a thin edge is beneficial in so far as it avoids a sudden change of section and achieves a smoother transmission of stress from tube to lug, with a profitable saving in weight. Another method of achieving these desirable aims is to scarf or cut the lug at an angle, or fish-tail the ends by cutting out two deep V-notches.

When heavy-gauge or butted tubes are used, a small saving in weight can be effected by taper-boring the ends to a depth about a quarter of an inch less than the amount which lies within the lug; this is never done commercially, but on racing frames it is possible to eliminate several ounces of weight by this method, with no loss in resistance to failure (Fig. 7.3).

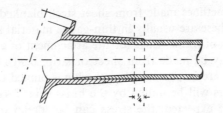

FIG. 7.3. Section through part of a steering-head joint, showing taper-boring of the top tube end.

MALLEABLE CAST IRON

Malleable iron is a peculiar material. Its ultimate tensile strength of around 24 tons/sq. in. is low compared to that of mild steel at 35 tons, but it is not very notch-sensitive; that is to say, it is not so likely to develop fatigue-cracks from local stress concentrations or surface defects as are stronger and harder materials. It can be cast in thicknesses down to $\frac{1}{8}$ in., and made in hollow or ribbed sections, according to requirements. It machines easily, either wet or dry.

Malleable castings are made first of all in "white" iron, an extremely hard and brittle material, and then subjected to a lengthy annealing process by which most of the combined carbon is either removed or converted into small graphite flakes. Distortion is likely to occur to some extent during annealing unless the parts are fairly simple and straightforward.

Unfortunately for the "special" builder, this manufacturing cycle almost precludes the use of malleable cast-iron for "one-off" castings, unless he is able to utilize some existing design, but one way out of this situation is to use Monel instead. Monel is a "natural" alloy of nickel and copper of equivalent strength, and can be machined and brazed just as easily as malleable iron. In fact, it is frequently used for experimental or show models when time is at a premium.

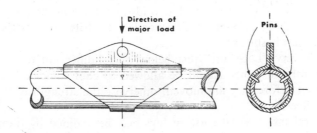

FIG. 7.4. A brazed wrap-round lug in side elevation and section.

93

Lugs are sometimes made from sheet steel, blanked out and folded to shape, but these are usually in thin-gauge material suitable only for the lighter class of frame. Lugs for the attachment of components such as oil tanks may be made from sheet or strip, bent into a circle with two ears which are in contact when the lug is pinned to the tube; after brazing, the ears will be united by the brass (Fig. 7.4). Where heavier loads are to be expected, the stress can be spread over the tube by making the lug much wider, tapering and scarfing the ends to eliminate useless weight.

FORGINGS

For heavier application and higher stresses, steel forgings are often employed; but as forgings cannot be cored like castings, but must be made solid, it would be a very expensive proposition to use them as raw material for, say, conventional head-lugs, since that would entail buying about twice as much steel as the finished part required and then going to the further expense of drilling or machining the excess metal away. Forged steel is, however, a good material for fork-ends, because these highly stressed components require only one fairly small short hole to accept the fork-tube, and consequently the waste of material involved is so slight that it can be accepted.

Occasionally simple lugs (such as those which form the forward ends of the side members of a built-up fork) can be machined from bar stock, with the ends either bored to fit outside the tubes or turned to fit inside them, holes being drilled centrally to avoid an abrupt change of section and to save a little weight. This procedure permits the use of a tapered tube at the expense of machining the spigot to a corresponding taper as well, whereas if the hole or spigot is parallel the last inch or so of the tube must also be parallel.

Incidentally, about two to five "thou" clearance should be provided between lug and tube. If there is less than this, it may be difficult to line up the components in the building jig when small errors are present; if more, there is the possibility that voids may form in the joint due to the brass tending, through capillary action, to drift towards the areas where the gap is smaller.

Brass is very "hot-short" just below its solidification temperature. Consequently all joints should be allowed to cool sufficiently for the brass to set before they are moved, otherwise the strength of the joint may be affected.

In several instances, the use of lugs may be avoided by trapping— that is, flattening—the tubes, which are subsequently drilled or punched for bolt-holes. The weakest point of a trapped tube is just where the flat section commences, and it is likely to break if subjected to much strain or vibration at right-angles to the flat portion.

One way of reducing the "notch effect" which is the prime cause of this type of failure is to flatten the tube in dies so that the change from round to flat section takes place over a finite distance, instead of abruptly, as it would if the tube were merely to be flattened in a vice (Fig. 7.5). Another method is to double-up the thickness by sliding a

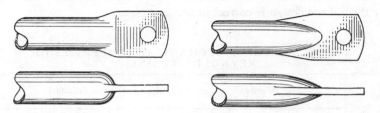

Fig. 7.5. Trapped tube ends. That on the right has a more gradual change of section giving greater strength under side loads.

second short piece of tube over the main one, then trapping the assembly and finally brazing the lot together. This makes quite a strong construction and is especially suitable for lightweight fork-ends in which slots are to be cut to provide axle adjustment.

MATERIALS FOR TUBES

Round, cold-drawn steel tube is by far the commonest form employed for brazed frames because of its simplicity in working and the ease of machining the lugs.

There are several grades suitable for brazing by the hearth or gas-torch method. In the Table 7.1, overleaf, reproduced by courtesy of the Reynolds Tube Co., Ltd., they are referred to as "qualities", but this term is rather misleading, as it gives the impression that "A" quality is superior to "B". Actually most production frames are made from "B" quality, which is a low-carbon, stable mild steel that can be brazed or welded by any method; whereas "A" quality, with a higher carbon content, *cannot be arc-welded* or even gas-welded with safety because local hardening and embrittlement occur due to self-quenching as the heat flows to the adjacent cold metal. It is, however, an excellent material for normal hearth-brazed frames.

It will be seen from the table that "B" quality tubing loses much of its "as-drawn" strength after brazing. This is because the higher figure is due to work-hardening of the steel during the drawing process, and the annealing which takes place during brazing removes the effects of cold working. In the "fully-annealed" state, to which tubes must be reduced if any tight bends are to be formed, the strength is reduced still further, and in this quality there is no possibility of restoring it by subsequent heat-treatment—even if such a course were possible on a complicated structure like a frame, which would inevitably distort beyond redemption. Where possible, therefore, bends which require full annealing should be avoided, and in fact there is rarely any necessity for them if the design is correct in the first place.

TABLE 7.1. MINIMUM MECHANICAL PROPERTIES OF REYNOLDS TUBING

Quality	"As drawn"			After brazing or welding		Fully annealed
	Yield stress	Ultimate stress	Elongation on 2-in. gauge length	Yield stress	Ultimate stress	Yield stress
	tons/sq. in.	tons/sq. in.		tons/sq. in.	tons/sq. in.	tons/sq. in.
"B"	26	28	12%	17	24	11
"A"	28	35	10%	25	30	22
"H.M."	40	45	10%	25	30	22
"C.M."	40	45	10%	30	35	25
"531"	45	50	10%	40	45	25

The chrome-molybdenum tubing termed "531" (a symbol derived from its chemical composition) is the strongest tubing available in the commercial range. It is quite suitable for ordinary brazing and loses very little of its "as-drawn" strength thereby. Even when fully annealed, it is almost as strong as "B" quality at its best, and this enables much lighter-gauge tubing to be used without decrease of strength. It must be remembered, though, that Young's modulus, which is a factor used in determining the deflection of a component under load, is almost constant at the figure of 30,000,000 for tension or compression and at 12,000,000 for torsion for *all* steels, *irrespective of their actual strength* —so that, size for size, a "531" tube is no stiffer than one of any other composition. However, as has been shown previously, a small increase in diameter increases the strength of a tube very greatly, and the best way of utilizing "531" is by specifying large diameters to maintain rigidity and light gauges to reduce the weight.

WELDING

As a method of joining frame-members together, autogenous welding, either by the electric-arc process or by means of the oxy-acetylene torch, has always had much attraction because it almost eliminates the use of lugs with their attendant weight and manufacturing costs. Of course, the ends of the tubes must be machined to the correct contours, and be accurate as to lengths, whereas, in most instances, square ends and quite wide dimensional tolerances are acceptable with brazed-lug construction. However, much of the attractiveness vanished in the early days of welded frames, partly because tube failure often occurred adjacent to the welds, and partly because of trouble with distortion during building.

Another objection was that if a welded frame broke it was not possible to remove the old tube and braze in a new one; furthermore, if the frame was repaired by re-welding, it often broke again at the same place. These objections were of special validity in countries where skilled service facilities were unobtainable and they contributed to the retention of brazed construction, especially on models which were exported in large numbers to places where frame-breakage was commonplace rather than exceptional. With better design, improved technique and a sounder selection of materials, the all-welded or partially welded frame can, however, be a perfectly satisfactory proposition and today many factories employ the process, which, in any case, is essential when sheet-metal components of considerable size are incorporated.

BRONZING

In addition to arc- and gas-welding, there is the process of bronze-welding, in which the filler-rod material, instead of being mild steel, is a copper alloy known under the trade name of "Sif-bronze". This material is applied with an oxy-acetylene torch, but owing to its low melting point the heat required is less than for true welding; the torch is fitted with a larger tip and the flame adjusted to give a less intensity of heat spread over a larger area than is the case with the former. Because of this, bronze-welding is considered by the people who should know best—the makers of the tubes—to be kinder to the steel and leaves it with more of its "as-drawn" strength; also the bronze supplies a ductile joint between the tubes, so helping to relieve any stress concentration.

When heated, bronze behaves quite differently from brazing-brass because, as it passes from the solid to the molten state it goes through

97

a transition stage during which it is semi-molten, a condition which permits fillets or bosses to be built up and holes or gaps between mating components to be bridged over or filled in. Brass, on the other hand, has a very short solidification range—it is either melted or it isn't—so that it cannot be built up in this way. Bronze, however, lacks the penetrative power of brass and will not flow into narrow gaps by capillary action so that it cannot satisfactorily be employed for making joints in which such areas of contact exist. Instead, joints intended for bronze-welding must be designed and prepared in much the same way as for oxy- or arc-welding, and it may be necessary to add gussets, ribs or straps to joints in heavily stressed localities so as to relieve the metal in the immediate vicinity of the welds from concentrated stress. Care must also be taken to ensure that no bending takes place while the bronze is molten, either through handling the components or through movement caused by thermal expansion. Otherwise there is a danger of inter-crystalline penetration by the bronze and subsequent tube failure such as may occur in similar circumstances with brass.

When using drawn tube, "A" quality, as previously mentioned, is unsuitable for gas- or arc-welding because, being a high-carbon steel, it hardens up locally due to the rapid flow-away of heat to the adjacent cold portions. This does not happen with the low-carbon "B" quality tubing and, although this type becomes softer and loses much of its strength in the portions which have been heated, it is commonly employed for parts where no great strength is required, or if cost of production is a point which must be closely watched. Where cost is secondary to excellence, "531" is the obvious selection, not only on account of its greater "as drawn" strength but because it retains 90 per cent. of that strength after brazing or welding. For cover-plates or gussets mild-steel is quite good enough, though some prefer to use 3 per cent. nickel steel for applications where strength as well as rigidity is required, as, for instance, at sidecar attachment points.

Non-circular Tubes

One advantage of welding or Sif-bronzing is that parts of irregular shape can easily be joined so there is no need to restrict oneself to round tube, as one has to when using brazed lugs on the score of easy machining of the latter. Tapered, oval or square tubes can be utilized or the sections may change along the length of the tube to suit the stresses encountered. Square tubing is available either in the solid-drawn form, or in the seam-welded variety, which is made by folding a strip into a square with rounded corners and continuously welding the joint as the tube is formed. Tube of this section can either be bent or notched and welded to form corners and can be welded or bronzed very conveniently to simple pressings made from steel sheet, blanked to size and with the edges folded at right-angles to provide rigidity, although it must be remembered that while a component of this nature is strong in bending, it has practically no torsional stiffness unless made into a box-section.

An example of using square tubes and pressings is to be seen in the D.M.W. frame, illustrated on page 68, Fig. 5.16, in which the front down-tube and the members which project rearwardly to carry the pillion footrests are curved and welded to the underside of a folded platform. Another folded pressing carrying the fork pivot-bearing, and also forming the rear engine plates, is welded to the upper side of the platform, providing a construction that resists transmission stresses in a very direct manner.

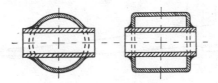

FIG. 7.6. Sections through bolt bosses formed by welding-in short cross-tubes. There is less interruption of the tube material when the original member is square instead of round.

One advantage of square tube is that lugs may be neatly incorporated with no loss of strength by drilling through and welding-in a short section of tube to accept, say, an engine or footrest bolt. This can, of course, also be done with a round tube but with less ease of drilling and at the cost of leaving less of the original tube material on each side of the bolt-boss to carry the applied stress (Fig. 7.6).

A Welded Rear Fork

When constructing a "special" it is not a difficult matter to fold up a pair of tapered square-section tubes to form the legs of a pivoted rear fork; these can be welded to a cross-tube either adjacent to, or forming, the pivot bearing and preferably strengthened locally by two plates at top and bottom formed into a box by a closing strip on the wheel side. Such a construction would be extremely strong in all directions even if made from steel of 16 or even 18 gauge, as the strength stems more from the size of the whole section rather than the thickness of material. In the schematic arrangement shown in Fig. 7.7, it would be preferable for the cross-tube to be of thicker section in order to cope with the high local loads encountered at the bearings—10-gauge tube (0·128 in. thick) would be about right, but this is one of the applications where it may be simpler to use a piece of mild-steel bar, bored out initially slightly under-size. Some distortion of the bore is inevitable during the welding process and after this part of the work is completed, the bore can be finish-machined or reamed to the correct size to fit the bearings employed; bar-stock is easier to machine than drawn tube, even in the soft condition, owing to the different grain-flow in the metal.

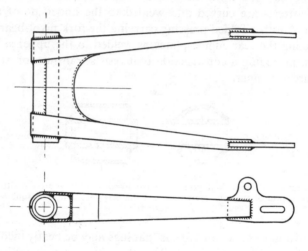

FIG. 7.7. Plan and elevation of a swinging fork with legs of tapered square-section tubes.

When building-up a structure of this nature, great care must be taken to avoid general distortion or warping during welding as it is a difficult matter to rectify it later without resorting to local bends in one or other of the legs. Given good machining facilities and a sufficient allowance of metal in the bore of the cross-tube, small errors can be eliminated when finally sizing the bearing housings by machining these absolutely true to the fork-ends and axle-slots.

HEAD LUGS

Welded head-lugs may be turned from bar-stock or made from a short section of heavy-gauge tube with two cups spigoted and welded thereto to form seatings for the head races. If the frame is of conventional form with a single straight top tube and either one or a pair of down-tubes, these should be machined to fit closely round the head-tube and then, if of heavy gauge, must be chamfered so that there is a V-shaped notch all the way round the joint in which the weld metal is deposited. If this precaution is omitted, the finished joint may not be welded all the way through, in which event it will be half-cracked before it even starts out in life and premature failure may easily take place under road loads.

In a structure built up in this manner the local stresses caused by these loads are borne directly by the welds, and even if these are perfect and there has been no under-cutting of the tube wall at the edge of the weld, as sometimes happens with badly executed arc-welding, the weakest parts of the complete joint are still the portions of tube adjacent to the point where the strength has been reduced through heating. Consequently, it is common practice to add gussets or stiffening plates, partly to ensure that at least some of the loads are carried by continuous metal and partly to distribute them over a longer length of tube, thus emulating the effect of a well-designed cast lug.

Local stiffening of a tube in a transverse direction can be accomplished by welding a single rib along it, as in the case of the "Featherbed" Norton, where the duplex rear down-tubes would be insufficiently rigid in the region of the pivot bearing without the help of the gussets which are carried round the lower bends to augment the corner-wise rigidity as well. This frame, when built for racing, is composed of "531" tubing, bronze-welded at all places including the points where the tubes cross over themselves just to the rear of the head-tube.

COUNTERING DISTORTION

Distortion to some extent is almost bound to take place in a welded frame and may be very difficult to eliminate if the structure is extremely strong and has no "open" or bolted joints which can be left temporarily free during the truing-up process. If cold-drawn, as opposed to welded or annealed, tube is used, advantage can be taken of the fact that, due to the compressive stress in the surface set up by the drawing process, heat applied locally to one side of the tube will cause it on cooling to take a permanent set towards the heated side. This is indeed about the only method which can be used when large tubes of over $2\frac{1}{2}$ in. diameter are used and, given the necessary setting fixtures, it almost eliminates the "brute-force" system of truing-up which is not always conducive to accurate results.

As a general rule, welds should not be subjected to what may be described as "tearing" loads; they are best located in areas where the stress is as nearly as possible pure compression or tension. Sometimes it is convenient to weld a short tube at right-angles to another, but the relative positions dictated by the circumstances are such that the centre-lines of the two are spaced some distance apart; the resulting weld is of an oval shape but if the short tube is carrying heavy loads which are varying in direction—as it would be if it formed, say, the pivot bearing housing—there is a great liability that the joint will fail, either through the weld or by tearing a piece out of one or other of the tubes. This contingency can be avoided by the addition of a cover-plate, running round the opposite side of the main tube and welded to it and the cross-tube, thus forming a strong triangulated structure and relieving the original weld of most of the applied load (Fig. 7.8). A different arrangement with the same function can be seen in the scooter fork crown (Fig. 7.9) in which a pair of simple plates are bronzed to

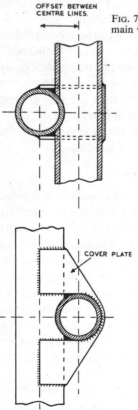

OFFSET BETWEEN CENTRE LINES.

COVER PLATE

FIG. 7.8. (Left) A welded-on sheet-steel cover plate relieves the main weld of stress at the intersection of two tubes with considerably offset centres.

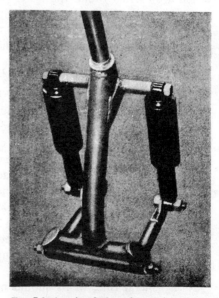

FIG. 7.9. A pair of plates bronzed to cross-tube and curved down-member serve the same purpose in a Reynolds scooter fork.

the cross-tube carrying the springs and the curved tube forming the support for the wheel-fork, thus tying the whole assembly together.

PRESSED STEEL

Pressed steel is used in many applications not directly concerned with the frame. Items which spring to the mind are petrol and oil tanks, tool-boxes, battery containers and chaincases which, with the exception of the first-named, can be made rapidly and cheaply from light-gauge, deep-drawing quality, sheet steel on small presses using relatively inexpensive tools.

Petrol tanks present their own problems. They are frequently made from a top section and two side-panels welded together in order to get some desired shape, and subsequently welded to a bottom section which usually incorporates the tunnel required to clear the top tube. Components of this nature are not subjected to frame stresses and, in fact, should be insulated by rubber mountings from them and from induced stresses due to relative movement of the attachment points, or engine vibration.

The petrol tank, especially the saddle pattern, can become the victim of vibration or frame distortion quite easily, because it is weakened very markedly in a transverse direction by the tunnel and may contain an amount of fuel equal to three times its own weight. Under the action of vertical vibration, the tank tends to hinge about the top line of the tunnel. If the natural frequency of this "tuning-fork" type of vibration coincides with a regularly used spot in the engine speed range, the tank will sooner or later split at one end of the tunnel unless the end areas are locally reinforced or steps are taken to prevent such vibration.

One method is to mount the front end of the tank in frame-brackets with two rubber-bushed bolts, spaced several inches apart, screwed into the tank-floor. This will hold the sides together, but the rear mounting must then be narrow or else quite flexible in order to avoid twisting loads being applied to the tank. Care must also be taken to stiffen the tank-floor adequately in the region of the front bolts, otherwise fatigue-cracks will occur due to the metal deflecting locally.

To provide a wide bracket is not convenient with some frame designs, and it may be much simpler to weld two ears to the tank tunnel-sides and bolt these to the head-lug. In this case it may be necessary to tie the halves of the tank together by a bolt and distance-piece, or some similar device, to prevent destructive vibration.

One of the outstanding features of the "Featherbed" type of frame is that it permits the use of a tank with a substantially flat floor, the weight of which is distributed evenly along the whole length of the top tubes. A single strap running along the upper mid-line is all that is required to hold such a tank in place, or it may even be retained by rubber bands attached to hooks on the underside.

When the frame design is such that the fuel container can be stowed away somewhere within it, the latter can be made cheaply and simply in two similar halves welded together. Ribs or depressions should always be pressed into the flat top and bottom, to tighten-up the metal and provide stiffness against "oil-canning".

PRESSED FRAMES

Quite apart from these hollow and relatively lightly stressed articles which are ideal applications of presswork, it has long been the dream of many designers to make the whole frame, or at least its major components, in sheet metal and do away with built-up tubular constructions entirely. Few motorcycle factories in the past possessed the equipment necessary for producing pressings of complicated shapes and several square feet in area at an economical price, but there were a few attempts to do so, or to make a complete pressed frame by welding together several smaller sections.

One example of a complete pressed frame was the Royal Enfield "Cycar" of 1933, though this was so designed that the side panels were folded rather than pressed, the resulting shape being necessarily rather angular and not outstandingly attractive. Even before that time there was the Beardmore-Precision, composed largely of pressings welded together, the basis of the design being a petrol-tank which was, in effect, also the top tube. Another design of the 'twenties was the Ascot-Pullin, in which some attempt was made to attain a clean external appearance by employing a sheet-metal frame incorporating the petrol and oil tanks. Tank leakage developed in the Ascot-Pullin and was by no means easy to rectify—an argument in favour of separate tanks as used on the Ariel "Leader" and the LE Velocette, which are not subjected to frame stresses and are well protected in the event of a crash.

The LE's frame is composed of two major components, a front portion extending from the head to the rear of the power unit and a rear portion, essentially an enlarged mudguard, welded to the front and incorporating slots for the upper attachments of the rear springs, which are adjustable for load compensation. The seating accommodation is bolted to the top of this guard so that the crew's weight is supported almost directly by the springs, and the pivot-bearings for the rear fork are located in the vertical sides of the front portion, which is strengthened partly by local plates, spot-welded to the thin main pressing, and partly by a bolted-in bulkhead which also carries the rear end of the power unit (Fig. 7.11).

At the front, the steering head is a built-up component attached by four widely spaced bolts to each side of the main pressing. Therefore, as in the region of the pivot-bearing, all major stresses are applied substantially in the plane of the sides—i.e., in the direction of greatest strength, a principle which is essential with sheet metal if undesirable flexure and early fatigue cracking is to be avoided.

Although a tubular assembly is used to support the front end of the power unit and the radiator, the pressed frame is complete in itself. Making it in two portions reduces the size of dies required and, to obviate a difficult deep-drawing operation, the rear guard is made in two halves, welded along the centre-line. These are initially pressed in one piece which looks rather like a large wash-bowl. The centre is then punched out to form the inner radius of the guard and the pair of blanks are finally welded together along the edges which previously formed the outline of the pressing.

The front guard is formed in a similar way and is bolted to the fork-crown only, being sufficiently rigid in itself not to require the usual stays. Most mudguard blades are made by a rolling process and possess little transverse rigidity in shallow sections, though the addition of deep integral valances helps considerably in this direction.

The most advanced application of press-work in British contemporary design is the Ariel "Leader", in which practically every component, including the front fork blades, are fabricated from sheet, suitably reinforced where necessary at points of major stress (Fig. 7.12).

The box frame is composed of two half-pressings, 20 s.w.g. thick, electrically welded along the centre line to form a very rigid structure. The appearance of this does not matter much because it is hidden from view by other (non-stressed) pressings of pleasing shape which blend well with the neatly styled tail portion, although the final appearance, to some eyes, gives an impression of heaviness which, however erroneous, is difficult to avoid in any design where much of the working parts are fully enclosed. Its derivative, the "Arrow", is almost free from this criticism.

PRESSED FORKS

Swinging forks can be constructed (as in the Puch, to quote one example) by making each leg of two similar half-pressings, welded along the edges to give a tapered oval section. The fork-ends are made from steel plate, punched to shape and welded, and the two legs are joined by a cross-tube, close to and just behind the pivot-bearing. This cross-tube is not welded merely to the inner side of each leg, which would be to court almost certain disaster, but is passed through holes pierced in each side and welded to both. Under lateral loads, which tend to bend the whole assembly out of square, the stresses induced in the thin metal of the legs are mainly tension or compression, whereas if the welding were on the inner side only, the metal would be subjected to intense local bending, with unavoidable flexure and eventual failure in that region.

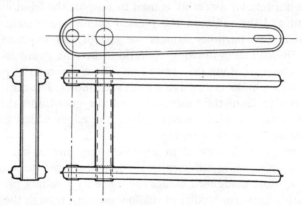

Fig. 7.10. Swinging fork of the Puch type, in which each leg is welded-up from two half-pressings.

Failure of this type is bound to occur in any sheet construction which is unthinkingly or unavoidably permitted or forced to flex at right-angles to its surface over a small area. Cracks will develop and radiate from rivet holes or around the bolt heads of components which vibrate laterally, and it may be necessary to reinforce such areas locally by the addition of large washers or shaped plates, which can easily be attached by electric spot-welding at several points without disturbing the temper of the steel to any great extent.

Stiffeners attached in this way should, however, always be placed so that the spot welds are not subjected to heavy tension, as they will sometimes pull through under that kind of treatment. Spot-welding is performed by passing a very heavy current through the tips of two copper electrodes, which are squeezed powerfully against the outer surfaces of the parts to be joined. The current raises the steel to welding heat in a fraction of a second, and the clamping pressure completes the weld which is in the form of a spot about $\frac{3}{16}$ in. in diameter or less.

Spot-welded joints are not watertight, but the process is sometimes used to tack two components together at several points before gas-welding or bronzing. Small dimples are created in the surface, and the edges of the sheets are often rendered ragged or uneven by local flow of the metal; these two effects go towards making an unsightly job which is difficult and expensive to clean up.

In car bodywork, where the process is used very extensively, this difficulty is overcome by fitting a U-section capping strip, either of

FIGS. 7.11 and 7.12. Modern practice. The stressed main pressings of the LE Velocette (Fig. 7.11) include the rear mudguard. In both this and the Ariel "Leader" (Fig. 7.12) the separate fuel tank is unstressed.

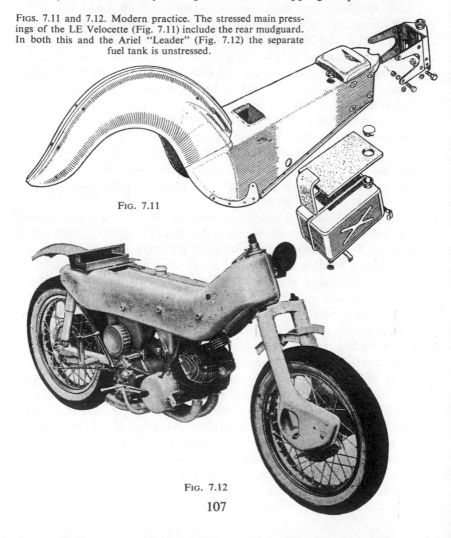

FIG. 7.11

FIG. 7.12

rubber or of some shiny metal. There are many places where this scheme can be used to advantage on motorcycles—as it is, for instance, on some B.S.A. tanks, which have two seam welds along the upper surface, covered by chromium-plated channel strip.

There is not much scope for presswork in conjunction with telescopic front forks, except for leadlamp nacelles, or even smaller items such as lamp or speedometer brackets. With the more complex bottom-link varieties, however, good use can be made of sheet steel by forming it to enclose the links, either partially or fully, so going a long way towards making an inherently "bitty" design look neat and attractive, while simultaneously shielding the mechanism from road grit.

Reference has already been made to the "Leader" fork (Fig. 7.12). This design is unusual, though by no means unique, in that the pressed blades are attached only to the lower end of the steering column, thus placing bending stresses upon this component to which it is not subjected when the blades are attached to both ends of the column, which is the more usual practice.

It does not follow that the idea is bad; it was used with great success on the very fast 120° Vee-twin Guzzi racers for several seasons. At first sight it appears that the column bending stresses would be extremely heavy during severe front brake application, but, by a fortunate combination of the forces brought into play, the stresses are not quite so great as might be imagined.

In the NSU leading-link forks, much of the mechanism is enclosed by pressings which are carried up and around the steering column, thus making a neat enclosure for what is normally an untidy area and eliminating bending loads at the base of the column.

Many years ago pressed blades were used to replace the tubular assemblies of some girder forks on the score of cheapness, but the blades were merely of open-sided channel section of no great depth. Consequently, they flexed laterally in service and crumpled up in a heart-rending manner under even a minor sideways impact.

In contrast to these designs, where virtue was sacrificed upon the altar of cheapness, the original Francis-Barnett "Cruiser" of 1933 employed fork blades each made from a D-shaped pressing, with a flat back welded thereto to form a closed section of pleasing appearance and adequate strength in all directions. Although this type of fork is now obsolete, the examples are quoted to indicate how the intrinsic good qualities of pressed-steel work can be turned to advantage, while failure to realize its limitations can result in designs which, though respectable in appearance, are functionally weak.

CHAPTER 8

The Power Unit

WHEN one considers the combinations and permutations possible with the factors involved in the basic design of the power unit—including the firing cycle, the number of cylinders, the manner in which they may be arranged, the type of cooling and whether or not the engine and gearbox shall be in unit—the designer's choice seems almost infinite. In practice, it is severely limited by commercial considerations.

From the sales point of view, the success of a new model—not necessarily in its first year, but within the next two or three seasons—may depend, and in fact almost certainly does depend, upon an intelligent appraisal of the trend in public taste. Strictly speaking this has nothing to do with engineering except in so far as, on more than one occasion in the past, engines or complete power units which failed commercially on their first appearances have been resurrected years later with resounding success. This could have been because the original edition, though sound in conception, possessed some defects in design or materials which outweighed its good features, or it may have been merely that at the time of introduction buyers were not prepared to accept something which differed radically from the ruling practice. But, whatever the cause, no one who is concerned with the commercial success of a new model can afford to ignore public opinion, however much praise is lavished on the product by those who are not likely to buy one anyway.

When constructing a model for some specific purpose such as racing, scrambling, or record-breaking, or a "one-off" special to suit one's personal tastes, the position is quite different. One is then at liberty to select the design which will provide the right tool for the job, irrespective of any other considerations—except that it may not be considered good policy for a factory which makes its living from, say, single-cylinder two-strokes to use a four-cylinder four-stroke or something equally exotic for its "works" competition models.

Coming down to cases, there are only three cylinder groupings worth consideration for general work, namely, the single, the twin and the four.

THE "SINGLE"

The single-cylinder has the great merit of simplicity, and even in the smallest capacities none of its components is ridiculously tiny. Size for size, in four-stroke form it gives more power than any multi-cylinder (unless the latter is built as a collection of singles, each with its own induction and exhaust system). On the reverse side, it lacks smoothness, partly because it fires only once in every two revolutions and partly because of its inherent lack of mechanical balance. It is true that both these defects can be made less obtrusive by good design and installation, but nevertheless they remain and must be accepted as part of the price paid for simplicity.

VARIOUS TWINS

The two-cylinder engine can be made in three ways—with the bores parallel to each other, arranged in V-formation or horizontally opposed to each other, on each side of the crankcase.

The most common arrangement today is the parallel twin—an outstanding case of a layout which made two or three premature appearances before it "caught on". This form of engine, in four-stroke guise, with both pistons going up and down together, is no better than a "single" as regards mechanical balance, but has a smoother performance because its power impulses occur once per revolution and are only half as great as those of a single of equal capacity.

Except for doubling the number of pistons, rods and valves, this layout entails no great increase in complication, and orthodox constructional and overhauling methods can be used. There are no difficulties in installation—in fact this may be somewhat eased by the reduced height, and the extra width is not much of a problem. Cylinder cooling can be as good as that of the single, and in some circumstances even better, because of the greater width of the fins, provided adequate precautions are taken to ensure a good flow of cooling air through the narrow space between the cylinder barrels.

By making a twin in the form of two singles, with the crankshafts geared together to run in opposite directions and fully counterweighted, a very well-balanced unit is obtained, possessing the equal firing impulses of the conventional type, but with the disadvantage that it can only be cooled well if the crankshafts are placed parallel to the frame, an arrangement which is suitable for shaft-drive but not for chain-drive unless a pair of bevels is interposed.

In the two-stroke form of parallel twin, the pistons move up and

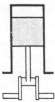

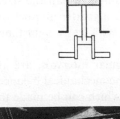

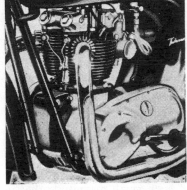

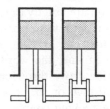

Fig. 8.1. The types which dominate the field today—the single and the parallel-twin four-stroke. Examples shown are the 350 c.c. A.J.S. Model 16 and 650 c.c. Triumph "Thunderbird".

down alternately in order to give a power impulse on every stroke, thus affording very smooth power-production and rather better balance than with the four-stroke arrangement. Balance, however, is still not perfect. Owing to the wide spacing of the bores a "rocking couple"—i.e., a tendency to oscillate the engine in relation to the centre-line—is present, and though its effect can be made quite unobtrusive by correct balancing and mounting, it cannot be completely eliminated.

The V-twin, once a very popular arrangement, is now out of favour with manufacturers, the main current production models being those of Harley-Davidson in the U.S.A. For all that, the layout has several points which render it attractive, especially for engines of large swept volume (Fig. 8.2).

It is very little wider overall and not quite so tall as a single of *half* the capacity, and though it is much larger at cylinder-head height the extra inches can be accommodated in corners which are not normally

111

fully occupied in a conventional frame. Owing to the circumstance that the pistons do not come to rest simultaneously at the end of each stroke, as they do in a twin or four, the flywheel weight for equivalent smoothness need not exceed that necessary for a single of half the size, and, one way and another, the V-twin will provide a greater number of working cubic centimetres in less block bulk and with less weight than any other arrangement.

The firing impulses, though not spaced at regular intervals, are at least as frequent as those of a parallel twin, and the mechanical balance is a peculiar compromise between good and bad which can be made to furnish an almost vibrationless performance, though the inherent balance is not as good as that of the horizontally opposed arrangement.

The h.o. twin is another time-honoured design which has fewer adherents today than it has had in the past. Mechanically there is a lot to recommend it, the outstanding feature being almost perfect mechanical balance due to the fact that the inertia forces generated by one piston are exactly cancelled out by equal and opposite forces from the other. If it were possible, without resort to complicated divided connecting-rods or twin geared crankshafts, to make the two bores actually in line, the word "almost" could be deleted; but with the conventional two-throw crankshaft there is necessarily a small offset, about an inch or so, between the cylinder centre-lines, and this gives rise to a rocking couple, fortunately of such small magnitude that it can be disregarded.

When the h.o. unit is installed in the plane of the frame, however,

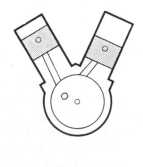

Fig. 8.2. Maximum c.c. in minimum space with minimum weight—the geometry of the V-twin fits snugly into a motorcycle's engine-space. Illustrated, a 1953 Vincent "Rapide".

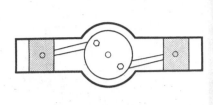

FIG. 8.3. Mechanical balance of the h.o. twin is almost perfect; installation geometry is not so good. The B.M.W. R69, above.

the cooling of the rear cylinder is bad because it is almost impossible to avoid severe masking by other components. If it is placed with the cylinders transversely the great overall width is a handicap on large-capacity units, particularly for fast solo work when the possibility of grounding the rocker-box covers becomes serious unless the whole engine is raised a long way above ground level.

Carburation is also a difficulty. Two instruments are preferable, but expensive and difficult to mount without getting in the way of the rider's feet; and the long induction pipes required with one carburetter have been known to give trouble with icing-up in cold climates. On the other hand, the cooling is about as good as it is possible to be, even in still-air conditions, and for medium and small capacities the type has some decided advantages, though the torque reaction brought about when the speed of a transverse engine is rapidly altered is not in its favour.

THE FOURS

When four cylinders are employed, the power impulses occur in an almost continuous stream and this affords very smooth running without the need for transmission shock absorbers. There are several possible cylinder arrangements—the "in-line" type (which may be mounted either longitudinally or transversely), the "square-four" type with two crankshafts geared to rotate in opposite directions, the horizontally opposed, with a pair of cylinders on each side of either a single shaft or two geared shafts, and the V-type with two pairs of cylinders set at any included angle that the designer wishes.

113

 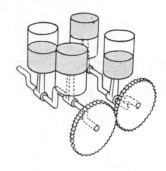

FIG. 8.4. The unique Ariel "Square Four": 1,000 c.c. in a very small space, the mechanical balance of a straight four, simple carburation.

Of these, the "in-line" or straight four with fore-and-aft crankshaft is the least suitable. It is difficult to house due to its length (although it is possible to crib a little space by mounting the gearbox alongside the crankcase of a small engine) and cooling of the middle two cylinders is very bad when normal air-cooling is employed.

If the "in-line" four is mounted across the frame, as in the Gilera and M.V. racers, the cooling is extremely good, which may be a contributory reason for the success of these makes in long-distance events. Constructional complications, however, are introduced by the fact that the only satisfactory form of primary transmission is the expensive central gear train which is a feature of these models (Fig. 8.7).

The "square four" arrangement gives a compact engine sufficiently narrow to permit the use of a normal offset primary drive to a conventional gearbox. As two pistons (on one diagonal) are at t.d.c. when the other two (on the other diagonal) are at b.d.c., the balance is exactly the same as that of a straight four. Since the induction strokes are equally spaced, a single carburetter feeding to a distributor-type manifold can be used if moderate power is the aim; but if it were desired to obtain racing power it would be difficult to install four carburetters, which can be mounted quite easily on a transverse "in-line" four. Cooling of the bores on the sides near the centre of the square also poses a difficult problem, and obtaining absolutely silent running of the crankshaft gears is by no means easy, especially in view of the change in centre-distance between hot and cold conditions which is unavoidable with an aluminium crankcase (Fig. 8.4).

The horizontally-opposed four is almost exactly the same as a twin of the same family except that with a single horizontal crankshaft the

114

cooling of the rear cylinders is not very good. Obviously, this form could be used only with the cylinders across the frame, and the problems of ground clearance and torque reactions encountered with the twin also exist in the four.

Using two geared crankshafts, one above the other, and arranging the pairs of cylinders with their common centre-plane vertical instead of horizontal produces an engine which is, in effect, two h.o. twins superimposed. The cooling of all four cylinders is then excellent, and the constructional details are not so complex as they might seem, because only a single crankpin is required on each shaft. The cranks are phased so that when the offside pistons are both at t.d.c. the nearside pistons are both at b.d.c., and in effect all four move backwards and forwards in relation to the crankshaft in a block. This would completely destroy the inherent balance of the single-crankshaft type, where the pistons move in and out together, but for the fact that the crankshafts are heavily counter-weighted so that they completely balance the piston inertia forces at the dead-centre positions, whilst at mid-stroke the centrifugal force from one counterweight, which in that position is unwanted, is exactly balanced by the force from the other counterweight. The result is an engine in which the balance is excellent, though it is obtained at the expense of placing heavy inertia loads on the main bearings. The subject of balancing is discussed much more fully in Chapter 16.

There is not the same objection to transverse mounting as there is with the single-crankshaft type, because the torque reactions arising when accelerating one shaft are balanced, at least in part, by reactions of opposite hand from the other shaft. From the installation viewpoint, too, this layout has some good points: as the cylinders in each bank fire at equal intervals, one carburetter per bank can be used, and whilst the main drive is taken off one crankshaft, the other can be utilized for driving the camshaft or electrical accessories. Nevertheless, it is an expensive form of motor to produce and it is doubtful whether it has sufficient advantages to justify its additional cost (Fig. 8.5).

The V-four consists essentially of two V-twins with a two-throw crankshaft, and is sufficiently compact to be mounted with the crankshaft either in line with or across the frame, the latter position being chosen for the Matchless and A.J.S. machines which utilized this form of engine for some time. In the Matchless, the included angle was reduced to 26° in order to accommodate all four cylinders in a single casting, and also to utilize a single overhead camshaft operating all eight valves; but such an arrangement is clearly not conducive to good cooling of the rear cylinders. On the A.J.S. racing machine, which started out in life air-cooled but was shortly afterwards converted to water-cooling, the construction was more conventional, the angle being opened out to 60° with one chain-driven camshaft situated in each pair of heads.

With one crankpin located at 180° to the other, the small out-of-balance forces present in a V-twin are almost cancelled out and very smooth running is obtained. Further, the engine occupies little space in relation to the swept volume. But with only natural draught to rely upon, proper cooling of all four cylinders becomes difficult, especially with the rearwardly disposed pair of exhaust ports (Fig. 8.5).

Of all these basic layouts, only the single and the parallel twin are

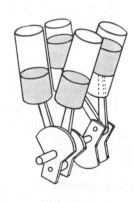
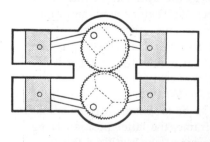

Fig. 8.5. Two fours. By the use of a narrow included angle the cylinders of the Matchless "Silver Hawk" of 1934 (top) were accommodated in a single block. Excellent cooling and good balance were secured—expensively—in the "double-deck" arrangement of the Brough "Golden Dream", of 1938 (bottom).

FIG. 8.6. The Guzzi V-8—the ultimate in compactness and complexity.

in general use today, with the flat twin in limited production and the V-twin only just existing. It is safe to say that only a bold man—or a concern with very big resources—would venture any large sum on endeavouring to introduce anything revolutionary, or even on reintroducing any of those which have failed to maintain their ground.

The position is quite different with pure racing models, where extremes in complexity, such as the V-8 Guzzi, have been produced. Engines with unusually-arranged cylinders, like the three-cylinder D.K.W., with one horizontal and two approximately vertical lungs, have also been considered worth trying—as in fact this particular example proved to be, so far as sheer power was concerned.

But racing and touring are, of course, very different things. In the first instance one is seeking the maximum power from a limited volume, with 100 per cent. reliability when driven under racing conditions by a very highly skilled rider, and with meticulous preparation by highly skilled personnel. In the second, a moderate amount of power is required with no particular limitation on capacity, but the engine has to be reliable under all sorts of conditions, from devouring motorways at "full bore" to plugging along at almost zero m.p.h. in heavy traffic, on surfaces varying from the ideal to deep sand or acres of mud and water. All these considerations affect the detail design of the engine, and the selection of the most suitable design for any particular motorcycle is governed therefore by the conditions in which it is to be used,

FIG. 8.7. A classic example of an engine designed and built regardless of cost for the specific purpose of winning races—the Italian M.V. "four".

the nature of the work to be done, and the permissible ceiling cost of manufacture.

In some instances, the third item may be of paramount importance. Shortcomings in the way of low power output or high fuel consumption may have to be accepted in engines designed for the very cheapest class of vehicle.

At the other end of the scale, for special racing or record-breaking power units the question of cost can almost be disregarded, provided that the success of the end-product eventually justifies the money laid out on its design and development. Engines for limited numbers of production, road-racing, scrambling or trials models fall into an intermediate category. A few pounds may justifiably be added to the cost if the improvement in performance so gained makes the difference between a potential winner and one which is virtually beaten before it starts.

Regulations imposed either by the law of the land or by competition rules also have to be considered. In some countries, models powered by engines below a certain capacity are granted tax relief or may be ridden without a licence, and the lion's share of the market in these areas will naturally fall to the maker who produces the most outstanding model of this restricted size.

In recognized international competitions, a series of capacity limits ranging from 50 to 1,200 c.c. has been adhered to for many years.

There are no limitations whatever on the general design, except that supercharging is prohibited and so is the use of additional charging pistons on two-strokes, both being devices which, in effect, defeat the purpose of the capacity limit. For record-breaking, however, these restrictions do not apply and you can do what you like in the way of forced induction or the use of special fuels provided the swept volume of the actual working cylinders is within the capacity limit.

Only in the U.S.A. is any distinction made between engines of differing designs. There, side-valve models up to 750 c.c. are permitted in certain types of races to compete against 500 c.c. overhead-valve models, and there is also a limit on the compression ratio permitted.

The number of variable factors in the basic design—the actual capacity, the number of cylinders, the type of valve-gear, whether two-stroke or four-stroke and so on—is so great that it is no easy matter to decide which combination is the best for any particular application. Several preliminary layouts may have to be prepared and investigated for cost and ease of manufacture before a final choice is made.

Frequently the size, type and accuracy of the machine-tool equipment available places some restrictions on either the general or the detail design. Changing public opinion must also be considered, especially in introducing a new model which is expected to continue in production for several years.

An example of changing status is the two-stroke engine, which not so very many years ago was acceptable only in small, inexpensive machines and was really no more than tolerated (except by true believers in the type) for its cheapness and simplicity of construction. Today, the position is quite different. Thanks to the development of the "loop-scavenge" principle, which eliminated the deflector-type piston, and better knowledge of port design, two-stroke performance figures are comparable with those of four-strokes of equivalent capacity, and a certain amount of mechanical complexity is acceptable if it yields a gain in performance or economy. The odd theory that once a departure is made from the essential simplicity of the two-stroke, you might as well make it a four-stroke, has gone by the board.

However, the two-stroke principle is seen to its best advantage only with cylinders of small capacity, partly because the ratio of port area to volume becomes less favourable as the dimensions are increased, and partly because cylinder distortion due to the unequal temperatures existing in the region of the ports becomes more serious with increase in cylinder diameter. For these reasons 200 c.c. per cylinder is near the desirable upper limit of capacity. Unless, therefore, one is prepared to go to the length of using three or even four cylinders, with their attendant difficulties of maintaining effective sealing between the various crankcast compartments, the four-stroke cycle is almost an automatic choice for air-cooled engines of over 400 c.c.

This leads us to a consideration of what size the engine should be. For racing, of course, this depends only on the category in which one wishes to compete, a promising line being to start off with a "125" designed in such a way that it can be duplicated to form a "250" later on.

For touring, a designer with wide terms of reference may well have in mind the adage that there is no substitute for litres. In other words, for certain jobs, such as fast touring on motorways or carrying heavy loads, a big engine, working well within its limits for most of the time, is preferable to a small one, screaming its heart out in order to develop the same amount of power.

While it is common practice to compare engines on the basis of peak power output, a much better yardstick is provided by ascertaining the specific output, or power developed per litre per thousand r.p.m. For example, the ordinary run-of-the-mill o.h.v. engine, with valve timing and compression ratio designed to give a good all-round performance for normal road work, has a specific output of between 8 and 9·5 b.h.p./litre/1,000 r.p.m. This figure is reasonably consistent for all engines, irrespective of capacity, *which conform to these requirements* (see table). A little engine can only be made to turn out as much power as a big one by making it turn over faster, or else by increasing its specific output.

This can, of course, be accomplished by the well-known expedients of raising the compression ratio, lengthening the valve timing, increasing the diameter and length of the carburetter choke and induction system, and fitting a resonant unobstructed exhaust system. But a price will be paid in loss of flexibility, erratic slow running and a tendency to raise the speed at which useful power is developed towards the upper end of the power curve—how heavy the price will depend upon the extent to which the aids to power-production have been exploited.

B.H.P. TARGET

These are serious disadvantages for normal road use and therefore it is not a good plan to aim at more than 10 b.h.p./litre/1,000 r.p.m. for this work. But for racing, where sheer power is the major requirement, they cease to matter much and it is possible to raise the specific power output to 15, though this is about the maximum which has so far been obtained from any four-stroke using atmospheric induction. If a quick check on the performance figures quoted for some engine indicates a specific output appreciably higher than this figure, either the claims are exaggerated or the test results have been obtained with nitromethane in the fuel (this compound provides a kind of chemical supercharging by the liberation of oxygen, thus enabling more fuel to be burnt per stroke).

Pursuing this matter of specific power a little further, the average side-valve engine can only achieve 8 to 8·5 b.h.p./litre/1,000 r.p.m., a figure which can be bettered by a conventional two-stroke with flat-top piston and designed for use on the road, complete with silencer.

A racing two-stroke with mechanical inlet valves of the rotary or

TABLE 8.1. CALCULATED PERFORMANCES

Make and model	Capacity	Claimed output	Specific output	Rear wheel size	Top gear ratio	Theoretical speed at 4,000 r.p.m.	Theoretical speed at peak r.p.m.
						Based on claimed output	
	c.c.	b.h.p./ r.p.m.	b.h.p./ litre/ 1,000 r.p.m.	in.			
Four-stroke Tourers							
Ariel "Square Four"	1,000	42/5,800	7·3	4·00 × 18	4·4	72	103
B.M.W. R69	600	35/6,800	8·6	3·50 × 18	4·9	62	106
B.S.A. B33	500	23/5,500	8·4	3·50 × 19	5·0	63	87
Gilera "Extra"	175	9·1/6,000	8·7	2·75 × 19	7·1	42	63
Panther 120 (solo)	650	27/4,500	9·2	3·50 × 19	4·6	68	77
Royal Enfield "Meteor Minor"	500	30/6,250	9·6	3·50 × 17	4·7	62	97
Triumph "Tiger Cub"	200	10/6,000	8·3	3·25 × 17	6·8	43	64
Triumph 3TA	350	18·5/6,500	8·1	3·25 × 17	5·3	54	87
Velocette "Valiant"	200	12/7,000	8·6	3·25 × 18	7·3	41	72
Velocette MSS	500	23/5,000	9·5	3·25 × 19	4·9	63	79
Vincent "Rapide"	1,000	45/5,500	8·2	3·50 × 19	3·5	90	124
Four-stroke Sportsters							
B.S.A. "Super Rocket"	650	44/5,600	12·0	3·50 × 19	4·5	70	98
Harley-Davidson XLH	900	47/5,000	10·5	3·50 × 18	4·2	73	91
NSU "Supermax"	250	17/7,000	9·7	3·25 × 19	6·8	45	80
Royal Enfield "Crusader Sports"	250	17/6,250	10·8	3·25 × 17	6·1	47	74
Royal Enfield "Constellation"	700	51/6,250	11·6	3·50 × 19	4·4	72	113
Triumph T100A	500	32/6,500	9·9	3·50 × 17	4·8	60	100
Triumph "Bonnevile 120"	650	46/6,500	10·9	3·50 × 19	4·6	70	113
Vincent "Black Shadow"	1,000	55/5,500	10·0	3·50 × 19	3·5	90	124
Two-stroke Roadsters							
Ambassador "Super S"	250	15/5,500	11·0	3·25 × 17	5·8	50	69
Ariel "Leader"	250	16/6,400	10·0	3·25 × 16	5·9	47	75
B.S.A. D1 "Bantam"	125	4/5,000	6·4	2·75 × 19	7·0	43	53
D.M.W. Mk. 9	200	8·4/4,000	10·5	3·25 × 18	6·2	48	48
Dot "Sportsman's Roadster"	350	22/5,000	12·6	3·25 × 18	Optional	—	—
Excelsior F10 "Consort"	100	2·8/4,000	7·0	2·25 × 19	7·4	38	38
Greeves 24DB (single)	250	11·5/4,750	9·7	3·25 × 18	5·7	52	61
Guzzi "Zigolo Mk. 2"	100	4·6/5,200	8·8	2·75 × 17	7·9	35	45
Messerschmitt KR200	200	9·7/5,000	9·7	4·00 × 8	4·2	43	54
Rumi "Junior"	125	9/7,300	9·8	4·00 × 8	5·4	44	81
Scott "Flying Squirrel"	600	30/5,000	10·0	3·25 × 19	4·1	75	94

reed type may record nearly double that figure if skilful use is made of the pressure-waves in a resonant exhaust system. However, the speed range over which this very high output is attained will be even narrower than in the case of the four-stroke with high specific output; the bottom falls out of the power-curve at around 8,000 r.p.m., making a six-speed gearbox essential for road-racing and rendering the engine useless for ordinary work.

The crux of the matter, where racing is concerned, is that everything, except reliability, must be subordinated to the need for obtaining power, though the shape of the power-curve must suit the kind of racing for which the engine is intended. Further, the reliability must be of the order which will withstand very high stresses for short periods under good conditions—rather than less intense duty for an indefinite time, possibly under the very adverse conditions, including neglect and poor maintenance, which fall to the lot of many touring engines.

For example, the speedway J.A.P., with its scanty finning, cast-iron cylinder head and drip-feed, total-loss lubrication system—but very rugged, simple and easy to work on—is an ideal example of a design built and developed for, and invincible in, a specialized sphere of operation. In this case, the demands to be met were a moderately high output allied to an ability to "hang on" at low speed and pull away from a momentary check without the help of a gearbox.

At the other end of the scale could be placed the 500 c.c. Guzzi V-8, in which complexity has been carried about as far as it can be in a two-wheeler, and to a degree which would render it useless for the knock-about work in which the J.A.P. seems to revel. In between there are engines like the double-o.h.c. Norton which, though not quite as fast as a highly developed multi-cylinder, is robust, simple to tune and relatively easy to maintain, and therefore probably a better proposition for the rider who has to do his own work, or at least does not have a flock of factory mechanics to do it for him.

There is another matter worth remembering, too. It is easier and less expensive in the long run to make a very fast, or potentially very fast, engine in the first place, and subsequently modify it or de-tune it for use on the road, than it is to start with a touring engine and then try to make it into a racer—as more than one factory has found out the hard way.

"Sticking strictly to the script" in embodying all the design principles essential to a top-flight racer may, however, result in a product which even when de-tuned is too expensive for the bread-and-butter market —as witness the present-day absence of the once-popular overhead camshaft in this field. A designer may, therefore, have to make some concessions in order to conform to the sales policy of his company.

This course of action has been discernible in the development of some models, especially for competing in events of the Clubman type. It is not by any means a bad thing, because the fruits of experience gained in racing can be almost directly incorporated into other models in the range which are substantially similar in design, whereas it may be difficult or even impossible to do so if the racing and production models are markedly different.

FIG. 8.8. An engine designed to give uttermost economy in production, consumption and maintenance. It is the 98 c.c. Villiers unit used in Britain's cheapest motorcycle—the Excelsior "Consort".

CRUISING SPEED

Whereas a racing engine is driven at or near its maximum all the time, it is more usual, on the open road at least, to drive a touring engine at its best cruising speed.

"Cruising speed" is one of those terms which everyone seems to understand, but nobody can define accurately; one possible description is the speed at which the vehicle appears to travel most happily. It will work up to that speed almost by itself, yet a conscious effort has to be made to push it along at any higher velocity. Some models do not exhibit this characteristic very strongly, but others do—in fact they almost "go to sleep" at some point in their speed range, buzzing along quite happily with the throttle rolled well back after the cruising speed has been reached.

123

It will be found that, provided the top-gear ratio is correct, the engine r.p.m. corresponding to this "best" speed is very close to 4,000 r.p.m. for all contemporary o.h.v. engines designed to produce around 50 b.h.p. per litre with good flexibility, irrespective of their cylinder capacity. The super-sports type of motor with higher compression ratio may cruise better at 4,500 r.p.m., whilst with side-valvers and two-strokes the speed may be more like 3,500.

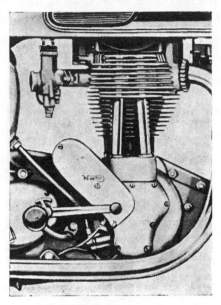

FIG. 8.9. A type once supreme in British motorcycle favour—the 500 c.c. o.h.v. single. The example seen above is that of the ES2 Norton.

"Cruising speed" is not necessarily—in fact it is unlikely to be—the most economical speed, but it gives the best return measured in miles per gallon per hour's running; and, after all, to many people time is of greater value than money, a factor which is sometimes overlooked when comparing the running costs of rival models.

The existence of a well-defined cruising speed is probably bound up with the fact that the peak of the torque curve also occurs at 4,000 r.p.m. in engines of average power output, and therefore at this speed both the combustion efficiency and the mechanical efficiency are of a high order.

To summarize: the easiest way to provide the tourist with more power and a high cruising speed without fuss is to use an engine of large capacity and of moderate specific power output rather than a smaller engine made into a semi-racer.

A 1,000 c.c. engine developing 45 b.h.p. at 5,300 r.p.m. will propel a solo model at over 100 m.p.h. on a top gear of 3·5 to 1 and will cruise at 80 m.p.h., at which speed the engine is turning over at only 3,800. This ability to lope along in an effortless manner is the main charm of the big engine, especially when it is in twin-cylinder form.

But the big—and consequently heavy—machine has been steadily going down in public favour for some years until today it is no longer built in Britain and is in production by only one maker in the U.S.A., a country which has produced more models of between 1,000 and 1,300 c.c. than any other.

It would appear that the 650 c.c. engine, turning out around 35 b.h.p., is fast enough for the majority of hard riders, especially for areas where high speeds cannot be sustained for very long periods. As it is possible to design such an engine in the form of a parallel-twin without incurring too much trouble from the inherent lack of balance of this type, it is understandable that it should have achieved considerable popularity in recent years.

How Many Cylinders?

This brings us to the thorny question—how many cylinders? From the mechanical point of view, the fewer the better. From the aspect of smoothness, the opposite is the case, but there seems little to be gained in this direction by using more than one "pot" in sizes below 150 c.c. for touring purposes. This is especially true of two-strokes, because it is more difficult to obtain good idling with a twin-cylinder two-stroke than it is with a single.

The single begins to lose its attractiveness in two-strokes, for reasons already mentioned, in capacities above 200 c.c. The same thing occurs in four-stroke form above 350 c.c., when its lack of balance and irregular torque commence to outweigh the merits of simplicity. Nevertheless, there is still plenty of scope for this type even up to 500 c.c., but above that at least two cylinders are required to furnish the degree of refinement which one expects nowadays.

Whether the four-cylinder engine will ever come back to favour except for racing is doubtful. However the cylinders are arranged, either with a conventional transmission or with shaft-drive, one is up against very tricky cooling problems—unless one resorts to a complicated construction with geared crankshafts, or the engine is mounted transversely, as in Italian racing practice.

In the transverse four, cooling is about as good as it is possible to be, but is gained at the cost of a complicated, expensive and potentially noisy geared primary drive, into which it would not be very easy to incorporate a flywheel large enough for touring purposes. A possible alternative would be to take a leaf from the scooter designer's book and use fan cooling with fine-pitched, small-diameter cylinder fins enclosed in close-fitting cowls, though a fan of the necessary diameter would not be an easy component to fit into the space available.

Water-cooling

Another possibility would be to adopt water-cooling. This method has been used sporadically for many years and is found today on the LE Velocette and Scott, but it has never really been held in much esteem and its overall cost and weight are both greater than that of conventional direct air-cooling, which works perfectly well with either a parallel-twin or a V-twin.

There is no doubt that water cooling does confer some advantages, particularly on an engine whose design is such that (a) adequate cooling fins cannot be provided at vital places, or (b) no draught can reach those fins which are there.

The first conditions may exist in a four-cylinder engine of the in-line or V type which has its cylinders closely packed together in order to

FIG. 8.10. The only V-twin of its capacity built today, but once a type frequently used by designers of machines intended for heavy work—the 900 c.c. Harley-Davidson, from the U.S.A.

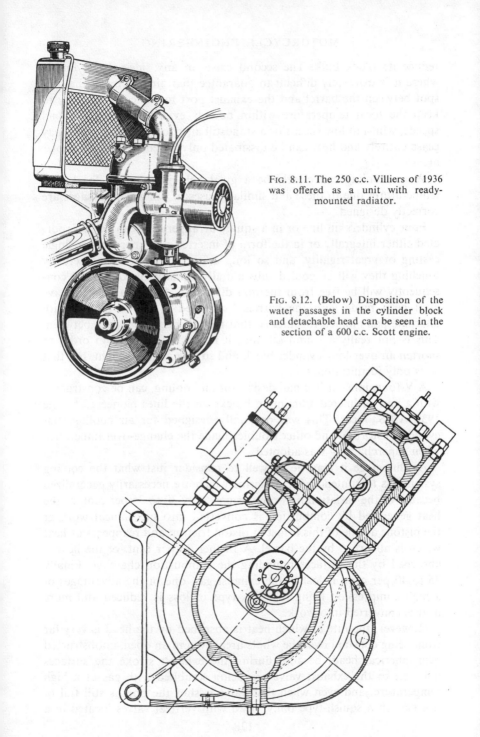

FIG. 8.11. The 250 c.c. Villiers of 1936 was offered as a unit with ready-mounted radiator.

FIG. 8.12. (Below) Disposition of the water passages in the cylinder block and detachable head can be seen in the section of a 600 c.c. Scott engine.

reduce its block bulk. The second exists in any side-valve cylinder, where it is extremely difficult to guarantee that air will reach the hot-spot between the barrel and the exhaust port in sufficient quantity to keep the local temperature within bounds even at perceptible road speeds, whilst at low speeds or a standstill air cooling at this point may cease entirely and heat can be dissipated only by conduction to cooler areas.

Water cooling can clearly be a great help in reducing local high temperatures due to these and similar causes, if the water passages are correctly designed.

Four cylinders, in line or in a square arrangement, can be incorporated either integrally or in the form of inserted wet liners into a single casting of great rigidity, and so long as the barrels are not actually touching they will be cooled substantially equally all round and consequently will be free from thermal distortion. Some car blocks have even been made with the barrels "siamesed"; that is to say, with alternate pairs joined together so that there is no water-space between. This is not really a sound scheme; it is usually adopted in order to shorten an over-long cylinder block and so save a little weight, but that is its only justification.

A V-four, inherently a bad design for air cooling, can be constructed with a pair of linered aluminium blocks on the lines pioneered by the 1939 A.J.S. racer. This was originally designed for air cooling, but cylinder distortion and other troubles made the change-over imperative when supercharging was adopted.

At this stage it may be as well to consider just what the cooling system has to contend with. In terms which are necessarily generalized because of the variation between designs, only 30 to 35 per cent. of the heat generated by combustion is converted into mechanical work at the piston; a little of this is lost in piston friction and reappears as heat which is absorbed by the barrel. A further 30 per cent. of the heat is absorbed by the surfaces bounding the combustion chamber. Finally 35 to 40 per cent. is lost in the exhaust gas, one of the advantages of a high compression being that this type of loss is reduced and more heat is converted into work.

However, the rate at which heat is absorbed by the head is very far from being constant over the whole area, even in an open, unobstructed hemispherical head, because during the exhaust stroke the surfaces adjacent to the exhaust valve are being scrubbed with gas at a high temperature, and even when that valve is shut the port is still full of hot gas. In a squish-type o.h.v. head with vertical valves located in a bath-tub-shaped recess, the flat squish area is largely protected from the worst of the combustion heat—or, to be more exact, is purposely designed so that little or no actual burning takes place in the narrow gap between it and the piston crown—so this area keeps very much cooler than the exhaust-valve region.

The area around the inlet valve in any shape of head is the coolest of all, not so much because it absorbs less heat as because it is kept cool by the ingoing fresh mixture and by conduction back to the cold inlet port.

Now what one requires in the combustion chamber is, as in many other instances, a compromise between two extremes—not too hot, not too cold, but just right. The colder the surfaces and the higher the conductivity of the metal, the greater the absorption of heat and the reduction of power (hence some of the sluggishness of an engine when first started up). On the other hand, if the walls or parts of them, are too hot, trouble will arise through (a) detonation, which causes "pinking" and can be very destructive; (b) pre-ignition, which may cause a dull knock and, even if inaudible, reduces power through excessive pressure-rise towards the end of the compression stroke; or (c) "running-on", i.e., an annoying refusal to stop when the ignition is switched off.

These faults, it must be borne in mind, are all due to *surface* temperatures, and it is clear that the local high rate of heat absorption around the exhaust valve is less likely to lead to uncomfortably hot surfaces in this region if the thermal conductivity of the metal is high, so that part of the excess heat can be conducted swiftly away towards the colder areas to equalize the surface temperatures, and part can be transferred rapidly to the external surface from which all the heat has eventually to be dissipated, irrespective of whether finning or water-jacketing is employed.

The exhaust valve, assailed as it is on both sides by hot gases, has to do what it can to keep cool by conduction through the seat and also down the stem and thence to the valve-guide, which itself is partly exposed to high-temperature gas. Conduction through the seat can only occur while the valve is actually closed, and the longer the valve-opening period the less the time available for the process; so, in racing engines particularly, cooling via the stem and guide becomes the main outlet and great care is necessary in the design of this locality to achieve valve reliability.

In any good water-cooled engine, care is taken to provide ample water-spaces round the valve-guide boss and adjacent to the seat, while pipes are often included to direct the flow of water towards these danger areas. Unless some such provision is made, or the jackets are skilfully designed to bias the water-flow in this direction, local boiling accompanied by the formation of steam pockets may occur.

There is then a grave danger that an iron head (or block, in the case of a side-valve) may crack, either simply through getting too hot or through rapid cooling off and contraction should conditions suddenly ease and the pockets rapidly fill with cold water. (There is a system known as "vapour-phase" or evaporative cooling, in which boiling followed by condensation outside the engine is intentionally allowed to occur; but this method can be used successfully only in power-units with water passages expressly designed or inherently suitable for it.)

Most water-cooled car and truck engines are fitted with a pump to provide a flow of coolant adequate for all demands, a thermostat to reduce the flow for quick warming-up and to avoid over-cooling under easy conditions, a radiator to transfer heat to the air and a fan to provide an air flow when the forward speed is insufficient. All these things, plus a pressure-cap on the radiator to raise the boiling-point slightly at sea-level and maintain it at the same temperature at altitudes, are necessary to cope with every possible set of running conditions.

On a four-wheeler there is usually enough space for these ancillaries. The situation is different on a single-tracker which is sufficiently cramped for space already unless the engine is either small in itself or has been arranged to leave some free space within the frame, as on the LE Velocette. This model was specifically designed for water cooling from the drop of the hat, because one of the primary aims was longevity —a feature which could not have been attained with small side-valve cylinders due to the difficulty, already noted, of eliminating local high temperatures and distortion between the exhaust ports and barrels. The problem is not present in the o.h.v. variant of this engine which is satisfactorily air-cooled.

Nevertheless, from time to time, designers have produced water-cooled models, some of which, notably the Scott, have been highly successful, utilizing only the simple thermo-syphon system.

A two-stroke barrel suffers very intensely from large temperature differences in areas which are close together and therefore prone to cause cylinder distortion. Differential cooling to cure this effect at least partially can be provided by the simple expedient of feeding the cool water into the jacket immediately adjacent to the exhaust port (or between twin ports) and, if necessary, deflecting the flow away from the transfer-port region by internal baffling or similar means. This scheme was adopted in the 250 c.c. Villiers of the mid-thirties which had two exhaust and four transfer ports; whereas the air-cooled version of the same engine could be overdriven on a hot day, it was impossible to tire the water-cooled model provided, of course, the radiator was adequate.

FIG. 8.13. Radiator of the 1959 250 c.c. Adler racer is placed high in relation to the cylinder block and equipped with a pressure-cap. Note large water passages and biasing of flow towards the exhaust-port side.

It is perhaps significant that nearly all examples of water-cooling in recent years have been two-strokes intended purely for racing, where the air-speed is high for most of the time and the lowness of the engine, and particularly of the exhaust system, not only allows enough space for a radiator large enough to handle a relatively modest horse-power, but permits it to be mounted at such a height that thermo-syphon circulation is adequate.

This system, which does away with the need for a pump, depends upon the fact that hot water is lighter than cold. It has the advantage that circulation does not commence until the engine itself is fairly warm, and thereafter automatically adjusts itself to demand. However, it will not provide a sufficiently rapid flow unless the top of the radiator is well above the outlet from the cylinder jacket. Even then, if for any reason the radiator ceases to reject heat as fast as it receives it, the water temperatures on the hot side and the cold side will tend to equalize, the thermo-syphon action will slow down and cease, and boiling will commence soon after.

The most probable cause of this condition is a lack of cooling air travelling in the right direction, which is of course, square to the main radiator surface, whereas the fins of an air-cooled cylinder can reap a benefit from whatever direction the breeze arrives. At a standstill, neither can keep going indefinitely, though the air-cooled cylinder is at an advantage, because the rate of pure radiation (as opposed to transfer of heat to the air in contact with the fins) increases as the fourth power of the temperature, and consequently a moderate rise in temperature results in a greatly increased rate of rejection by this means, which is quite evident to anyone astride a machine in traffic on a hot day.

A radiator, despite its name, cannot make use of this phenomenon because it cannot rise above boiling-point, and this it may attain very quickly in the absence of air from straight ahead. One method of assistance is to incline the radiator forward so that air can move through the core by natural convection; this is a feature of the Scott, but if overdone may reduce the efficiency at high speed.

The whole problem could be solved by fitting a fan. This, however, is bulky, difficult to drive on a conventional motorcycle and, unless carefully guarded, is likely to inflict physical injury on an unsuspecting mechanic—altogether something to be avoided in this application, although it is a perfectly feasible proposition when flywheel-mounted and cowled, as is now common practice on many scooters.

Thermo-syphon circulation operates with only a few ounces per square inch pressure differential, and therefore requires large areas in order to promote an adequate rate of flow. These can be provided easily in a two-stroke, but not so easily in a four-stroke, especially in the danger areas round the exhaust valve and sparking-plug boss.

By fitting a pump the water can be forced to go where it is most needed, and it even becomes possible to use ethylene-glycol, which is more viscous than water, to keep the general temperature of the engine higher. This circulation system was used on the A.J.S. racer but, besides providing an extra component to drive, it complicates the pipework and is a potential source of water leaks.

The geared-twin, supercharged racing Velocette ("The Roarer"), which was at the paper stage when the A.J.S. first appeared in its water-cooled form with twin radiators, was originally intended also to be water-cooled, but Harold Willis was so horrified by the apparent bulk and complexity of the Woolwich product that he instantly reverted to air-cooling, despite the fact that the exhaust ports were at the rear and thus deprived of any direct air-blast. He did not know, at the time, that only one of the A.J.S.'s two radiators was in use and that the apparently enormous pump-casing contained an impeller of exactly the same size as the one he had intended to fit.

On the score of cost, water cooling is probably the more expensive, partly because a radiator with the stylish appearance necessary on an open motorcycle is not a cheap item and some extra parts and work are entailed in assembling and coupling-up the cooling system. Some benefit is to be expected in mechanical silence because the water-jacket acts as a sound-deadener, but advances in cam and valve-gear design and the adoption of pistons which can be run with very close clearances have resulted in some air-cooled engines being so quiet that there would be little gain from water-cooling them.

All in all, therefore, it would appear that for everyday use with conventional o.h.v. engines, in single or twin-cylinder form, air cooling is as good as, and in some respects better than, water cooling. It also results in a motorcycle which is easier to build and subsequently to work upon; and it has no freezing troubles in winter-time.

Fig. 8.14. Water cooling for performance: the very fast 500 c.c. A.J.S. supercharged V-four racer of 1939. Only one of the twin radiators was actually used.

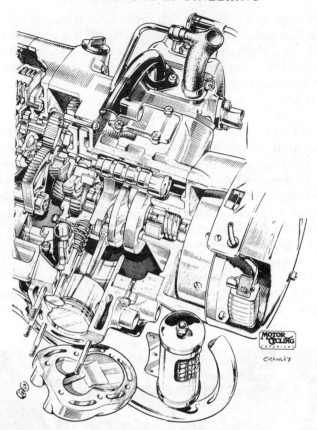

FIG. 8.15. Water cooling for longevity; engine section of the 200 c.c. Velocette LE power unit. The LE is the only two-wheeler now in large-scale production to be designed specifically for water cooling.

For racing, water cooling is unnecessary except for engines with tightly packed cylinders, but it may be of great advantage for two-strokes of very high specific output. Another worth-while application might be for a record-breaker using a very compact, heavily super-charged four-cylinder unit with a skin-surface radiator forming part of the shell and offering very little extra air resistance; the idea has been tried on cars and aeroplanes and certainly offers possibilities which have not so far been exploited on a two-wheeler.

COMPETITION POWER UNITS

This is the age of the specialist and therefore of specialized machines. Gone are the days when one model of motorcycle was expected to serve as a tourer, a racer, a hill-climber and a scrambler merely by adding or subtracting odd bits such as guards, lamps and silencers, and pouring different-smelling liquids into the tank, according to the requirements of the moment. A private owner can still get a lot of fun

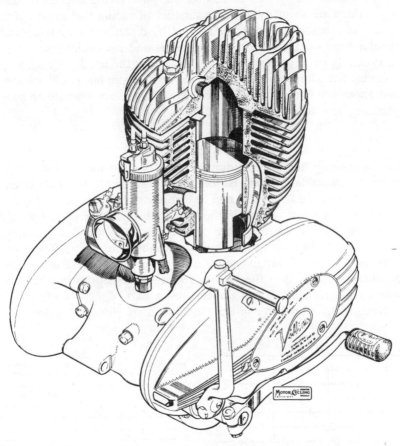

FIG. 8.16. During the past few years small two-stroke engines have made immense strides in the competition world. Here is one of the most popular, the 250 c.c. Villiers 33A/4 scrambles unit. The 32A/4, for trials, is similar in general design.

that way—especially if he is not upset by running last most of the time with an occasional "blow-up" for good measure—but the matter assumes different proportions to the executives of a factory which depends for its well-being and commercial prosperity upon success in the competition field.

Much can be, and has been, accomplished with a basic engine more or less modified to suit the conditions; but, generally speaking, an engine designed specifically with one object in view will out-perform one which has merely been modified.

The classic example is, of course, the pure racing engine, though again there are so many different varieties of racing that invincibility in any one branch can only be assured by directing all thinking and development towards the special problems and difficulties peculiar to it. Probably the prime exponent of this art was the late Joe Craig, who regarded the winning of the T.T. as the highest aim one could achieve, and about five minutes after collecting one Island event would be busy planning how to win it again next year.

THE ROAD RACER

Let us consider the prime requirements of a road racer. First of all, it must be reliable (the late Harold Willis' dictum, "They only count the winners at the finish", should be emblazoned on the walls of every drawing office)—but reliable in the sense that it has to keep going only for the distance of the race, after which it can be overhauled by skilled mechanics. There is no need to build-in reliability of the "50,000 miles between overhauls" variety; but, on the other hand, there is no time nowadays to pull into the pits to repair some pettifogging trouble which a tourist might accept as being just a part of the day's fun.

Next, it must be faster *in lap speeds* than its rivals. This does not

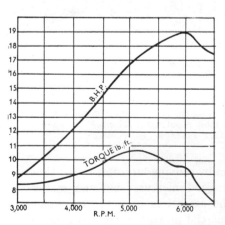

FIG. 8.17. Output curves for the "scrambles" Villiers 33A/4.

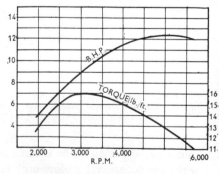

FIG. 8.18. Output curves for the "trials" Villiers 32A/4 Thermometer and barometer corrections have been made in respect of both this graph and that in Fig. 8.17.

necessarily mean that its flat-out maximum must be higher, though that is obviously an advantage, especially on a very fast circuit or one containing a long straight where an ultra-quick model can build up such a lead that the rest of the field cannot catch it on the twisty bits.

Three or four extra horse-power at the top end of the speed-range may be dearly bought if they can be obtained only by sacrificing much power lower down, especially on difficult circuits, even if the gearbox has five, or even six, ratios to enable the rider to keep the revs. in the useful range at all times. The availability or otherwise of such a box has an effect on the shape of the power curve to be aimed at, and also on what might be termed the minimum useful speed. However, even if there are only four ratios, they can be so close for any of the courses used for today's International events that there is little need to bother about what happens below 6,000 r.p.m. to an engine which peaks at around 8,000.

Reliability and the ability to sustain power for long periods is bound up very closely with good cooling which, in turn, may be completely nullified by matters external to the power unit. In road racing, there is almost always plenty of cooling air available somewhere in the vicinity, but the problem is to utilize it effectively when it is deflected away from the engine by the wheel, forks and (in most cases) frame which lie in front of it.

The answer with unenclosed vertical singles was to widen the fins until they reached out into the air-stream, but the situation has been radically changed by the advent of frontal streamlining. A thorough investigation into its effects might conceivably lead to a return to shallower and therefore lighter fins, enclosed within ducts fed by air from the front of the shell—a scheme which, though it might work very well on racers and record-breakers, would be of little use for tourers, where the air-speed might often be down to nothing or even reversed in direction.

Power/weight Ratio

For maximum acceleration, a high power/weight ratio is essential, but it is a false move to endeavour to save weight on the power plant if this entails any loss of performance or stamina. On the other hand, as manufacturing cost is of little moment, expensive steels and high-strength light alloys can be freely used, or components which commercially would have to be made from castings might be made, at very many times the cost, from solid forgings machined to shape. Even so, it is bulk, rather than absolute strength, which determines the rigidity of a component, and racing engines of this variety are, if any-thing, heavier than they used to be, despite the employment of materials of high specific strength.

Part of the weight of a touring engine is accounted for by the fly-wheels, which, even on a multi-cylinder engine, must have a considerable mass for the sake of flexibility and good manners when changing gear. In racing, with compulsory push-starts, strictly one-way traffic and very close, easily-changed gear ratios, neither of these attributes is necessary to any marked extent, and flywheels, as such, can be almost dispensed with, the mere mass of the smallest discs which can just accommodate the crank-throw being sufficient in itself where rotational speeds approaching five figures are concerned. It is then up to the rider to avoid either stopping the motor or bursting it through inaccurate co-ordination of two hands and one foot when changing gear. This is not such a dreadful matter as it sounds, since the road surface is usually good, while gear-change points can be discovered in advance during practice and in any case are indicated by the tachometer, which the rider usually has the opportunity to observe.

It is sometimes said that powers have not increased as rapidly as they might have done over the years; but it must be remembered that we still have only 14·7 lb./sq. in. air pressure and the calorific value of petrol has remained substantially constant. That being so, the only really practical way to get more urge, in the absence of supercharging, is by increasing the rotational speed and designing the valve-gear so that it can accept these higher revs. This means the adoption of the double-overhead-camshaft principle, which is bulky, heavy and expensive, or even the "desmodromic" or mechanically returned valve-gear, which is even more complicated but enables fantastically high engine speeds to be achieved. With these developments goes the utmost utilization of pressure-waves in the exhaust and inlet systems, especially in two-strokes, a practice which is fast approaching the point where the realms of acoustical engineering are entered.

Fuel Consumption

Contrary to what might be imagined, the specific fuel consumption (i.e., pints consumed per b.h.p. per hour) is not at all bad on racing four-stroke engines—and neither can it afford to be, for an engine with an insatiable thirst needs either an enormous weight of fuel on board or an extra pit-stop and the time-loss occasioned by whichever expedient is chosen may put it right out of the winning bracket. Here is another case in which an unbridled search for more power regardless of other things may defeat its own object. The trouble was particularly prevalent years ago with two-strokes, but of recent times it has been overcome to a large extent by the development of ports and exhaust systems which do not cause so much charge-loss as the older designs.

Thus we see that the trend in road-racing design has inevitably been towards robust but high-revving engines, which have good cooling, a high degree of stamina and reasonable consumption, but are expensive, mechanically complicated, not particularly light, and deficient in flexibility and low-speed pulling power.

SHORT-DISTANCE ENGINES

Most of these characteristics are unsuitable or even undesirable for short-distance work such as grass-track or speedway racing, and the designer's approach to engines for such uses must be coloured by quite different thinking. Power is, of course, essential, but it must be there in plenty from perhaps 2,000 r.p.m. upwards. To be more accurate, high *torque* at low and medium speeds is required, because either the machines are single-geared or they should be capable of "holding" a gear at times when a change would not be practicable; in a sliding turn, for instance, continuous traction is essential and you cannot change gear in the middle of it.

These considerations limit the extent to which "long" valve timings and resonant inlet and exhaust systems can be exploited and so automatically reduce the ultimate power output; but this limitation is not wholly bad, because the mechanical and thermal stressing are thereby kept down to reasonable figures. This permits the design to be directed towards lightness, which is essential in the interests of easy handling as much as for acceleration, but as the majority of such engines will be sold to the public in quantity and not just built in small handfuls to be owned and maintained by the factory, manufacturing costs must be considered, and so must ease of maintenance. The gritty atmosphere usually present promotes rapid wear of barrels, rings and valve-stems (if the latter are exposed), but this assumes less importance if stripping down and reassembly is quick and easy, and replacements are relatively cheap, which implies that they are light and of inexpensive materials.

For grass-tracking and speedway, alcohol fuels are permitted. This factor permits compression ratios as high as 14:1 to be used, and goes some way towards solving the cooling problem because the fuel possesses a high latent heat of evaporation—that is to say, it takes a lot of heat to convert it from liquid to vapour and this heat must be extracted either from the ingoing air or from the interior surfaces of the engine. To obtain an efficient combustion chamber shape at very high compression, it is best to make the stroke perceptibly longer than the bore, and this in turn makes for less area in contact with the gas at maximum temperature, thus further assisting cooling. Valve sizes may be restricted compared with those of a "square" engine, but will be adequate for speeds up to 6,000 r.p.m. or so, and will be better than the large valves for maintaining torque at low speeds—a matter which is also assisted by a considerable angle of offset of the inlet port, though this has an adverse effect on power as the speed rises.

Although an aluminium-alloy head is lighter than one of cast iron, it is not strictly necessary for this work, because iron warms up more rapidly—an advantage with alcohol when no extensive warm-up periods are allowed—yet will keep cool enough for short events even with scanty finning, a point which applies to the barrel as well. Push-rod operation of the valves is adequate and is lighter, less bulky and much easier to overhaul than any form of o.h. camshaft. Also, there is no necessity to circulate vast quantities of oil through the motor for cooling as well as lubrication, so even the "total-loss" system will serve.

Probably the best example of a true short-distance engine developed along these lines is the 500 c.c. J.A.P. which, though it has changed to some extent through the years, is fundamentally the same as when it started life. Weighing only about 70 lb. and developing some 42 b.h.p., it achieved pre-eminence in the speedway world and, together with its 350 c.c. brother, supplies the power for many a successful grass-tracker. A comparison between this motor and the double-o.h.c. Norton clearly shows how two lines of specialization have been brought to their logical conclusion; though the Bracebridge Street product is, of course, outmatched by the Italian multi-cylinder engines, which are even better examples of the pursuit of the ultimate for the job in hand.

SPRINT ENGINES

An engine designed for short-distance racing makes a good jumping-off place to the construction of a real sprinter, intended for standing quarter-miles and kilometres, or hill-climbs which rarely take more than 40 seconds. Here, however, one can go to even greater extremes in cutting down areas or weights to save ounces, even at the expense of drastically shortening the life of the components concerned. But this is a field for the owner rather than the designer, since an individual can take risks with his own engine which a factory would not dare to do with units sold over the counter to anyone who comes along. It is worth noting, though, that sometimes the designer was right in the first place, and cutting down the original weight of some components at the expense of rigidity may lose far more than it gains, whilst reducing strength too far may result in a blow-up in the first hundred yards.

SCRAMBLES ENGINES

Scrambling, or moto-cross, confronts the designer with a very difficult set of conditions. A high power/weight ratio as well as low total

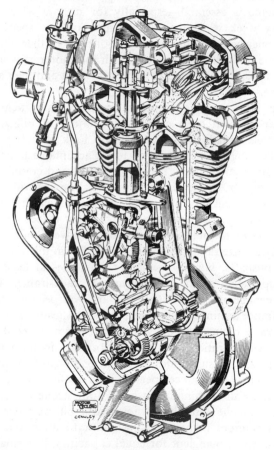

FIG. 8.19. The 350 c.c. Velocette "Viper"—an engine equally at home in scrambles or on the highway.

weight is highly desirable, but tractability is almost as vital, partly because fairly wide gear ratios are demanded on some courses and partly because a rider may not always be in a position to change into the correct gear precisely when and where he should. An ability to withstand unintentionally high revs. without bursting anything is necessary, because the motor may on occasion find itself flat on its side screaming its heart out, with the rider temporarily detached and picking himself up some yards away.

The general conditions are often filthy in the extreme, with clods of earth or streams of mud flying in all directions, and therefore efficient air cleaning and complete protection against entry of dust or water into the engine is essential—especially for motors which are raced almost every week while the intervening days are spent largely in travelling somewhere else to wear them out yet further. Cooling also presents some difficulty because, although the motor is working hard most of the time, the air-speed is never very high and may at times be down to zero.

Dry-sump lubrication is of assistance here, as it achieves some internal heat removal by a copious circulation of oil. Aluminium-jacketed barrels with light-alloy heads can look after the air-cooling side whilst keeping the weight down to an acceptable figure—so long as they remain clear of mud. The fewer nooks and crannies there are around the cylinder, the better on this score. The fins will still clog up in time, of course, but they will at least be less difficult to clean out.

The valves of o.h.v. engines are always likely to become entangled with each other or to foul the piston crown above a certain rev. limit. Push-rod engines are rather more likely to suffer in this way than those with o.h. camshafts, but, in the larger capacities at least, the extra bulk and top weight of the latter layout is undesirable. A push-rod motor can be made proof against momentary overspeeding by providing enough clearance around and between the valve heads to avoid fouling even above valve-bounce speed, even though this may entail a lowering of the compression ratio. These precautions are in the nature of an insurance, and are not substitutes for ensuring, by careful cam and valve gear design, that valve-bounce speed is high enough in the first place.

In general, an all-aluminium push-rod four-stroke of solid internal construction fills the scrambling/moto-cross bill very well, but the two-stroke has more than a passing claim to attention. It has no poppet valves to be mangled; for equal capacities, it is smaller than a four-stroke and so can provide a greater ground clearance for less top-weight; and it can usually be made to develop as much power per c.c., though it is difficult to make it maintain this equality over the whole speed range. A two-stroke with very good top-end power is even more likely to be "gutless" at low speed than a four-stroke; but with greater attention being focused upon port design and the development of rotary or reed inlet valves this deficiency may be redressed.

Scrambles engines suffer more than most from violent shocks due to the machines repeatedly taking off over bumps and landing. The effort of the flywheels to accommodate themselves to the rapid changes of speed encountered by these circumstances is apt to pull a built-up assembly out of alignment, especially if the flywheel is located on the side opposite to the primary drive (as it often is on two-strokes because of the difficulty of placing both on the same side and also fully enclosing them). This means that great care should be taken in the design to see that there is no possibility of the crank-webs moving on the pin; this can be done by allowing plenty of high-tensile material around the hole and providing the largest possible crankpin with the correct amount of interference.

Basically, the Scott layout, with overhung pins and a central flywheel, is very good in this respect, as even if the two halves of the shaft did move they would still remain in alignment, while the flywheel's central position ensures its protection without excessive width or liability to strike the ground on corners or in ruts. The parallel-twin four-stroke with centrally placed flywheel is also good in this respect; furthermore, its crankshaft assembly cannot be pulled out of line, because it is either cast in one piece or built up with the components located by dowel pins on large diameters, instead of merely by frictional grip.

TRIALS ENGINES

Engines for trials of the mud-and-rock-climbing variety beloved of British organizers require two outstanding characteristics—tractability from the maximum right down to tick-over speeds and invulnerability from mechanical damage, either self-inflicted or from external causes. Minimum width at or near ground level, to give clearance over rocks, is of prime importance. This and the "mechanical damage" item just about rule out the transverse h.o. twin and put a premium on the inherently narrow four-stroke single, for solo use anyway.

Tractability, vital when negotiating very difficult terrain, is gained by the use of "slow" valve timings and small carburetter sizes and the elimination of peaks or hollows in the power curve through wave-action or resonance in the inlet and exhaust systems—just the reverse of racing practice. Either flat spots or surges of power would obviously be very disconcerting to a rider picking his way carefully up a steep, rocky gully by skilful use of the throttle.

Sheer power is not of much importance, as any lack in this direction can be offset by a wide-ratio box, in which a "dreadnought" bottom gear can confer the ability to climb the side of a house, even if at a very low speed. In trials of this nature the ability to "get there" is paramount, and overrides any consideration of how fast you can go in the process.

But though the average speed from point to point may not be high in terms of m.p.h., in terms of physical effort it may be very high indeed—so much so that towards the end of the day fatigue begins to take its toll and undermines the rider's ability. Broadly speaking, a lightweight is less exhausting to handle than a heavyweight, and this would in some measure account for the increasing success of small machines in exceptionally severe events such as the Scottish Six Days Trial.

CHAPTER 9

Choosing the Valve Layout

THE first four-stroke motorcycle engines used mushroom or poppet valves for controlling the flow of gas to and from the cylinders. Since then, despite shortcomings which have prompted the invention of many other types, the poppet valve has maintained its top position in the popularity poll, and today it is unchallenged in the automotive field.

The ways in which these valves may be installed and operated, however, are legion, and from time to time almost every possible arrangement has been tried. At present, inclined overhead valves operated by push-rods and rockers are practically universal, but it was not ever thus. For many years, side-valve engines held pride of place, and the inlet-over-exhaust arrangement has been used on several very successful engines.

Especially in the formative years, when it was hard to make a reliable engine at all without bothering about combustion efficiency or high specific power, the simple side-valve was often the designer's first choice. In this scheme (Fig. 9.1. (a)) the valves are located parallel (or approximately parallel) to each other and alongside the cylinder barrel, which

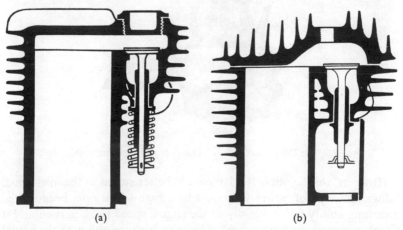

(a) (b)

FIG. 9.1. The early fixed-head side valve (a) was detonation-prone and irregularly cooled. Far better combustion-chamber shape is provided by the detachable-head layout (b) on the right.

145

can be made as a complete unit by casting a lateral extension wherein the valves operate, and which includes the inlet and exhaust ports.

Originally, screwed valve-caps were provided to permit assembly of the valves and their lower faces were approximately level with the upper surface of the combustion chamber, which extended right across the bore about half an inch above the piston crown at t.d.c. This shape was adopted partly because it assisted in machining the blind-ended bore, and partly because it was not then realized that it was about the worst possible shape from the detonation point of view—a fact which called for a skilful and knowledgeable hand on the manual ignition control lever, which was almost as important as the throttle.

On the credit side, as the valves were opened by short tappets operated by cams either directly or through lever-type followers, the mechanism was about as simple, light and direct as it was possible to be, and was potentially capable of running at very high revolution rates, as witness the 250 c.c. J.A.P.—produced *circa* 1920 and reputed to be capable of 8,000 r.p.m.

Fig. 9.2. The 250 c.c. J.A.P. (*circa* 1920). Note "Fir-cone" valve caps.

However, this layout is fundamentally better suited to the low-speed, "slogging" type of power unit than to a high-speed one, because the breathing ability falls off badly as the engine speed rises, particularly if a high compression ratio is used. This is so because although the actual ports can be made with the smooth curves and easy contours conducive to good gas-flow, the ingoing mixture has to undergo *two* changes of

146

direction after it negotiates the valve-seat and before it can enter the cylinder proper. Also there is a considerable interference with gas-flow through the proximity of the combustion-chamber wall and "ceiling" around and above the valve-heads; any endeavour to raise the compression ratio by reducing the clearance volume causes greater interference and reduced volumetric efficiency, so that beyond about 8:1 the loss from one source cancels out the gain from the other.

The discovery by Sir Harry Ricardo that "pinking", or detonation, arose through uncontrolled and instantaneous combustion of the last portion of the charge within the cylinder head considerably altered the side-valve picture. Ricardo's solution was to concentrate the greater part of the clearance volume over the valves, leaving a flat portion of the head extending over most of the bore diameter, with only a very small clearance over the piston crown, which was also flat (Fig. 9.1. (b)).

In the Ricardo layout, the space between crown and head is so small, and the surfaces so cool in relation to combustion temperatures, that the gas trapped in this "quench area" does not detonate. This, however, is only one of the merits of this head, which was so effective that the side-valve engine was able to hold its place against the overhead-valve in the car world for many years.

The additional advantages are: (a) more space and smoother internal contours can be provided round the valve-heads, giving better breathing; (b) the stream of gas "squished" out from the quench area at the end of compression creates a violent turbulence in the charge which promotes rapid, thorough burning and permits a moderately high compression ratio to be used without the excessive juggling with ignition timing which the older sort of head demanded. However, the restriction on breathing created by reducing the clearance volume, and also the area of the throat between the cylinder itself and the combustion space, still limits the highest useful ratio to about 8:1. The designer is in a somewhat similar predicament with valve sizes; if these are increased for better breathing, either the heads are masked by the walls or the ratio has to be lowered.

Owing to the difficulty of boring and honing a cylinder right up to a square corner, the Ricardo design necessitates a detachable head, with its attendant gasket and several studs; but this proved a blessing in a very thin disguise, because it did away with the old valve caps which, except in the case of the J.A.P. aluminium "fir-cone" variety and its imitators, were built-in hot-spots. It also opened the way to aluminium heads with deep diagonal finning for better cooling. Maintenance became easier, and so did manufacture.

Unfortunately, however, it did nothing to eliminate the main defect of the air-cooled side-valve cylinder, which is extremely difficult to overcome and which, in the last analysis, sets a limit to the power that can be obtained for any length of time. This is the fact that the area between the cylinder wall and the exhaust port receives heat from both sides and is almost impossible to cool effectively, even if a fan and cowling are fitted. In the days of belt-driven, clutchless models the self-generated cooling air speed was to some extent proportional to the throttle opening, except when hill-climbing—an exercise which brought on a loss of power loosely attributed to "overheating", but actually caused by valve-seat and cylinder distortion which at times was severe enough to cause temporary seizures.

The first man to detect this Achilles' heel was J. L. Norton, who attacked the problem by separating the exhaust port from the barrel wall and providing an air space between them so that cooling was a trifle better and there was far less likelihood of the port pulling the cylinder out of round. This feature alone went a long way towards explaining the outstanding success of his B.R.S., 16H and "Big Four" engines. Blackburne and some A.J.S. engines employed detachable heads with integral ports which did not distort the barrels.

Cooling difficulties became even more acute with the advent of geared transmissions and heavier machines, and were even accentuated by some later developments aimed at enclosing and lubricating the valve gear which, when run open, suffered from too little oil on the stems, leading to rapid wear, and too much oozing out of the tappets, leading to a messy exterior.

The English system of enclosure was to cast a box, with a detachable cover, on the side of the barrel—an expedient which cured the lubrication problems, but at the expense of placing an air-blanket over a quarter of the barrel area, which manifestly is a bad idea. There were, it is true, efforts by some designers to reduce the ill-effects in minor ways, but the better system was that developed in America, whereby the operating mechanism of each valve was enclosed in a tube which did little to impede air-flow.

Transatlantic designers also took the sensible course of swinging the exhaust port well away from the cylinder instead of keeping it in a plane parallel to the centre-line of the machine. Some American side-valve engines are capable of very high sustained speeds thanks to this attention to basic principles—and also, of course, to a desire to hang on to the type, although it had ceased to have much attraction in England after the advent of o.h.v. designs which were just as reliable and silent as the side-valve design but which developed much greater power.

There could still be a field of application for the side-valve, however, in water-cooled form, where the local overheating problem can be solved by correct design of the water-passages. The LE Velocette is the only example of the type now in production, but it is possible to envisage a very neat, compact in-line 500 c.c. four, producing about 20 b.h.p. at 5,000 r.p.m., which would be small enough to mount transversely— even, possibly, just in front of the rear wheel, scooter-fashion, and with the radiator built into the leg-shields.

INLET OVER EXHAUST

Another type of valve gear, which had a considerable following for many years, is the "inlet-over-exhaust" (i.o.e.), with its inverted alternative, "exhaust-over-inlet".

In its earliest versions, the i.o.e. had a cam-operated side exhaust valve, with an automatic inlet valve located co-axially and vertically above it; the inlet valve was contained in a cage and the exhaust valve could be extracted through the opening left when the cage assembly was removed.

From this rudimentary scheme it was but a short step to adding a

FIG. 9.3. Two pre-First World War examples of i.o.e., both with full mechanical operation —the 327 c.c. NSU of 1912 (left) and the 293 c.c. Velocette which appeared in the following year.

rocker and push-rod to operate the inlet mechanically, and a very worthwhile engine resulted. The Rudge which won the 1914 Senior T.T. was a good example of the type, which the firm retained until discarding it in favour of the four-valve o.h.v. model. Other famous users were the Swiss M.A.G. and the American Harley-Davidson, one of which was the first machine officially to attain 100 m.p.h. at Brooklands. (D. H. Davidson, 100·76 m.p.h. over the flying kilometre on April 28, 1921.)

Advantages of this layout as compared to the s.v. are that quite large valves can be used without unduly increasing the volume of the combustion chamber, and the cylinder cooling is better because the airflow between the barrel and the now-isolated exhaust port is greater than it can be when both valves are at the side. For somewhat the same reason, the degree of skill involved in moulding and casting the cylinder is less.

Another advantage is that the valve chamber can be narrower than the cylinder. This factor was of value for in-line four-cylinder engines such as the automatic-inlet F.N. as far back as 1910, and the later American Ace, Henderson and Excelsior.

However, the necessity of a cage for the inlet valve was a hindrance to obtaining smooth internal contours for easy gas-flow, while cylinder distortion due to unequal metal sections and differing local temperatures was still a problem. This was attacked by one or two makers by placing the exhaust valve overhead and the inlet valve below (e.g., the Martinsyde "Quick-Six"), while ex-R.F.C. "types" may recollect the V-eight R.A.F. engine which employed this valve arrangement and looked remarkably like a collection of motorcycle cylinders bolted to a common crankcase. It is interesting to note that possibly for reasons of accessibility, each sparking plug of the R.A.F. was fitted to the valve chest on the side remote from the cylinder—and about all one can say of this location is that, however hard you tried, you could not choose a worse one.

There are a few examples of i.o.e. engines still extant in the car world, and one or two conversion sets are available to convert a s.v. to i.o.e. with a sizeable increase in power, but these all make use of a detachable head and relatively large inlet valves located over, or nearly over, the bores. This method of construction suits a four- or six-cylinder engine, but if it is applied to an air-cooled single the result is more complicated than a side-valve and less efficient than an overhead-valve, so it is not surprising that there are no examples of i.o.e. or e.o.i. engines in production today for motorcycles.

Overhead Valves

Since an internal combustion engine operates by converting energy in the form of heat into mechanical energy, the less of the former that is lost during the process by being absorbed into the surrounding metal, the more efficient the engine will be. In simpler words, the smaller the surface area of the combustion chamber, the better.

Fig. 9.4. The engine which did so much to put "o.h.v." on the map—the original "Big-port" A.J.S. Large, inclined valves and light rocker gear were its most significant features.

This fact was recognized very early, and put into practice by inverting both valves, seating them directly in the head above the cylinder and operating them by means of rockers and push-rods. However, the first examples of this type, now commonly referred to as o.h.v., did not necessarily prove to be much faster than rival s.v. or i.o.e. engines, because they all suffered from identical limitations in other directions, such as inefficient port shapes, poor cooling, "slow" valve timings and detonation due to the wrong shape of combustion chamber and incorrect plug location.

In addition, vertical valves seated directly in a fixed head were necessarily less than half the bore in diameter, whilst they could be larger than that in either of the other types. This limited their breathing ability, but a worse defect was the ever-present bogy of a wrecked engine resulting from failure of the exhaust valve—a frequent occurrence before the development of high-hot-strength valve steels, and not unknown even today. When the exhaust valve is located in a pocket to one side of the cylinder, its decapitation is rarely attended by serious mechanical consequences, but these could be disastrous in an o.h.v., especially one with a fixed head and a cast-iron piston, even to the

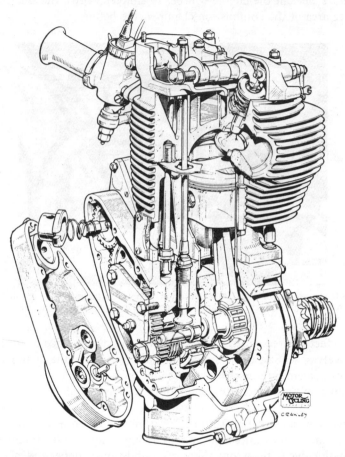

FIG. 9.5. Modern o.h.v. practice in a high-performance single. This view of a 500 c.c. B.S.A. "Gold Star" engine shows clearly the large valve area, advantageous combustion chamber shape and relatively clear porting obtainable with a good inclined valve layout.

extent of wrecking the whole top half of the engine beyond redemption if the catastrophe took place in the heat of battle.

Because of this weakness, designers were loath to employ strong valve-springs, so the inherent ability of the o.h.v. engine to maintain a high volumetric efficiency at high r.p.m. was largely lost. This fact enabled the side-valve to continue to win long-distance races for far longer than it should have done (the last major victory was the Sunbeam's Senior T.T. win in 1920), while the o.h.v.'s lack of reliability frightened off the man-in-the-street to a degree which militated against any manufacturer being game enough to stake his all by restricting his range solely to o.h.v. models.

Credit for ending this situation must go largely to the Stevens Brothers of Wolverhampton, who produced the "big-port" A.J.S.— which, thanks to its nickname, is remembered more for its one bad feature than for its good ones, of which the large, inclined valves and light rocker gear are the two most noteworthy for the purposes of this argument. With only 350 c.c. to play with, this little giant-killer was able to vanquish any contemporary engine up to twice its size, and did so with such regularity that the superiority of the o.h.v. principle was established beyond argument.

The reasons for this are not difficult to see, yet it has taken many years of painstaking work by knowledgeable technicians to realize all their implications and to translate them into physical form. Briefly, the use of inclined valves permits the valve-head size to be considerably larger than half the bore whilst making the combustion chamber approximate to the desirable part-spherical shape which has the least surface-to-volume ratio. Further, the contours of the inlet pipe and port can be of a shape favourable to gas-flow, the sparking plug can be placed in a situation which does not tend towards detonation, and (a most important point from the reliability aspect) waste heat inevitably absorbed by the exhaust-port walls does not effect the cylinder barrel, which can be a simple, symmetrical component with good all-round cooling and no built-in hot-spots.

Whilst not *absolutely* essential with this layout, a detachable head is desirable in the interests of easy assembly and maintenance. Although there may be more total work required to manufacture a separate head and barrel than a single component, the operations involved are simplified and subsequent repair work such as reboring is facilitated by the ability to handle each part separately. Foundry work is considerably simplified and there is no necessity to use the same metal for both parts; instead, the barrel can be made from an iron with outstanding wear resistance, while the head can be made from an iron possessing specially good fluidity when molten, or of aluminium-bronze or high-strength aluminium alloy with inserted or cast-in valve seats, according to the designer's own ideas on the matter.

With one or two exceptions, the o.h.v. engine has been developed with the accent on speed and power—a circumstance which has given it a reputation for roughness that is not really deserved. Whatever may be said in favour of alternative arrangements, the fact remains that the o.h.v. is capable of out-performing them in *any* particular—power, fuel economy, flexibility and even long life—provided that the design is correct in the first place and directed primarily at whichever of these attributes is the main aim. The conclusion, therefore, is a verdict in favour of the o.h.v., but a wide field of choice remains, for there are many ways in which the valves may be installed or operated while still coming under this general heading.

Overhead Valve Layouts

A clear majority of the car engines which use this kind of valve gear have all the valves located in a single row, usually offset by a small amount from the centre-line of the cylinders. The valves are vertical and operated by rockers and push-rods from a long camshaft carried in the block near the base of the cylinders.

This is, in essence, the same layout as that employed on the old "90-bore" J.A.P. V-twin of hallowed memory, except that in the latter engine the cylinder heads were non-detachable and were virtually merely plates or discs cast integrally with the barrels (Fig. 9.6). Ports and valve-guide housings were formed in a separate casting bolted to the flat outer face of the head, an arrangement whose sole merit was that it made the job of casting the cylinders much simpler.

It might, of course, be argued that it was better to have a poor design

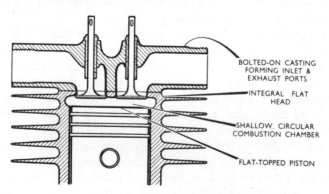

FIG. 9.6. Layout of a typical early o.h.v. design with parallel valves and integral flat head. Inefficient combustion chamber shape set a severe limit upon compression ratio.

which could be manufactured rather than a much superior design which could not be made at all, and in fact that position has always existed in engineering. The designer, especially in commercial work, is always limited to what the available materials will stand and what the available methods can accomplish.

In experimental and racing work, the more forceful type of designer tends to override these limitations, thereby spurring the metallurgist on to develop better alloys and the machine-shop and foundry to employ techniques of a more advanced nature, almost irrespective of their cost. Once the practicability of a special technique is established, it is the province of the production engineer to reduce the cost to an acceptable figure and rarely does he fail, although the process may take several years.

For example, the modern die-cast high-strength aluminium-alloy cylinder head, now accepted as commonplace, would have been an impossible dream not many years ago, but it has come into being through the racing designers' insistence on light-metal heads at all costs and the foundryman's skill in eventually evolving methods by which they have become a commercial proposition. However, this is not strictly germane to the issue, which is the design of the valve gear and combustion chamber.

To return to the vertical overhead-valve layout—the combustion chambers of the early air-cooled engines resembled a boot-polish tin in general shape, and detonation, though not so serious as on contemporary side-valves, was a problem which severely limited the usable compression ratio. The development of "squish" heads, following Ricardo's pioneering work on non-detonating side-valve heads, largely cured this trouble. The scheme was to locate the valves in a recess and machine the head so that portions of it were separated from the piston-crown at t.d.c. merely by the thickness of the gasket (Fig. 9.7). Near the end of compression, mixture was "squished" out from the narrow gap into the recess, thus creating the amount of turbulence necessary for rapid combustion, while the quenching effect of the cool surfaces in close proximity to each other eliminated detonation in the unburnt gas lying farthest from the plug.

Great—and sometimes exaggerated—claims were made for some of the head shapes developed along these lines for car engines. While they did permit the use of moderately high compression ratios with excellent economy and high torque at low and medium speeds, their breathing ability was restricted by the 90° bends in the ports and the close proximity of the valve-heads to the combustion-chamber walls, so their high torque could not be sustained at high r.p.m. and their maximum power development was therefore limited.

Nevertheless, from the production point of view, application of this head to an in-line multi-cylinder engine produced a layout so simple and straightforward that, with slight variations between makes, it is almost standard practice on cars today, excepting high-performance models. But the mechanical situation is different on engines with only one or two cylinders.

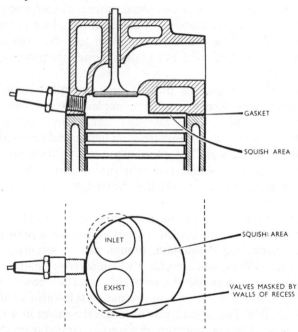

FIG. 9.7. A water-cooled o.h.v. head of the type employed in many car engines, showing how the valves are masked by their proximity to the combustion chamber walls.

In such cases, where the camshafts are quite short and the cylinder heads are usually individual castings, there is not much extra work involved in inclining the valves at a considerable angle, although it is a little more expensive because the size of the rockers and rocker-boxes is increased and any such increase must add to weight and therefore to cost.

Inclined Valves

Inclining the valves confers a number of benefits, in addition to permitting larger diameters to be used without exceeding the confines of the cylinder bore. The bend in the induction port is less acute, which is beneficial to good cylinder filling, and the exhaust port can be short and smoothly contoured, which helps in getting the spent gas away.

Possibly of even greater value is the reduction in the amount of waste heat absorbed by the walls of such a port as compared to a long,

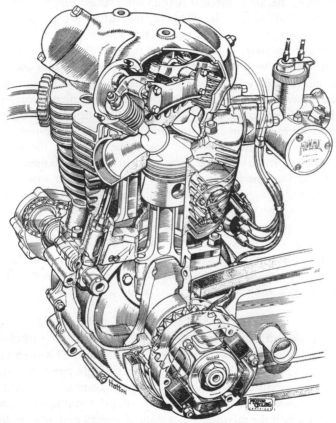

Fig. 9.8. A sectioned drawing of the Norton "Dominator 99" o.h.v. engine showing short, smooth, exhaust port.

square-cornered port in which the gas flow is erratic and turbulent. It has been estimated by research workers into cooling problems that about 45 per cent. of the total amount of heat absorbed by the head is picked up by the exhaust-port walls. Clearly, everything possible should be done to reduce this effect, as it leads to local high temperatures in the region of the valve-guide boss and causes the valve to run excessively hot, even to the point of failure.

157

Another advantage of inclined valves, especially in conjunction with aluminium heads, is that each valve is, or can be, disposed along an axis which is radial to the spherical portion of the combustion chamber. Presupposing that each valve is accurately in line with its seat when assembled cold, it will remain so when the whole head is at running temperature, because thermal expansion takes place substantially equally in all directions. If, however, the valves are parallel to each other, the seats, which are located in the hottest portion of the head, will move apart under the influence of thermal expansion and will become out-of-line with the valves, which are guided from a cooler area.

This effect leads to lack of gas-tightness and also accentuates any tendency towards valve breakage, because the heads do not seat squarely and the stems are consequently subjected to continual bending loads which, in time, they may fail to withstand. It is, of course, affected considerably by dimensions—the larger the cylinder, the worse the effect. Though it may not be very great in even the largest cylinders likely to be used in motorcycle work, nevertheless it can exist, and where engines of high power output are concerned it is best to eliminate it by disposing the valves radially. This was done in the very successful four-valve Rudges and the "Mechanical Marvel" Excelsior, about the only four-valve engines which ever managed to vanquish the conventional two-valver in road racing, where stamina is an essential attribute of success. However, the special aspects of heads with more than two valves is a wide subject which will have to be deferred.

TURBULENCE

Reference has already been made to the necessity for turbulence or "swirl" in the mixture to ensure rapid combustion. This is so because the rate of travel of a flame starting from a single point in stationary or quiescent mixture is so low that complete combustion could never be achieved in an engine operating at speed, but the process is speeded-up enormously if the mixture is in a state of violent agitation, preferably of an orderly kind which can be controlled in direction or intensity by the detailed configuration of the head or ports.

In "squish" heads, the size, position and minimum width of gap between the areas concerned are the main factors determining the amount of turbulence. Each of these can be modified easily in the experimental stages to obtain the optimum results, but in hemispherical heads with only one inlet valve, reliance is placed upon the angle of entry of the inlet gas-stream to establish a rotary "swirling" action of the whole charge (Fig. 9.10).

158

It has been clearly proved that once this induction-directed swirl has been established, it will continue in being for the whole of the three remaining strokes. As the rate of rotation of the mixture may be several times as fast as that of the engine itself, it is difficult to see how the swirl could possibly die out before the exhaust valve opens, though, of course, by that time its intensity has been considerably reduced.

The intensity of this mass turbulence depends mainly upon two things —the speed of the ingoing gas (which at full throttle is approximately proportional to engine speed) and the angle and direction at which the stream enters the cylinder. The least swirl—and, incidentally, the best volumetric efficiency—is given by a port lying in the plane of the valves (that is to say, directly fore-and aft in a conventional single) and with a large down-draught angle. Conversely more swirl is afforded by off-setting the port so that the gas enters tangentially to a greater or lesser degree according to the angle of offset, the amount of down-draught and the internal contours of the port; a "flattish" shape has more effect than one with a curve which brings the general direction of flow more in line with the axis of the valve.

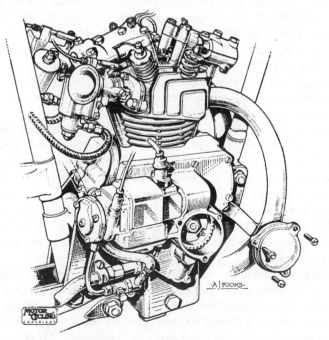

FIG. 9.9. Four radial valves and twin carburetters on splayed inlets—the Excelsior "Mechanical Marvel" of 1933.

In addition to this mass effect, local turbulence is set up by eddy-currents created by the ingoing gas tripping over its own feet as it passes the edges of the port and valve. This effect is quite valuable, especially at low engine speeds when the mass-turbulence is not very great, but the larger the valve the less it becomes, all other things being equal.

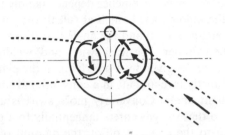

FIG. 9.10. Plan view of a cylinder head, showing how swirl can be produced by offsetting the angle of the inlet port. The exhaust port in this example has no offset.

It will, therefore, be appreciated that, for good tractability and an ability to pull well at low and medium speeds, a small valve fed by a port with a large amount of offset is required. But if one wishes to go higher up the speed range in order to get good top-end power, larger valves and straighter ports are required in the interests of volumetric efficiency; even ports with no offset at all and the largest valves that can be accommodated will provide enough natural turbulence for clean combustion at very high revolution rates.

This is another example of not being able to have one's cake and eat it. The features which are essential for good low-speed power are in opposition to those required for high-speed power and, in practice, a compromise between the two is necessary, with a bias in either direction according to the type of performance required. In general, an offset between 12° and 18° with an inlet valve of diameter equal to half the bore and lifted an amount equal to one-quarter of its diameter, will give very good all-round results in an engine whose bore and stroke do not differ greatly.

To keep manufacturing costs down, it is common to make both valves of the same dimensions and material, and therefore interchangeable. This scheme is of doubtful merit because, for various reasons, the exhaust can be, and should be, smaller than the inlet, and it requires a much more heat-resistant and expensive material. If both valves are identical, either the material is not quite good enough for the exhaust, or else unnecessary expense is incurred by making both valves from expensive steel. Making the valves dimensionally identical but of different steels is a practice fraught with grave consequences, because inevitably someone will put a valve in the wrong place and find himself faced with an expensive repair bill, for which without doubt (but with some degree of justification) he will blame the maker of the machine.

The better method, if the most costly, is to regard each valve as doing a different sort of job and to design it accordingly. The inlet is automatically kept cool by the ingoing charge, to which it must offer the least obstruction, because for every pound of difference between the pressure in the cylinder at the start of compression and that of the surrounding air there will be a reduction of one-fifteenth in power output. On the exhaust side, the bulk of the burnt gas is expelled by its own pressure, and a pound or so per square inch of pressure on the exhaust stroke will reduce the power by only about 1 per cent.

EXHAUST VALVE PROBLEMS

Being in contact with hot gas for most of the time, the exhaust valve runs very hot, even to the extent of glowing a dull red, and the surface of its head constitutes a possible source of self-ignition of the mixture before the spark is timed to occur. This hotness is not wholly detrimental, as it acts to vaporize the fuel, which enters the cylinder as minute droplets, and thereby promotes good combustion. Carried to excess, however, the effect is bad, but it can be limited to an acceptable amount by reducing the head diameter to 90 per cent. of that of the inlet, using a larger stem diameter and taking care to see that the valve-seat and guide are kept as cool as possible, because it is only through those two areas that heat absorbed by the valve can be dissipated.

Exhaust valves are liable to attack by lead through the products of combustion present in the exhaust when tetra-ethyl-lead has been added to the fuel as an anti-detonant, the villain of the piece being lead bromide. Austenitic steels such as KE 965 or Jessop's G2 or any which conform to the English specification D.T.D. 49b or EN54 are much more resistant to attack, which causes severe pitting and channelling across the seat, than are other less highly alloyed steels; they also possess much more strength at high temperatures, and so are safer all round. "Nimonic 80", a non-ferrous alloy, mainly composed of nickel and originally developed for the turbine blades of jet engines, is also coming into use and, in fact, is now standard equipment on the Velocette "Venom".

The Exhaust Port

A view down the exhaust port of an engine under load would show the hot gas impinging on the underside of the head, then bouncing off, striking the exhaust port walls and generally tying itself in knots before issuing from the port. This is bad for the valve, bad for gas-flow and bad because the violent scrubbing action causes much heat to be absorbed by the port walls and valve-guide boss, which is precisely what one wishes to avoid in the interests of valve cooling.

There is no way of eliminating this eddying entirely, but the effects can be reduced by widening the port considerably in the areas on each side of the guide-boss, so that it is actually wider than the valve throat. This is of especial value in those designs where the port has to be kept flat in order to reduce overall height, or to give enough clearance for valve springs in a limited space.

It has been thought that the angle of offset of the exhaust port, if any, is immaterial because it cannot affect combustion conditions in the same way as offset of the inlet port. A little reflection, however, will show that if there is a large amount of horizontal swirl in the gas it will be as well to humour it by offsetting the exhaust port in the same direction; in fact experimental work has proved that this is true. If one considers the residual gas whirling past the valve-head, it must obviously object to being forced to change direction through 90° in order to escape through the port, and this may well be part of the reason why engines designed with an excessive amount of swirl fall off in power at high speed.

CHAPTER 10

Head Design and Materials

UNTIL recently, cylinder heads and barrels shared with lamp-posts the distinction of commonly being made from cast iron. This is one of the most versatile of materials; not only that, it is also cheap, it can be cast into the most intricate shapes provided one possesses the necessary know-how, and it can be drilled, turned, bored and ground with little difficulty.

Furthermore, it is about the only metal that can be run against itself without seizure or rapid wear, even under conditions of great heat and scanty lubrication. A cast-iron piston will run satisfactorily for years in a cast-iron cylinder, but a mild-steel piston would fail rapidly if run in a mild-steel barrel.

Cast iron's major defects are low tensile strength and extreme brittleness. Even these deficiencies, however, have been largely overcome by metallurgical methods, so that irons with a high degree of ductility and shock resistance are commercially available; their applications include overhead rockers and crankshafts.

In any case, low tensile strength and brittleness are not of very serious consequence except in engines where light weight is an essential feature. The earliest cylinders and heads were made, usually integrally, from ordinary grey cast iron with a little phosphorus added to give fluidity at pouring temperature and so assist the metal to flow into the narrow spaces in the mould which formed the fins.

Moulding technique was not very advanced at that time, the practice being to use wooden patterns, split into halves, and rammed up with "green" (i.e. damp) sand into moulding flasks. Extracting a pattern with a great number of deep, closely-pitched fins from the green sand was quite a problem and, hence, designers were forced to put up with inadequate fin area in order to simplify the work in the foundry.

Today the method is still somewhat the same, but for production work the patterns forming the outside shape, and the core-boxes in which the cores for the ports are made, are constructed of metal and the moulds are dried in ovens or hardened by injecting carbon dioxide into the sand before the iron is poured in. Filling and ramming the

163

moulds is usually accomplished on machines in a fraction of the time taken by hand moulding, and in one way and another the process has been developed until there is now no difficulty in casting fins up to 2 in. deep and spaced $\frac{3}{8}$ in. apart.

With the advent of the detachable cylinder head, moulding became a little simpler, and it also became possible to use a different grade of iron, or an entirely different material, for this component.

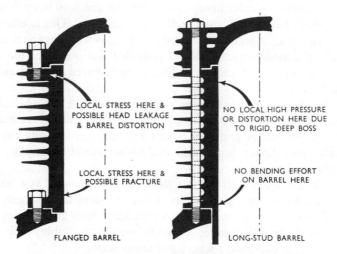

LOCAL STRESS HERE & POSSIBLE HEAD LEAKAGE & BARREL DISTORTION

NO LOCAL HIGH PRESSURE OR DISTORTION HERE DUE TO RIGID, DEEP BOSS

LOCAL STRESS HERE & POSSIBLE FRACTURE

NO BENDING EFFORT ON BARREL HERE

FLANGED BARREL

LONG-STUD BARREL

Fig. 10.1. Part-sections comparing a flange-type barrel with one secured by through-bolts. The second form is superior structurally but more expensive.

The main quality desired in a cylinder iron is freedom from wear; some grades of iron are better in this respect than others, mainly on account of their differing grain structure. It was once thought that rapid wear was due to insufficient hardness, and one or two makers adopted irons which could be hardened by heat treatment after all machining operations, except final grinding or honing, had been performed.

However, while a hardened barrel may have a lower rate of wear than a soft one under abrasive conditions—for example, when an engine is run in dusty surroundings minus an air cleaner—it is not necessarily any better, and may even be worse, than a softer iron of the correct analysis under the corrosive conditions which exist every time the engine is started up from cold.

At such times the upper end of the cylinder wall is almost free from oil, and the fact that it is cold causes the water vapour, formed as part of the products of combustion, to condense thereon. Partly because of the cold conditions and partly because of the usual enrichment by flooding of the carburetter or closing the air slide, combustion of the mixture is not complete and this results in the formation of acids which are dissolved in the condensed water vapour and attack the cylinder walls.

Fortunately, air-cooled cylinders warm up so quickly, especially if the engine is allowed to run for a few moments before setting off, that corrosive wear is not so serious a matter as it is with water cooling. Cars used by doctors, or on short-distance work of the "stop and go" variety, can wear out their cylinders with astonishing rapidity unless precautions are taken to raise the temperature of the block quickly and to maintain it at the correct heat, whereas taxi engines, which rarely stop long enough to cool down, will accomplish very great mileages without serious wear.

Plating the cylinder with a deposit of hard chromium, which resists both corrosive and abrasive wear, is an attractive solution—with two drawbacks. One is that it is expensive, partly because chromium is dear stuff and partly because internal plating requires a specialized technique. The other reason is that oil does not "wet" a polished chrome surface.

To overcome the latter trouble, it is necessary to provide microscopic oil reservoirs in the surface, either by making the deposit porous or by "back-etching" with a reverse flow of current towards a specially-formed cathode, which forms tiny depressions in the plating. Even if, as is possible, the plating is confined to the top one or two inches of the barrel, where the greatest wear occurs, the process is generally considered too costly to be justified in commercial work. After all, provided that the grade of iron employed has been selected primarily for good wear-resistance and not on account of its low price or especially good "machineability", cylinder bore wear is not a serious problem—at least, when an efficient air cleaner is employed.

High-grade cylinder irons usually have small percentages of nickel or chromium added, as these elements refine the grain, distribute the graphite more evenly and in smaller flakes and increase the tensile strength. The microstructure of the material is then referred to as "pearlitic", but there is another type of iron, containing more nickel and also copper as alloying elements, which is known as "austenitic".

Austenitic iron differs in being non-magnetic and highly resistant to corrosion. It also work-hardens with use—that is to say, it develops a hard skin under the rubbing action of the rings and piston skirt. This would seem to make it a highly desirable barrel material, but it is

165

Fig. 10.2. Large-area fins, drilled for fixing studs, on a two-port o.h.v. J.A.P. of 1928.

costly and does not lend itself well to being cast into intricate fin shapes; also, there is some reason to think that it is not such a good material as pearlitic iron from the lubrication aspect. Some years ago, a famous racing factory ceased to use it after experiencing trouble through excessive smoking at high r.p.m. with pistons and rings which ran perfectly in standard cylinders.

Some makers have, however, used austenitic iron for liners in aluminium jackets because of its high coefficient of thermal expansion: 0·000019 in. per degree Centrigrade, as compared with 0·000012 in. for ordinary cast iron. There is obviously less tendency for the jacket to lose contact with the liner when the high-expansion iron is employed.

BARREL FIXING

Because of cast iron's low tensile strength and lack of ductility, barrels which are retained by a base flange and four or six studs have, on occasion, broken off just above the flange. This distressing occurrence is most likely when the flange is located close to the bottom of the cylinder, and may be aggravated by a combination of a flexible crankcase and a rigid head-steady, as described in the section on torque reactions in Chapter 16.

FIG. 10.3. Meagre barrel finning on two early engines—the 1¼ h.p. French-built Werner of 1899 (top) and a 1901 Minerva; both have automatic inlet valves.

Forming the barrel with a long skirt projecting into the crankcase, and thereby raising the flange into a position much closer to that occupied by the gudgeon pin when the rod is at its maximum angularity, reduces the bending moment on the barrel very considerably; but, of course, the tensile stress due to gas pressure loading is still present. The best solution is therefore to use long studs which extend right through the barrel and head and hold the whole lot together, so relieving the barrel of tensile stress and the inevitable local loading at the flange studs which is a possible source of distortion under load.

This construction is more expensive because, in addition to the use of longer studs, it entails drilling through all the fins (casting the fins with slots to clear the studs, as has been done sometimes, is prone to make the cylinder go "square" under running conditions). However, it opens the way to using bi-metal barrels, formed of aluminium jackets and thin liners, with perfect structural safety, even on big singles. The position with vertical twins is not so critical, because the area of the flange, embracing, as it were, both cylinders, is twice as large in relation to the piston thrust as in the case of the single.

"AL-FIN" BARRELS

For a time it was fashionable racing-engine practice to cast a finned aluminium jacket round an iron cylinder, more in the interests of lightness than for better cooling. In fact, as it was difficult to guarantee close contact between the surfaces at all temperatures, there was little if any reduction in temperature of the liner, but this position has been altered by the development of the "Al-Fin" process by which liner and jacket are metallurgically bonded together (Fig. 10.5).

In this process, which is the subject of patents and took a long while to perfect, the iron components are first "tinned" in a bath of almost pure aluminium, which has a great affinity for iron, and, while still hot, are transferred to a mould into which the aluminium is poured. There is thus no heat-break between the two metals such as exists between two unbonded parts, and very efficient cooling at an overall weight about half that of an equivalent iron barrel is obtained.

The resulting component, however, is not altogether perfect. On cooling down after pouring, the aluminium contracts and so subjects the iron barrel to a high compression stress. When the cylinder is at working temperature on the engine, the greater thermal expansion of the light metal relieves this compression and the barrel, if originally machined truly cylindrically, then expands at the upper end and becomes tapered. The effect may be serious in large-bore engines, but is less so in small ones, and may be guarded against to some degree by proportioning the fin area so that the barrel temperatures are as nearly as possible equal from top to bottom.

FIG. 10.4. Exposed valve gear meant relatively free airflow over the head, whether pillar-mounted as on this 250 c.c. four-valve Rudge (top) or with side-plates on the 1931 T.T. Raleigh (bottom).

169

Fig. 10.5. Contrast in T.T. practice. (above) The bronze-head Royal Enfield Senior machine of 1935 and (below) the modern "Manx" Norton, with its deeply finned and spigoted Al-Fin barrel and light-alloy head with seat inserts.

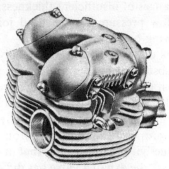

FIG. 10.6. Light-alloy cylinder head of the 1960 Norton "Dominator" twin.

THE CYLINDER HEAD

We come now to the more interesting part of the assembly, the cylinder head. The design of this was also influenced very largely in the early days by what could be accomplished in the foundry, and what little finning existed was often placed in the way which was easiest to make, rather than where it would provide the best cooling. Nevertheless, the overall effect, as compared with some later designs with enclosed valve gear, was reasonably good, as it was the usual practice to mount the rockers either between sheet-steel side-plates or on separate brackets, so permitting a good movement of air over the head (Fig. 10.4).

Some of the methods employed for bolting the head on were not so happy, however, and blown head gaskets and leaking joints were not unknown.

The big-port A.J.S. was one of the designs exempt from these troubles, as its head was retained by a U-bolt which fitted into a slot cast in the vertically placed fins, so providing an equal distribution of pressure over the small-section copper-and-asbetos washer which formed the gasket. Slotting the fins formed a heat-break between the hot exhaust side and the cool inlet—a very desirable feature, the value of which was, apparently, not recognized, because in later models the U-bolt was discarded and replaced by a strong steel bridge-piece which bore on a single button right in the centre of the head. This would appear to be an ideal arrangement, but was not, because the intense local pressure was sufficient to distort the head and cause the valves to leak.

This illustrates the cardinal importance of locating head studs so as to avoid local high stresses. Such stresses can also be generated by head

171

studs screwed into flanges of insufficient thickness, so creating areas of alternate high and low pressure on the head joint, with a resultant liability to joint-blowing or head-distortion.

The best method is undoubtedly to use equally spaced studs which run right through substantial bosses to a height somewhat above the top of the combustion chamber. Although the pressure at each one of the nuts is high, the load is well distributed down at the joint face, and if the head is of aluminium a gasket is not strictly necessary.

Whatever its good properties may be, cast iron has one shortcoming —low thermal conductivity. This means that it is likely to develop internal hot-spots; also, the exhaust valve has difficulty in getting rid of heat through its seat and stem. Therefore the use of cast iron places a limit on the compression ratio employable on petrol without trouble through detonation or early self-ignition.

Bronze Heads

The first attempt to overcome this limitation was to employ an aluminium-bronze alloy, composed of copper alloyed with about 10 per cent. of aluminium, which could be cast to the same proportions

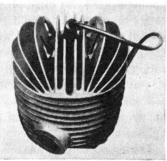

Fig. 10.7. Two-stroke heads lend themselves to radial finning. The Villiers sports engine of the mid-1930s (left) employed light alloy for both the head and the muff round the upper barrel. Very deep and almost ideally disposed are the fins of the modern Zündapp alloy head (above).

and with the same pattern equipment as for iron. This development took place rather later than it might have done—Ricardo had already pointed the way by using this material for the heads of the racing three-litre Vauxhall he designed in the early 'twenties—but it rapidly became standard practice for racing machines and a number of sports models.

Aluminium-bronze permitted an increase in compression of about one ratio due to its higher conductivity. It was, however, far from popular in the machine shop, because it is an awkward material to work, especially when drilling long holes; it is also about one-eighth as heavy again as cast iron, as well as more expensive. Another defect found in road machines was a tendency towards rapid wear of the inlet valve seats. All things considered, the bronze head had little to recommend it except the increase in power of perhaps 5 per cent. or 8 per cent. which it conferred, and the next step was to investigate the possibilities of aluminium as a head material for o.h.v. engines, as it was already in use on s.v. and two-stroke engines,

Aluminium Heads

The employment of aluminium alloy for the cylinder heads of side-valve and two-stroke engines presents few problems, because in neither type are there any valve seats, guides or ports to worry about, and the fin design can be quite simple and straightforward—even though at times it is somewhat less effective than it appears to be.

To be of any real use as a heat dissipator, a fin should spring from the hot metal actually surrounding the combustion chamber. Placing vertical fins on a horizontally projecting fin is of very little use except to make the head impressively large and to provide a symmetrical appearance. The original Villiers system, with some vertical and some radially disposed fins, avoids this situation, but does not lend itself well to die-casting in permanent moulds, which is probably the reason why it has been discarded on some models.

Almost any aluminium alloy can be employed, provided it is not too soft and ductile, otherwise it will distort between the bolt-holes and may also eventually give trouble through wearing or stripping of the sparking-plug threads. For racing use, however, with compression ratios running well into double figures, it is advisable to use an analysis such as Y-alloy or RR53, both of which possess great strength at high temperatures, otherwise cracking may occur round the plug-boss.

FOUR-STROKE O.H.V. PROBLEMS

Four-stroke o.h.v. heads are a different kettle of fish, partly because of the necessity for providing durable valve seats and partly because the structure is complicated—and, in places, weakened—by the presence of the ports.

One method of providing suitable valve seats and retaining rigidity was the original Norton system of first casting an aluminium-bronze "skull", forming the entire wall of the combustion chamber and the first inch or so of both ports. It also had two projecting bosses through which the valve-guide holes were subsequently drilled, and was provided with a number of small ribs which formed keys for the aluminium shell cast round the skull after the latter had been placed in the mould.

This method permitted deep cooling fins to be used without the weight penalty incurred by an all-bronze head, while the contact between the skull and shell was so intimate, and the heat conduction consequently so good, that a compression ratio of 10:1 could be employed with pre-war 50-50 petrol-benzole mixture. The head was, however, costly to manufacture in small quantities and did not lend itself to quick production methods in the foundry. Further, the cast metal of the skull was prone to rapid inlet-seat wear which, moreover, could not be repaired by welding and re-machining, as could a solid bronze head, because of the almost certain liability to melt the aluminium shell locally and thus destroy the vital close contact between the two components.

Another approach aimed at reducing weight and making better use of the high-conductivity aluminium was to cast in a pair of seat-rings, either of aluminium-bronze or of austenitic cast iron, relying upon the cooling contraction of the light metal to ensure gas-tight joints between the rings and the head. Unfortunately this was not always achieved, and pressure leakage took place down the sides of the rings, while the thin metal between the rings, or between the plug-hole and the exhaust ring, sometimes cracked, rendering the head useless because repair was impossible.

A more satisfactory solution to these difficulties was found by combining both the seat-rings and the plug-boss into a single iron casting resembling a pair of "spectacles"; the design employed in the later models of the 500 c.c. Ariel "Red Hunter" single is a good example (Fig. 10.8). The ring portions are formed with a reverse taper, so that circumferential contraction of the aluminium pulls them firmly back against the rear surface, and the exterior shape of the iron is relatively smooth and not broken up by the ribs which were originally thought to be necessary. In fact, the smoother the surface, the better the contact will be, and it is the general shape rather than the surface finish which

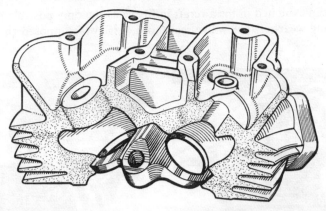

Fig. 10.8. In the light-alloy heads of the later Ariel "Red Hunters", valve seats and plug boss formed a single cast-iron insert of "spectacles" shape; its edges had a slight reverse taper.

retains the whole thing in place.

The construction is, however, rather a tricky one from the foundry angle. The iron casting must first be heated before being placed in the mould, and the latter must then be closed and the metal poured very quickly, otherwise there is a chance of poor contact between the parts or, in extreme cases, voids existing between the two due to water which has condensed on the iron flashing off into steam when the aluminium hits it. Such defects, unless of a gross nature, are difficult to detect.

Still, the "spectacles" plan does at least localize most of the production difficulties within the walls of the foundry, and improved methods have made the process satisfactory both technically and pricewise. But the machine-shop still has to overcome the difficulty of machining the sphere nicely, since austenitic iron should be turned at a low speed with a heavy depth of cut, whereas aluminium is just the opposite and requires a high speed and light cut to obtain the smooth surface finish desired. This, in fact, is one of those situations mentioned in an earlier section, where the demands of the designer temporarily outrun normal production procedure, which eventually catches up with the demand.

Separate Inserts

Another school of thought preferred to keep all its troubles under its own control by adopting separate valve-seat inserts, fitted mechanically (instead of by casting) into recesses machined in the head. This scheme had been exploited in the aircraft industry as the only possible method of fitting wear-resistant valve-seats to a forged (as opposed to a cast) head.

Fig. 10.9. Sand-cast barrel of a 1948 Triumph "Grand Prix" engine (left) contrasted with one of the same maker's early die-cast barrels on a touring engine, some four years later. Note the much closer fin spacing.

Holding the Inserts

All sorts of fancy methods have been devised and used to retain the rings—such as screwing them in with the head at a high temperature, or pressing-in below the surface and peening the soft head metal over the edge—but the least expensive *and* best method happens to be simplest. It consists of machining the recesses accurately parallel and square to the bottom with the finest possible finish, and machining the inserts with similar accuracy and finish to a diameter sufficiently large to ensure that the rings will not come loose at running temperature (which in a well-designed head should not exceed 250°C.).

The first engine to be built on these lines was the Mark V KTT Velocette. As a precaution, the recesses and inserts in this motor were formed with a very slight reverse taper, amounting to two or three thou. on the diameter—just sufficient, in fact, to permit the large rear ends of the inserts to pass through the small outer ends of the recesses when the inserts were cold and the head heated to 200°C. This stratagem provided an insurance against the inserts dropping out, but boring back-tapered holes to an accurate size is an awkward proposition. Further, if a seat ring *does* come loose you are in trouble, whether it can drop out or not; it just goes on getting looser with continued running. So eventually parallel holes were employed, as also by Norton (Fig. 10.5).

A parallel ring in a parallel hole will never—well, hardly ever, as W. S. Gilbert would have said—come loose if the machining standard is high, the interference (or tightness) correct in relation to the metals employed, the general proportions of the ring are right and—a final but quite valuable detail—the ring, when fitted, is slightly "under flush" with the sphere surface instead of being level or standing proud.

Aluminium-bronze and austenitic cast iron have approximately the same thermal coefficient of expansion, but the former has a higher conductivity. Austenitic iron has a low rate of seat-wear, and while wrought aluminium-bronze in the form of extruded tube is better in this respect than cast metal of the same analysis it is not so resistant as iron, especially on the inlet side. Consequently, in racing engines it is usual to employ the yellow metal for exhaust seats, while austenitic iron is used for the inlets. On sports engines, where long life is of more importance than high conductivity, austenitic iron is frequently used on both sides.

Regarding proportions, a shallow thin-walled ring holds in better than a thick, deep one, partly because it has a little more "give" in it to accommodate variations in the fit which are bound to occur with changes of temperature, and partly because, for a given valve size, there is more parent metal surrounding the recess. Occasional cases of ring-loosening have been traced to the excessive tightness of a thick-walled ring, which, when it has expanded under heat more quickly than the head, has stretched the recess permanently, so destroying the original interference. The opposite thing can happen with a bronze ring, which may shrink under excessive compressive stress, but the final result is the same.

In general terms, the radial wall-thickness of a ring should be around 10 per cent. of the port diameter, and its depth should be about 1·6 times the radial thickness. The exact proportions are not vital, but those quoted produce rings which will hold in well, without occupying too much of the combustion-chamber area or making the amount of metal between the two inserts dangerously small. Fortunately, with inclined valves the recesses diverge sharply, so there is always more metal between them than there appears to be on the surface.

However, as the inserts must be larger than the valves, separate inserts impose a greater limitation on the maximum sizes of the valve heads than does the "spectacles" pattern of cast-in insert or the now disused "skull" arrangement. This limitation could be serious in a long-stroke small-bore engine, but becomes less so as the cylinder proportions become square or over-square and there is more room for the valves.

As an interesting sidelight on this facet of head design, it may not be generally known that the A.J.S. racer which subsequently came to be known as the "Porcupine" was originally intended to be supercharged and to be able to run at manifold pressures of up to 20 lb. above atmospheric. To handle over twice as much air as when normally aspirated without incurring too much pumping loss, the largest possible valves would be required; and to minimize the ill effects of the much greater heat-loss to the walls, a head material of the highest available conductivity was essential.

One solution, which received much more than a passing thought, was to cast the head in silver, the thermal conductivity of which is three times as great as that of pure aluminium, and to utilize thin-walled, shallow inserts, silver-soldered in position to provide both a thermal and a mechanical bond with the head without, in themselves, placing any restriction on valve size.

This project even got as far as a visit by Joe Craig to Hatton Garden, from which two major facts emerged. One was that the head casting alone would cost about £350, though the silver merchants were prepared to buy back any machining swarf and scrapped or unwanted heads at the ruling market price for the metal.

The other revelation was that in order to be castable in the intricate sections demanded by the general construction, and to be hardened sufficiently for mechanical strength, the silver would have to be alloyed with a high proportion of copper. This would have the effect of dropping the thermal conductivity to a figure not much better than that of aluminium, though size for size the silver head would have been three and a half times as heavy as an aluminium one!

So the idea was smartly abandoned as impracticable (even if the frantically high price could have been accepted) and the head reverted to Y-alloy. In any case, the whole head design had subsequently to be drastically altered, since the porting system adopted for supercharging was totally unsuitable for atmospheric induction with normal carburetters.

A Choice of Materials

Y-alloy, containing 92 per cent. aluminium and 3½ per cent. copper as its main ingredients, was one of the first high-strength light-weight casting alloys to be discovered and it is still one of the best materials available, particularly as it retains its strength well at high temperatures.

This invaluable property is shared by RR53, which some consider to be easier to cast, and many high-performance heads made in England have been manufactured from one or other of these two metals.

Both have to be heat-treated to bring out their full strength. This means that should any repair work, such as welding-up holes caused by over-enthusiastic port enlargement, be carried out by oxy-welding, the metal in the vicinity of the weld will be only in the annealed or soft condition and its strength will have gone down from 18 tons/sq. in. to about 10 tons/sq. in., which may have serious effects. Small welds can, however, be made by the argon-arc process without deleterious results, as the welding heat is applied only locally and very briefly.

As can be seen from Table 10.1 on page 181, the coefficient of expansion of these two alloys is fairly high, so they tend to expand away from aluminium-bronze or austenitic iron inserts. An interference of 0·002 in. per inch of diameter is, therefore, necessary to retain them without loosening at running temperature.

Alloys containing a high percentage of silicon, such as "Lo-Ex" or L33, have a coefficient almost identical to those of bronze and austenitic iron, so slightly less interference can be used. For "Manx" Nortons,

FIG. 10.10. Silver was too expensive. . . . Complex head of the 1948 A.J.S. "Porcupine" racer.

179

which employ this variety of light alloy, a *total* interference of 0·003 in. is quoted.

After allowing for the thicker sections required in stressed areas, an aluminium head scales about half the weight of an iron head of the same overall dimensions. Even so it is more expensive in material cost, especially when the high-strength metals just discussed are used.

However, it has been found that except for out-and-out racing these are not really necessary, and less-expensive commercial alloys, particularly DTD424, which came into use during the war as a general-purpose metal, can be employed satisfactorily. Moreover, DTD424 can be die-cast in permanent metal moulds with a reduction in labour cost, greater dimensional accuracy and a better surface finish than can be obtained with conventional sand moulds.

These factors, allied to the high speed at which aluminium can be machined, all tend towards bringing the overall cost down to a figure which is low enough to permit the use of light-alloy heads on touring

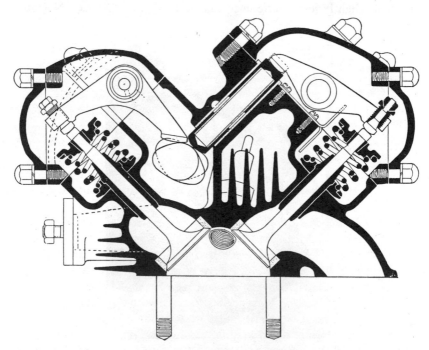

FIG. 10.11. Disposition of shrunk-in valve inserts is clearly shown in this section of an experimental Sunbeam alloy head.

engines, with benefits to the rider which not so long ago were enjoyed only by those who could afford the more exotic types of motorcycle, and in the past few years there has been a very noticeable trend towards greater adoption of the scheme by all manufacturers.

TABLE 10.1. PHYSICAL PROPERTIES OF LIGHT ALLOYS

Commonly used nomenclature	British Standard (B.S. 1490)	Ultimate tensile strength tons/sq. in.		0·1 % Proof stress tons/sq. in.		Ultimate tensile strength at 250°C. tons/sq. in.	Coefficient of expansion (20°C. − 100°C.)
		Sand cast	Chill cast	Sand cast	Chill cast	Sand cast	
DTD424	LM 4	9·0	10·0	5·0	5·0	8·1	21 × 10⁻⁶
L33	LM 6	10·5	12·0	3·5	4·5	5·0	20 × 10⁻⁶
Lo-Ex	LM 13WP	11·0	16·0	12·0	17·0	10·0 (Chill cast)	20 × 10⁻⁶
Y-Alloy	LM 14WP	14·0	18·0	13·0	15·0	14·2	23 × 10⁻⁶
RR 53	LM 15WP	18·0	21·0	16·0	19·0	13·8	22 × 10⁻⁶
RR 50	LM 23P	10·0	12·5	7·0	8·0	6·2	22 × 10⁻⁶

Fin Design

Before commencing to design the fins of such a complex casting as a cylinder head it is first necessary to lay out the positions of the valves, seat inserts (if any), ports, sparking plug and the bolts used for attaching the head to the barrel or crankcase.

Enough metal must be provided around each of these localities to cope with the mechanical and thermal stresses likely to be involved, not merely from the aspect of sheer strength, but more with the idea of eliminating deflection or distortion, either of which may lead to blown head-joints or leaking valves.

One should studiously avoid skimping the weight of metal used in highly stressed areas on the score of cost. In any case, the finished article will weight several pounds and the small percentage saving achieved by carving off an ounce or two of material here and there may make all the difference between a mediocre article and one which will withstand full power for long periods without distress. "Penny wise, pound foolish", must be the designer's motto here.

Obviously, there are many vital details such as the valve angles and diameters, plug location and so on which need very careful consideration before they can be finally settled, and some compromises may have to

181

be made in order to obtain satisfactory locations for the head bolts. Four of these are quite sufficient if they are correctly disposed, although five or even six have been fitted on occasions, usually because the porting or the valve-gear layout has demanded it.

However, in conventional two-valve heads the general disposition and proportions of the ports do not vary very greatly and can be taken as substantially constant for the purpose of this section, which is to discuss the general design of the fins. On the other hand, the method of operating or enclosing the valve-gear does vary significantly from one design to another and may have a very marked bearing on the effectiveness or otherwise of the cooling.

As an example, in the early days when valve-gear was exposed and lubricated scantily, if at all, it was common practice to keep the rockers well clear of the head and mount them either on slender posts or between side-plates, which were often liberally pierced to assist air-flow. The general obstruction to air-flow over the fins was then far less than it is in some later fully-enclosed push-rod designs, or with an overhead camshaft, and the matter became largely one of putting on fins wherever they could be accommodated, provided that moulding and casting were within the existing capabilities of the foundry. Even then, some avoidable mistakes were made which led to lack of stamina, cracked valve seats, burnt or broken valves, and a general state of what is now known as "customer dissatisfaction".

Air cooling is a complex process involving the absorption of heat by the internal surfaces, the transfer of that heat through the metal by conduction to the external surfaces and to the fin-roots, and finally

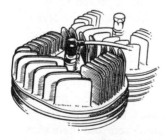

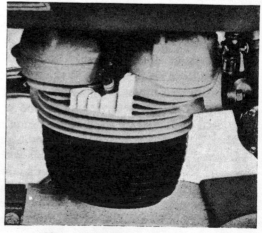

FIG. 10.12. Deflector-type finning directs air towards the plugs on the racing M.Z. twin two-stroke (above) and the 250 c.c. touring A.M.C. engine (right). In the second case, it also aids cooling of the shielded area between the rocker-boxes.

its transfer to the air. There is also the matter of conduction across the mating surfaces of the valve guides and seat inserts (if used) where the fit, though close, nevertheless constitutes a heat-break, and the areas where less intimate contact occurs, namely the valve seats and the portions of stem within the guides.

To give some inkling of the principles involved, it may be worth noting that a hot metal surface dissipates its heat in two ways—by radiation and by convection.

In the radiation process, heat is transmitted through the surrounding air *without warming it up*. The heat does not reappear until it strikes some other body—for instance, a tiny frozen hand held, even at some distance, in front of an electric fire.

Radiant heat behaves in a very similar manner to light; it travels in straight lines, and is reflected by a polished surface and absorbed by a dull black one. The latter process is reversible, and therefore a polished surface emits less heat by radiation than a black one. The rate of emission from a polished surface is approximately one-tenth that from the same surface covered with a thin film of lamp-black, and the emissivity of a cast-aluminium surface is increased about 10 per cent. by a *thin* coating of black paint.

Radiation takes place only at right angles to the surface. Even if that surface is somewhat rough, as in commercial sand castings, the general direction of the total heat being given off is square to the main surface.

Strictly speaking, when a body is very hot in relation to its surroundings the radiation varies as the difference between the fourth powers of the absolute temperatures concerned. When the difference in temperatures is only a few degrees, Newton's law of cooling applies and the rate of heat-loss is then directly proportional to the temperature difference between the body and its surroundings. However, in practice this still means that the loss by pure radiation is low at low cylinder temperatures, but increases very rapidly if the cylinder gets much hotter than it should be.

Since air takes no part in the process, radiation goes on just the same whether there is any wind present or not, so it is of most value as a safety-valve at zero air-speed. Under normal circumstances it accounts for only one-sixth to one-tenth of the total heat loss and cannot be greatly increased by the addition of fins, whose only effect is to increase the effective radiation area from that of the bare head and barrel to that of the general outside shape enclosed by the fin-tips.

This is so because adjacent fin surfaces merely radiate heat from the hotter one to the cooler, or not at all if both are at equal temperatures.

The effective radiating surface is perhaps doubled or trebled by the addition of fins, whereas the area of surface in direct contact with the air may be eight to twelve times that presented by the bare components.

But there is a second source of heat dissipation which *can* take advantage of this increase in area—convection. It consists of a direct transference of heat to the layer of air in immediate contact with the surface; this layer then expands, becomes lighter and, under natural conditions, rises and is replaced by cold air which is heated in its turn.

Air is an extremely poor conductor of heat, its resistance being some 3,500 times that of iron, and little heat would be removed were it not for the setting-up of these convection currents, which to quote a homely example again, can be felt rising from a hot-water room-heater (incorrectly called a "radiator", whereas "convector" would be a more descriptive term).

The greater the surface in contact with air, the greater the heat-dissipation will be, provided that the air movement is sufficient. Even if the fins are substantially vertical and unshielded (as on a B.M.W. flat-twin) natural convection, though a distinct help when the model is at a standstill, would be insufficient at high power; and, of course, it can scarcely be of any benefit at all on a vertical single-cylinder or twin engine with horizontal fins.

It is therefore necessary to rely on the forward speed of the machine to provide a forced circulation or, in the case of those with enclosed engines, to employ a fan. The fan has the advantage that its air-delivery bears some sort of relationship, even if a rough one, to engine speed and power output.

Without a fan, the air velocity over the cylinder is totally unrelated to engine speed, to power or even to road speed, because a strong side or tail wind will alter both the rate and direction of the resultant wind; nevertheless, under most circumstances this will be blowing from the front and in a horizontal direction, unless seriously deflected by some external fitting.

To take full advantage of this type of flow, the fins on a vertical barrel should be horizontal—or reasonably so, for there is reason to assume from the behaviour of V-twins and singles with sloping cylinders that an angle of inclination of up to 25° from the vertical detracts little, if at all, from the effectiveness of the fins, and may even be of some assistance at very low speeds in permitting natural convection currents to form between each fin.

The general direction of the head fins should be either horizontal, or vertical and parallel to the centre-plane. They should be disposed in the manner best calculated to allow moving air to penetrate right down to the fin-roots and to eliminate pockets of stagnant air which, if undisturbed, act as insulators.

Head-bolt bosses in close proximity to ports sometimes create such pockets. The effects can be made less serious either by separating the bosses from the port wall, even though this may be a tricky job for the foundry, or by going to the opposite extreme and using very generous fillets between boss and port which in effect, fill up the unwanted pockets with metal (Fig. 10.13).

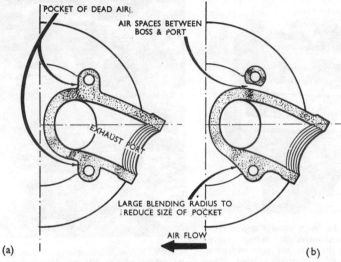

FIG. 10.13. (a) Section through head, showing pockets of stagnant air behind bolt bosses. (b) Two methods of improving this condition.

The areas below and behind a steeply offset exhaust port are other badly cooled places. It is in such localities that aluminium scores over cast-iron, as, although it is only two-fifths the weight, its thermal conductivity is double, so that generous sections can be employed without a serious weight penalty in order to conduct the heat out to a region more exposed to the air-flow.

Heads have occasionally been designed with a bank of vertical fore-and-aft fins lying between the valves. This arrangement is bad in two respects. One is that the ventilation is bound to be poor and deepening the fins makes matters worse, if anything. The other is that differential expansion of the hot head-metal between the valve seats and the cold fin-tips sets up stresses which have been known to create valve-seat distortion and gas leakage.

185

One palliative is to cast a transverse slot through the bank of fins, partly to assist air circulation and partly to remove any restraint on free expansion of the head, but a better solution is to arrange the fins at an angle so that air is collected on one side of the head and guided through to the other. On vertical twins, especially those with integral or bulky bolted-on rocker-boxes, inclined fins may materially assist in feeding air through into the badly ventilated area behind and between the two cylinders.

Fig. 10.14. With careful design, the bulky enclosures of hairpin valve springs do not prevent adequate cooling of a light-alloy head. The example is a 1949 350 c.c. T.T. Velocette.

Fig. 10.15. Vertical fore-and-aft fins between the valves of the 125 c.c. Honda racer are pierced and air is directed towards them by a sheet-metal deflector (not shown).

ON THE EXHAUST SIDE

Since most of the heat extracted from the exhaust valve is transferred to the head via the guide, it is essential to pay particular attention to this region, although it is not always easy to achieve anything like perfection. The space taken up by hairpin valve springs necessarily cuts down the area of finning close up to the guide, whilst prominent fins springing from a long exhaust port do little more than handle the heat absorbed in the port itself.

Any heat which escapes in the exhaust gas is simply a waste product and as such should be dismissed down the pipe as soon as possible and not allowed to embarrass the head any more than is absolutely unavoidable. To that end, the port should be short and of the smallest diameter consistent with good power production.

Largely on the score of weight, but also in some cases because it was a refinement added to an existing open-valve design and later retained for manufacturing reasons, valve enclosure on cast-iron heads is frequently carried out by using a bolted-on light-alloy rocker-box with separate oil-tight housings for the valve springs. Some of these devices are well clear of the head and do not interfere too greatly with air flow; the J.A.P. design is good in this respect, though others are not so happy.

The bevel-box and housing of a single overhead camshaft can create a much more serious situation, especially with an engine which is so tall that the cambox must be kept close down between the valves in order to fit into the frame. But the whole picture is altered when light alloy is used, because then it becomes possible to cast the cambox and head in one unit without excessive weight, and to employ copious lubrication without smothering the exterior with oil. Either coil or hairpin springs can be used; even the bulky enclosures required to house the latter are not so detrimental as they might appear, since the high-conductivity material will transfer heat quickly to fins applied to the spring-box walls (Fig. 10.14). Probably the outstanding examples of this construction were the "Works" 350 and 500 c.c. Velocettes, which were notable for their enormous fins, approximately 10 in. square in plan view, though the unit camboxes used previously with coil springs were made separate to accommodate hair-pins.

The size and shape of these fins were developed not only to furnish a larger area than the conventional circular outline, but also to get their tips out into fast-moving air. Experiments prove that at high speeds a region of comparatively dead air, extending as the speed rises, exists behind the shelter of the front wheel and forks; this can lead to the cooling becoming progressively worse instead of better.

Incidentally, a comparison between the head assembly of the pre-war push-rod Velocette, the K.T.T., and the post-war aluminium component with integral rocker boxes provides a very good example of the way in which design progresses by utilizing ideas from every source available. The later example is lighter, simpler to make and better cooled than the original version and, moveover, it can be die-cast in permanent moulds which, besides reducing the component cost, furnishes cleaner and more accurate castings and increases the strength of the material, in this instance Y-alloy.

Avoiding Slots

Fin area is sometimes lost through having to provide clearance for the sparking plug and the push-rod tubes or cam-shaft drive; these gaps cause discontinuities in strength or conductivity which are best avoided. If, say, the head has several horizontal fins, it may be possible to adjust the plug angle so that, while the firing points remain in the correct position, the top fin need not be cut away much, if at all, to miss the

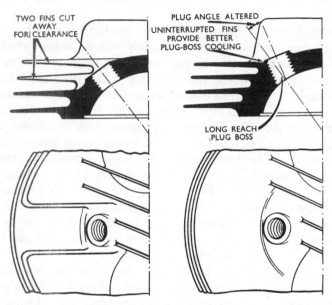

Fig. 10.16. (Left) Section and plan of head with two fins cut away to provide plug clearance. (Right) Use of a long-reach plug at a modified angle provides uninterrupted finning with the same firing point.

body and give spanner clearance (Fig. 10.16). A long-reach plug thread helps the situation, as the boss can be in direct contact with one or even two fins.

On the push-rod side it is possible to cast a tunnel up through the barrel and head fins, provided that there is space for air to pass through behind the tunnel. Rudimentary fins may be applied to the visible side for the sake of appearance, but overcooling in this region can do more harm than good, the ideal being to aim for equality of temperature all round. However, this is entering the province of barrel design.

Fin Proportions

In practice fins are usually of plain tapered section, spaced somewhere between $\frac{3}{8}$ in. and $\frac{5}{16}$ in. apart. Although this shape was adopted simply because it is the easiest to make in the pattern and foundry stages, it is, by a happy chance, a very efficient section on the basis of weight in relation to heat dissipation when the air-speed is low and its direction is erratic.

Ideally, a fin should have concave sides and sharp tips and be blended into the base metal by circular fillets. Such a shape is difficult to make, but a good approximation can be attained by using a double taper on the sides (Fig. 10.17) and rounded tips $\frac{1}{16}$ in. wide.

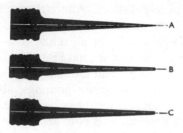

FIG. 10.17. (*A*) Ideal fin section for constant temperature gradient. (*B*) Double-taper section, a practical form of *A*. (*C*) Conventional single-taper fin. The root fillets play an important part in providing a heat path.

The fillets present no difficulty, though they are sometimes inadequate in size, or even omitted, because their value in feeding heat into the fin-roots is not fully appreciated. The limiting factor in casting is the depth of fin in relation to the pitch, but fins up to $2\frac{1}{2}$ in. deep can be sand-moulded in aluminium by specialists in the art.

Lately, die-casting has become a serious rival to sand-moulding for production models where the design is sufficiently well established to warrant the high initial die cost. Excellent examples of this class of work are to be seen on Triumphs, and even the Japanese Honda racing models had die-cast heads and barrels in 1959.

With die-casting, there has come about a tendency towards using a larger number of thinner fins than is customary, or even expedient, with sand-casting, though this is by no means general. Some makers, though adopting die-casting for production reasons, have maintained the fin dimensions previously used for sand, a procedure which has much to commend it on machines cooled only by normal draught. When fan cooling is employed high-speed air can be directed by cowls which embrace the fin-tips closely, and for these conditions the ideal is a large number of thin fins.

Anyone wishing to delve still further into the relative merits of various fin sections can find much to interest them in a paper written by P. V. Lamarque, entitled "The Design of Cooling Fins for Motor Cycle Engines" (*Proceedings*, I.A.E., 1942–3: see Bibliography, page 321).

COOLING THE BARREL

Considered as an engineering proposition, the cylinder barrel (or block in the case of some multi-cylinder engines) comes into quite a different category from that of the head because the duties which each has to perform, and the thermal and mechanical stresses to which they are subjected, are completely distinct. Although the head has much the smaller internal area, the amount of heat absorbed both internally and through the exhaust-port walls in an o.h.v. four-stroke is, as a first approximation, 80 per cent. of the total heat absorbed from *all* surfaces and, with the exception of a small amount which may be removed by oil flowing through the valve-spring housings, all this heat must be dissipated through the fins; the head has, as it were, to stand on its own feet in the matter of keeping itself cool or at least avoiding becoming too hot. On the other hand the barrel of the same type of engine has only to get rid of the remaining 20 per cent. of the rejected heat and a sizeable proportion of this need not be handled by the fins at all but can be removed internally, either in the lubricating oil or by the air-displacement which can occur if a large breather pipe is fitted; another path for waste heat can be provided, in spigoted barrels, by conduction to the relatively cool crankcase.

AVOIDING DISTORTION

The head has only to maintain gas-tightness of the valves and, provided the design is good, it can achieve this end even at temperatures which are high near the exhaust valve and low near the inlet; the barrel, however, has to remain round and straight under all conditions if blow-by past the piston-rings or the upwards passage of oil into the combustion chamber is to be avoided; also, any severe distortion, especially if accompanied, as it usually is, by local hot-spots, is prone to cause piston-seizure unless excessively wide clearances are used, with resultant noisy running. Barrels which are distorted when hot always wear unevenly, and after reboring will not work well until they have again developed the unequal wear which is necessary to provide some semblance of circularity under running conditions.

Resulting from the absence of actual inlet and compression strokes as such, which means, in effect, that the cylinder always contains hot gas, the heat-loss to the walls of a two-stroke is much greater than in a four-stroke; it is not actually doubled on that account, because the gas-temperatures, in general, are lower. The actual increase is of the order of 70 per cent.—an amount which is sufficient to make the cooling of a two-stroke something of a problem which is further complicated by the presence of ports and passages in the lower half of the barrel. The exhaust port (or ports) naturally absorbs heat in much the same way as its counterpart in a four-stroke, and the shorter it can be kept the better; even so, the exhaust side of the cylinder is bound to be hotter than the side containing the transfer ports, and usually the induction port also. This, in conjunction with the unavoidably irregular metal thicknesses in that region, predisposes the cylinder towards distortion which is especially unwelcome because, for optimum performance, the piston which also acts as a valve must run at the closest clearances possible. The smaller the bore, the less the actual departure from true circularity will be. For that reason and also because the ratio of cooling area to heat rejected to the walls becomes more favourable with decrease in cylinder size, two-strokes give better performances in small capacities, whereas four-strokes are not quite so sensitive to dimensions.

On vertical—or near-vertical—cylinders, plain circular barrel fins are the simplest to manufacture and afford the most effective cooling at high speed. When inclined to the air-flow, as in V-twins or sloping engines, their cooling efficiency is actually increased at low and medium speeds, though this effect diminishes as the fin-spacing is decreased; sloping fins are also a help when the air-speed is down to nil, because natural convection currents can then form between the fins to provide an amount of cooling which, though limited, is at least something on the credit side. In this respect horizontal, transverse cylinders are the best of the lot, since they can take full advantage of either speed-induced draught or natural convection. Moreover they are not hampered by frame components or tanks which may interfere with air-flow from the front, or oil tanks or battery boxes which can have a surprisingly large adverse influence by hindering the freedom of exit of heated air from the rear; this last point is one which is not always given sufficient attention when laying out the installation of vertical engines.

Circular fins would not be very effective on a forward-facing un-cowled horizontal cylinder at speed and hence such cylinders are usually equipped with radial fins, although some very small two-strokes, capable only of low road-speeds, have worked well enough with circular fins.

At first sight radial fin arrangement appears to be much superior to the circular one because the air-space between adjacent surfaces becomes greater as the fin depth is increased and any one fin does not become blanketed by its mates on either side which happens when circular fins are made of excessive depth. But, while this is true, it is not such a real advantage as it may look. For one thing, you can only apply a certain *total* length of fin, measured at the roots, to the curved surface of the barrel regardless of which way the fins go and for any given thickness of root, there is a maximum depth of about eight times this thickness above which there is no gain in cooling, provided that the *whole* fin is exposed to the air-blast.

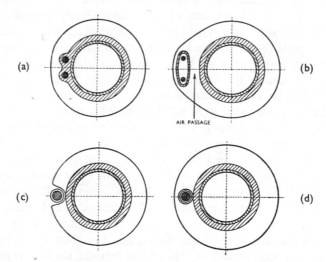

FIG. 10.18. Providing for push-rod operation: (a) Holes drilled in solid bosses. (b) Cast-in tunnel. (Bottom) Camshaft vertical drive through (c) break in fins and (d) drillings in fins of larger diameter.

Circular fins have the added and very real advantage that they provide a high degree of circumferential stiffness and thus resist any tendency towards ovality, as long as they, themselves, do not distort appreciably; being so much deeper radially than the cylinder wall, the fins are the real masters of the situation. For that reason they should, so far as possible, be continuous; for instance, if long holding-down bolts are used holes should be drilled for them instead of casting deep slots into the fins. This latter process has been carried out on occasion and invariably leads to piston trouble through the barrel assuming a four-sided shape, not necessarily during running, but even after a pit-stop of a duration sufficiently long to allow the cylinder to cool off, which it does unequally due to the vertical gashes in the fins.

A detail design feature worth mentioning in passing is that small, flat bosses should always be added to the tapered flanks of any fins which are to be drilled; unless this precaution is taken, the drill has a tendency to wander, especially where iron fins are concerned, and the holes will not be true. If the bolts are so located that they are almost touching the actual wall, as they often are with thick aluminium jackets, it is better to employ cast-in bosses so that the drill goes through solid metal all the way; the bosses need be very little larger than the bolts (as an occasional break-through into air will not matter) and will cause only a little more obstruction to air-flow than the bolts on their own.

Camshaft Drives

The housing containing the overhead camshaft drive, whether it be by shaft, chain or gears, is another encumbrance, as it always entails some reduction of fin area and loss of symmetry, more especially in large engines where the drive has to be kept relatively close in order to avoid making the whole thing too wide.

The deep slot in the fins, which is necessary to clear a vertical drive-shaft is clearly undesirable and one way out is to make the fins bigger still and either cast-in a tunnel or drill a large hole for the drive-housing; these expedients cause less reduction in area than the slot, but the main advantage lies in maintaining equality of circumferential stiffness.

Fig. 10.19. (Left) B.S.A. "Gold Star" o.h.v. barrel offers an excellent example of cast-in push-rod tunnel. (Right) Completely circular M.Z. "250" 2-stroke barrel finning showing the unusual location of the exhaust port at the rear.

Push-rod enclosures can also be a nuisance, though to a somewhat less degree, and do nothing towards improving the appearance. Some makers, notably B.S.A. and Royal Enfield in England, provide tunnels cast integrally with the fins, in which case the tunnels should be either tight in against the jacket, with plenty of fin on the outside, or kept sufficiently far away to allow air to flow through and then the outside wall of the tunnel can be supplied with just enough fin-depth to give a smooth appearance. In the first method there is not a great deal of reduction in cooling efficiency, especially with aluminium; with iron there is a possibility of a hot streak being caused down the barrel. In the second method, overcooling of the outer tunnel wall may give rise to differing amounts of thermal expansion causing undesirable internal stresses and a chance that the whole barrel may even bend slightly, hence the endeavour to keep the temperatures equalized by making the visible fins short (Fig. 10.19).

Fin Effectiveness

Because the breeze on any cylinder other than one which faces horizontally forward must, of course, impinge mainly on the front side, the rate of heat dissipation is bound to be greater on this side than at the rear, and it may even be slightly higher still at the sides. Experiments on cylinders placed in a direct airstream and heated uniformly by internal electrical elements, described in the N.A.C.A. Report No. 488, entitled "Heat Transfer from Metal Cylinders in an Airstream", indicated that the difference in temperature between fin and the air in front, at the sides and at the rear, given a speed of 58 m.p.h., was of the order of 95°, 140° and 130°F. respectively, with tapered fins of 0·3 in. pitch, 1·32 in. depth and 0·13 in. average thickness; these are about average proportions for motorcycle work and it is interesting to find that thinner fins of closer pitch created a greater variation—55°F. as opposed to 35°F.—while thicker fins of coarser pitch caused about the same variation, but the average temperature went up at air speeds from 30 to 150 m.p.h.

This leads to the conclusion that experimentally-developed conventional fin proportions are not very far wrong, although the results of this test are not strictly applicable; for one thing, due to the presence or close proximity of exhaust ports, the internal heating in practice is not uniform, and for another, the air-flow is not straight but largely consists of a mass of eddies, while a proportion of the front side of the cylinder is shielded from direct blast. Nevertheless, there is obviously good reason for locating the exhaust at the front, or if this is not practicable, at the rear rather than at the sides, as is done indeed on the M.Z. two-stroke. Considerable lengths have been gone to in this engine to reduce the pick-up of heat in the exhaust-ports; although there are two cut in each cylinder, they merge quickly into a single outlet, the length from bore to flange-face being less than two inches (Fig. 10.19).

Although this design necessitates a thin piece of liner $\frac{1}{4}$ in. wide and 1 in. long between the ports and supported only on the outside by a streamlined bar, this practice has clearly been deemed to be preferable to that of using twin outlets with their inevitably greater surface area and a space between which would be bereft of any cooling whatever except by conduction to neighbouring cooler areas. This problem exists even with forward-facing twin ports.

HEAT FLOW

One elementary law governing the behaviour of heat is that it always travels from a warm area towards a cooler one; if it is desired to keep an area such as the inlet port cool, it is useless to connect it to any hotter places by continuous fins, which will merely conduct heat to just where it is not wanted; an early example of avoiding this is to be seen in the de-finned inlet port of the Model P Triumph, and many two-strokes might benefit from having the barrel-fins separated, even by thin slots, from the inlet ports. Conversely, the law operates to good advantage in attaining some degree of equality in temperature all round the barrel especially if thick, continuous, circular fins are used; these then act as channels to transfer heat to well-cooled areas.

The better the heat conductivity the more pronounced this effect will be; the conductivity (K) is measured in British Thermal Units per square inch (of area) per inch (of thickness or depth) per degree Fahrenheit per hour, representative figures being 2·12 for iron, 7·66 for Y-alloy and 18 for copper. So aluminium fins will conduct heat at $3\frac{1}{2}$ times the rate which iron ones of the same section will, for the same temperature difference, but are only two-fifths of the weight. Put in another way, for the same *weight* they can be 50 per cent. thicker and 72 per cent. wider and will then be able to conduct heat at nearly *nine times* the rate of the smaller iron ones.

The rate at which heat is dissipated to the air is, however, practically independent of conductivity, but depends upon the surface area, the air-speed actually traversing that area and the condition of the surface. For those reasons, iron fins of the same dimensions as the very deep, aluminium ones used on racing barrels will dissipate nearly as much heat but would be prohibitively heavy and more likely to suffer from wide temperature differences at various points on the cylinder wall. If the air-flow could be induced to follow the entire fin surface instead of breaking away from the sides and merely becoming a turbulent mass at the rear, better cooling could be effected for less weight or bulk; this can be achieved to a considerable degree with fan-cooling by cowls fitting the fin tips, and can also be obtained with natural draught by partly enclosing the fins with shrouds which merge into an outlet of rectangular section, and three or four inches long. When correctly proportioned, such cowling may provide a reduction of 30 per cent. in the temperature of the rear wall and may well be worth investigating for racing machines, particularly when fitted with fairings. The scheme would not, however, be of much value for touring models.

Cooling the Multi-cylinder

In some respects, a multi-cylinder engine is better off than a single in the matter of cooling. Broadly speaking, for any given capacity it presents a greater area of wall on which fins can be placed; small cylinders are easier to cool than large ones anyway; and when the cylinders are spaced wide apart, as in a transverse horizontal twin, a 120° twin or even a conventional V-twin with an included angle of around 50°, there is no or little interference by one cylinder with the other and they can be designed on straightforward lines.

Even the three-cylinder D.K.W. racing two-stroke enjoyed the last of these advantages by virtue of its unique layout, and it shared with the wide-angle twin Guzzi the distinction of having the horizontal cylinder equipped with radial fins. Laying the D.K.W.'s centre cylinder down flat helped to make a compact unit but was not really a good arrangement, because there was a heavily shielded area between the downward-facing exhaust port and the crankcase which could be a source of trouble; the two upright cylinders with circular fins were much better in this respect and were out in the breeze as well (Fig. 10.21).

The V-twin

Although the cylinders of a 50° twin are wide apart, the rear cylinder is shielded by the front one at speed and what air it does get is already heated to some extent. At one time it was usual to point the rear exhaust port backwards, partly, one supposes, because it looked symmetrical and partly to get out of the difficulty of making the rear exhaust pipe miss the front head. It is hardly surprising that engines built in this way, particularly those with side valves which are prone to run hot in the exhaust-port region even at the best of times, were unable to stand up to long periods at full power except under racing conditions when alcohol fuel could be used.

It is, in fact, rather strange that in the heyday of the big twin nobody ever installed one of these engines with the rear cylinder vertical as in certain early NSU twins. This would be good for cooling and was considered as a possibility during the gestation period of the post-war Vincent "Rapide". In the event, the more conventional arrangement previously used in the pre-war edition was adopted, but with both exhaust ports facing forward and the rear cylinder offset by $1\frac{1}{4}$ in. to

FIG. 10.20. The transverse V-twin—British and German. A Brough Superior prototype of 1937 (top) and a production tourer, the 1951 Victoria "Bergmeister".

197

the right of the front one. In practice, both cylinders appear to be cooled equally well.

This installation, however, serves to show that one cannot be too dogmatic about cooling, nor can theory be applied too rigidly because

FIG. 10.21. Horizontal front cylinders, radially finned, on two Continental racers, the 1954 three-cylinder D.K.W. two-stroke (top) and the "wide-angle" Guzzi twin of 1950.

FIG. 10.22. More uniform temperature distribution is the object of the side-mounted exhausts of the R.C.A. twin two-stroke.

FIG. 10.23. (Right) Full exposure of the horizontal twin's cylinders is well shown in this view of a 1954 B.M.W. racer.

of the unknown and variable factors which abound. At speeds around the three-figure mark there is actually a *forward* current of air in the region of the front head—a fact which became known only when oil leaking from a loose valve-cap during Clubman's T.T. practising spread along the top of the front mudguard. A similar phenomenon was observed on the flat-engined 250 c.c. Guzzi, where oil was carried across a gap of several inches between the rocker-gear and the guard.

A V-twin placed with its cylinders transversely should not suffer from such capricious behaviour of the air, and symmetrical engines of this type have performed very well in three-wheelers when placed at the front. Although the arrangement appears to be very attractive for a two-wheeler also, it has been tried and dropped by several English factories, partly because it has inherent transverse out-of-balance forces which, though not very large, operate at a point where the frame is most susceptible to vibration (Fig. 10.20).

THE PARALLEL TWIN

The most common layout today is another which was tried and dropped several times before it was finally accepted both for touring and racing.

This is, of course, the conventional parallel twin with the crankshaft at right-angles to the frame, an arrangement which is intrinsically good for cooling because it moves each cylinder out towards the regions of high-speed air.

This virtue existed to an even greater extent in the geared Velocette racing and touring engines (strictly "one-off", each variety) in which the crankshafts lay fore-and-aft and were coupled by spur-gears very similar to those used in the Ariel "Square Four". The crankshafts were necessarily over 5 in. apart, which, besides moving the cylinders outwards, provided plenty of space between them. This space was still further increased in the touring version by off-setting each one by a quarter of an inch in relation to its crankshaft. There was then enough room available, without too much restriction of airflow, to locate the push-rods in a central integral housing which was almost undetectable unless its position were known.

Inter-cylinder spacing is different in the conventional layout with a single two-bearing crankshaft because, in the interests of rigidity of this component, it is essential to have the cylinders very close together. The alternative is to gain more air space by using a three-bearing shaft, a more costly arrangement which is currently found only on A.M.C. products and, of course, on twin two-strokes, where a central seal is essential between the two crankcases.

In this connection, the R.C.A. engine is interesting. Realizing that the inner cylinder walls will be hotter than the outer walls and, as a consequence, the cylinders will tend to distort into the shape (though not quite to the same extent) as a banana, the designer has moved the exhaust ports from the front round to the side in an endeavour to equalize the temperature and so eliminate such an undesirable effect, though possibly at the expense of creating a hot area just abaft each port (Fig. 10.22).

With the close cylinder spacing essential if a two-bearing shaft is used, it is advisable to form both cylinders in one block, otherwise the fins would be of such a pronounced D-shape that distortion would be almost inevitable. The standard practice is to continue the fins across the narrow gap, and as the inter-cylinder space is roughly of venturi shape, the air collected at the front will pass through the centre at a fair velocity and in close contact with the surfaces. So although the actual area presented is small, the heat removal will be effective—provided, of course, that neither the entry nor the exit is badly obstructed.

Modern Parallel Twins

The Triumph design, to which must go the credit for the resurgence of the parallel twin, has the push-rods enclosed in a pair of small tubes, nestling in deep slots in the fins ahead of and behind the block. This idea would appear to entail the loss of some fin area and obstruction

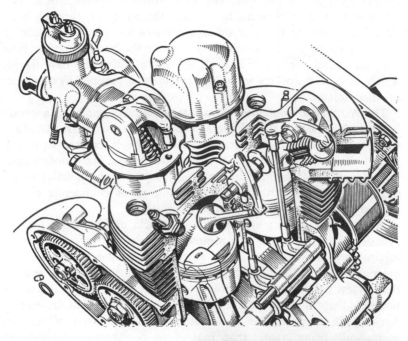

FIG. 10.24. Modern parallel-twin practice. Push-rods are located within the cylinder walls of the A.M.C. engine (above) and centrally behind the cylinders in the B.S.A. (right).

to the flow of both entering and leaving air, but since it has been retained for many years on several editions, it is not presumably, a source of trouble in practice.

In B.S.A. twins, all four push-rods are grouped in a single integral tunnel at the rear of the block, so that there is no obstruction to entering air but some on the exit side. The least obstructed passage of all was obtained on the Ariel twins, by running the push-rods through holes drilled in bosses at the four outer corners of the block—positioning which would be difficult to improve, because the bosses interfere little with the barrel cooling and they also act to stiffen the base flange, which, as in all the others with block cylinders, is retained by a number of small bolts.

The A.J.S. and Matchless twins, as we have seen, have a centre bearing which permits the cylinders to be spaced farther apart. Although the fins are of a distinct D-shape, separate barrels are used with with long bolts running through the separate heads. An unobstructed central airflow is obtained by housing the push-rods in holes in the cylinder walls, and with this construction either cylinder is free to expand without disturbing the other (Fig. 10.24).

When both cylinders are cast in one block, any tendency for one cylinder to distort along the common centre-plane through thermal expansion is resisted to an equal extent by a similar tendency in the other (as long as the temperatures of both are equal), so in general there is less liability for "monobloc" cylinders to go oval in this direction than there is with separate cylinders. But either might distort in a fore-and-aft direction due to circumferential expansion of the hot centre walls being greater than that of the cooler outer portions. In practice there appears to be little to choose between the two designs on this score.

The original design of the A.J.S. twin racer was intended for supercharging; the cylinders were almost flat, being inclined at 15° from the horizontal, and the inlet ports lay between the valves (rather in the manner of the Bristol car engine) so that fresh charge would blow directly into the barrels with less chance of driving straight out of the exhaust valves during the overlap period. Since this was a double-o.h.c. design with the rocker-boxes running from the offside right across both heads, the barrels could only receive whatever air managed to squeeze between the rocker-boxes, the inlet ports and the major diameter of each head—a condition which obviously left the inner sides of the barrels in jeopardy.

Radial finning all round was not much good, because the adjoining central fins would simply form pockets with no exits; and circular fins could only work by the inadequate means of natural convection. So a compromise was made by designing spiral fins which could receive air at the upper ends and screw it out, in a manner of speaking, into the open again lower down the barrels. At the time, it seemed that casting such fins was not possible, so they were broken up into a number of radial sections, rather like turbine blades and giving somewhat the same effect. Hence the soubriquet of "Porcupine" which, like many inaccurate nicknames, has remained long after its origins have been forgotten. In later editions of this engine, normal radial finning was used but only after the overhead inlet ports had been discarded in favour of normal ones to suit atmospheric induction.

The head of this model was a one-piece casting, and the obvious course was to use continuous transverse fins, which then lay almost edge-on to the air-stream. However, as they were several inches deep measured along the central plane, their root-thickness at the joint-face was so great that there was very little space for air to get through into the danger area between the barrels. One (unused) suggestion was to cast-in a block of sheet copper fins, 0·030 in. thick and 0·140 in. apart, which would have doubled the fin surface while offering very much less restriction in area. In the upshot, and again after the inlet ports had been moved out of the way, normal finning broken up by a large number of slots was used (Fig. 10.10).

In any event, this is not an easy type of engine to cool and is not nearly so simple in this respect as a horizontal single, in which the rocker boxes obstruct only half the head area instead of most of it.

In vertical push-rod twins the rocker-box, if common to both heads, can be turned to good effect by contouring its lower surface so that air is collected and diverted into the central space, and the head-finning can then be arranged to take advantage of the flow so created. A good application of this principle is to be seen on B.S.A. designs in which the vertical fins on the upper surface of the head are curved outwards at the rear, following the contour of the Y-shaped inlet pipe which otherwise would constitute a severe obstruction. The separate exhaust and inlet rocker and valve housings used on A.M.C. engines preclude this treatment, but it is notable that the greater part of the finning is concentrated on the exhaust side, where it should be (Fig. 10.24).

CENTRAL-DRIVE TWINS

Recently, it has become a trend in racing design to construct tiny twins as two individual single-cylinder engines attached to a central component containing the primary drive and (in four-strokes) the drive to the valve-gear. This is of particular advantage for cooling in such designs as the twin 250 c.c. M.Z., and is still useful in the case of a four-stroke, though to a lesser extent because of the presence of the drive housing between the barrels. Since overall width-reduction is not vitally important, adequate air spaces can be provided and at least the drive-housing is cooler than the cylinders and can therefore receive radiant heat, which is then carried away internally by the oil.

This scheme can be considered in some ways as a derivative of the arrangement introduced on the four-cylinder Rondine and retained on its ideological descendants, the Gilera and M.V. fours. M.V. cylinder blocks, however, contain all four bores, plus an integral camshaft-drive tunnel in the late models, whereas the Gilera, at different stages of development, used either the block system or four separate barrels with long through-bolts.

In the block system there is not much air space between the tunnel and the bores on each side of it, though there is sufficient between each of the two outer pairs of cylinders. All the barrel fins are horizontal and continuous and are made of aluminium alloy; any tendency towards unequal cooling is largely smoothed out by conduction.

The lower half of each cambox, though integral with the one-piece aluminium head, is kept sufficiently far away to allow air to pass through the fins which connect the two—a valuable contribution to cooling which is possible because, with such a short length from crankshaft to head-joint face, there is plenty of room above the head to elevate the camboxes just that little bit which makes all the difference between getting some air-flow and none. Of course, the transverse mounting of the block is almost ideal for utilizing the model's forward speed effectively, and these engines can function satisfactorily with less weight of fin per horse-power than any other design (Fig. 8.7).

With more than four cylinders, however they are arranged, the matter becomes almost insuperably complicated unless fan cooling, with its attendant bulk and power loss, is employed. In fact, when Moto-Guzzi constructed the V-8, they simply went straight to liquid cooling, since it would have been impossible to cool the rear bank of cylinders adequately by natural airflow (Fig. 8.6.).

CHAPTER 11

The Timing and Valve Gear

THE correct functioning of a four-stroke engine depends very largely upon the precision with which the mechanism controlling the motion of the valves is designed and made. This mechanism, referred to under the generic heading of "timing gear" may embody spur gearing, bevel gearing, chains and sprockets, or even some form of eccentric drive, either singly or in combination—the choice resting on many factors besides the predilection of the designer for any particular system.

As with many other things, the relative importance of these factors varies with conditions.

For racing, accurate operation irrespective of speed or load is a prime consideration and freedom from friction is also very important, but noisy operation and high manufacturing cost are not of much moment, provided the first two aims are achieved. For inexpensive touring engines, low cost becomes the chief item, provided that reasonably accurate operation and a moderate degree of silence is obtained; while for road-going sports engines a combination of all three attributes is required, coupled with ease of maintenance, as so many engines of this type are cared for by their owners.

FUNDAMENTALS

The simplest form of valve timing gear consists of a pinion mounted on the main-shaft; a gearwheel, with twice as many teeth as the pinion, fixed to a single cam; and a pair of cam-followers, oscillating on a single pin and transmitting motion either to a pair of tappets sliding in guides or to the lower ends of a pair of push-rods. The magneto can be chain driven from a sprocket carried on the end of the camshaft, and the construction lends itself to either side-valve or push-rod o.h.v. layout.

With only a single cam, the angular duration of opening of both valves is usually the same, and the relationship between their timing is determined by the angular disposition of the respective cam-followers. If different durations are thought to be necessary, it is possible to make one follower with a plain radius on the foot, and the other with two radii joined by an arc of the same radius as that of the cam base-circle.

205

However, good results can be obtained without resort to expedients of this nature, as evidenced by the Ariel "Red Hunter", a comparatively modern example which, besides being extremely simple, has the merit that the cam and followers are very wide. This benefits the latter from the wear point of view, but does nothing to help the cam, which has, in effect, twice as much work to do as if it were one of a pair (Fig. 11.2).

Despite its simplicity, the single-cam system places limitations on design which are not always acceptable. In fact it is far more common to use two cams, either on a single shaft in conjunction with lever-type followers, or on separate shafts, in which case direct-acting sliding followers or tappets are commonly employed.

With lever followers, the push-rods can either be located close together and housed in a single tube or tunnel, or be spaced one or two inches apart and enclosed in separate tubes or in holes drilled through the cylinder jacket. The last arrangement, if properly executed, interferes less with barrel cooling and permits shorter and lighter overhead rockers to be used, but there is little to choose between the systems on either score.

As far as possible, however, followers should always be designed so

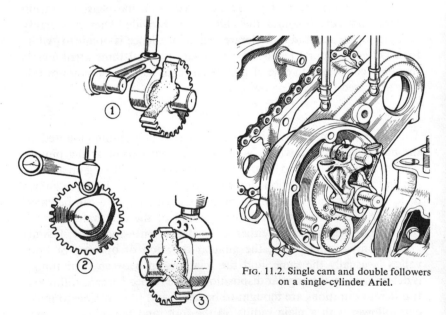

FIG. 11.2. Single cam and double followers on a single-cylinder Ariel.

FIG. 11.1. Types of cam follower: (1) the simple lever, (2) the roller-foot lever, (3) the direct-acting "mushroom".

that the major stress in the steel is compression, rather than bending. They can then be made quite light without danger of fatigue failure, which occurs only in the presence of bending or tensile stresses, but never under simple compression loads.

Even then, followers lead a very strenuous life, especially in engines which are carelessly permitted to run with excessive tappet clearances, and should be made from a high-quality nickel-chrome steel, heat-treated to give a tough core, with the wearing surface case-hardened to a depth of 0·040 in. The case obtained with nickel-chrome steel is not likely to "spall" or flake away from the core, and it does not soften quite so quickly as the case on mild steel under the influence of the high temperatures which may be generated if the lubrication is insufficient, which it usually is when starting from cold.

Roller Followers

Some designers prefer to eliminate rubbing contact by using rollers instead of solid feet, in spite of the objections that the overall weight of the follower is increased and that the rollers sometimes develop flats through skidding on the cam-surface.

The roller does not rotate at constant speed, but is spinning faster as it passes over the nose of the cam than it is when in contact with the much smaller base circle, and the force necessary to accelerate or decelerate the roller tends to promote momentary skidding. For that reason, a cam used in conjunction with a roller follower should have a large base circle radius to reduce the percentage difference between it and the nose radius; if the followers are solid, on the other hand, the overall size of the cams should be as small as possible in order to reduce the rubbing speed.

Direct-acting followers are usually of the "mushroom" type, with flat contact surfaces, disposed slightly off-centre to the faces of the cams so that they will rotate and thus distribute the wear evenly; there must, of course, be room to accommodate the large-diameter followers, as there is if two separate camshafts are used, as in the A.M.C. singles. As the reaction to any force applied to a body acts at right angles to the surface concerned, there is very little side-loading to contend with and the diameter of the tappet stem can be quite small. There is *some* side-thrust present, of course, partly due to the load being applied eccentrically and partly through friction, which acts along the line of the contacting surface; but wear from this cause is not serious and it is quite practicable to run a mushroom or cylindrical follower direct in the metal of the timing chest, as, in fact, is done in the small Triumph singles.

Flat followers are used in conjunction with "harmonic" cams, i.e., those with contours composed of three (sometimes more) circular arcs. Though this type of cam furnishes highly satisfactory results and is very simple to design and make, some designers prefer to utilize curved follower-feet, which provide a little more latitude in the selection of the most suitable cam contours and enable a pair of cams and followers to be accommodated in a relatively small space. This is a matter of importance in some engines; a good example of compact design is to be seen on Triumph twins, in which pairs of followers are carried side by side in common bushes spigoted into the cylinder base-flange (Fig. 11.3).

With tappets or followers of the Triumph or similar types, it is logical to use ball-ended push-rods running direct from the top of each follower to the appropriate overhead rocker. In the days of exposed valve-gear, it was the practice, even with lever-type followers, to fit tappets running in reasonably oil-tight guides between the followers and the lower ends of the exposed push-rods, but tappets became unnecessary when push-rod enclosure came into use. The push-rods could then run directly from the followers to the rockers, thereby eliminating all frictional drag and effecting a worth-while reduction of weight—a matter of vital importance in valve-gear, since at high speeds the inertia forces generated will amount to several hundred times the weight of the components concerned.

The extra length of the direct-acting push-rod is, however, a disadvantage. A push-rod is, in effect, a long, slender column loaded in compression and it has a tendency to fail by buckling which increases as the square of its length. Even if a rod does not actually fail, it can whip laterally, an action which is fostered by the fact that the ends are moving in arcs which themselves are different, and as a result the actual valve-motion will not agree absolutely with the motion which the cam theoretically imparts to it.

To a certain extent this is bound to happen, due to the cumulative effects of springing or flexure in every one of the components from the camshaft up to the valve, and allowance has to be made for it when developing high-speed cams; but whereas it can be reduced in most places by attention to stiffness and rigidity of mounting, push-rods must of necessity be kept light, without any trace of whippiness.

The solution is to employ thin-walled steel tube, $\frac{3}{8}$ in. diameter by 0·030 in. thick, or high-tensile aluminium tube of the same diameter, but approximately 0·060 in. thick, with very light ball-ends or cups sweated to the steel tubes or pressed into aluminium. Ball-ends need not be of large diameter—$\frac{1}{4}$ in. is ample, and $\frac{3}{16}$ in. is sufficient for

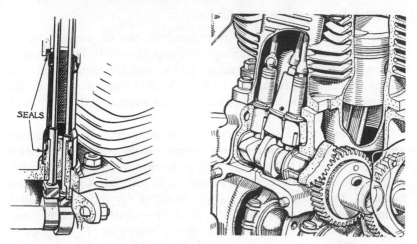

FIG. 11.3. (Left) On Triumph twins, pairs of followers are carried side by side in common bushes spigoted into the cylinder base-flange.

FIG. 11.4. (Right) All valves are operated from a single rear-mounted camshaft on the B.S.A. twins.

small engines—and there is no necessity to locate the cups hollow side up to retain lubricant. Provided there is some oil or oil mist present, the oscillating motion of the rod will ensure that enough enters the cup to prevent wear, especially if the diameter is kept to the sizes given and the actual amount of relative sliding movement is therefore small.

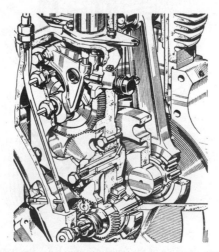

FIG. 11.5. The Velocette "high camshaft" gear; a detail from the 350 c.c. "Viper" engine.

The High Camshaft

The "high camshaft" idea, introduced on the M series Velocette engines, overcame the disadvantage of long push-rods by interposing an idler wheel between the mainshaft pinion and the cam wheel, thus raising the camshaft centre almost to the level of the base of the deeply spigoted cylinder so that the push-rods were short and therefore both light and stiff (Fig. 11.5).

This scheme was also adopted on Vincent engines, but in these an unconventional rocker arrangement permitted the rods to be so short that there was little to be gained by making them tubular; instead, they are of stainless-steel rod, 0·280 in. dia., with integral, work-hardening ball-ends. In engines of this marque modified for sprint work, solid aluminium-alloy rods are found to work satisfactorily, running direct in the steel cups; the weight saved is only of the order of $\frac{3}{4}$ oz. per rod, but even this is worth losing if it can be done without sacrifice of strength.

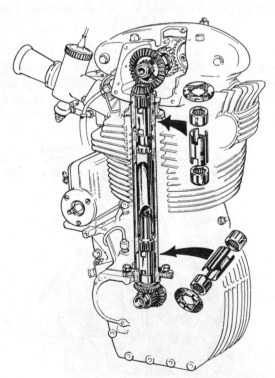

FIG. 11.6. Classic example of the bevel-driven o.h.c.—the "Manx" Norton.

210

It is possible to operate all four valves of a parallel twin from a single camshaft, as on the B.S.A. products, using a train of only three gears, but the general rule is to use one shaft at the front to operate the exhausts and another at the rear for the inlets, so introducing an extra gear-wheel which may, however, be used to drive the generator and thus eliminate a chain-drive.

An alternative scheme is to use a "triangular" chain-drive to both shafts, as on the Ariel twins, but in this particular design it has been necessary to resort to two extra pairs of gears, one set to drive the generator and the other to drive the magneto, so that any benefits the chain-drive might have conferred in the way of silence are largely lost, and the design would have been much simpler if a single idler wheel had been used, as in the A.J.S. twins.

Magneto Drives

Chain-drive is frequently used for magnetos, and it is undoubtedly a cheap and effective way of transmitting motion between shafts which are some distance apart. However, there are grounds for thinking that the slackness or play which must be provided in the chain to allow for centre-distance variations at differing temperatures, plus the inherent springiness in the whole drive, may permit inconsistency of spark-timing to occur. This, though of little importance in a touring engine, might be detrimental in racing engines which are much more sensitive to ignition timing than they are to valve timing.

It was said that the Rudge engines with chain-driven magnetos were slower than their counterparts with gear drive; and although the most successful English racing single has always had its magneto chain-driven, some pains have been taken in the 7R A.J.S. to provide gear drive to this component, while retaining a chain for the overhead camshaft. In general, it has been found that centrifugal automatic-advance devices function best with gear drive; in fact they cease to operate with a chain should it by any chance become tight, and the trend with touring engines is therefore towards gear drive.

Obtaining Silence

Because of the irregular torque required to drive a shaft with only one or two cams, obtaining silent running is something of a problem, aggravated by the fact that the gears are usually made of steel with a rate of thermal expansion much less than that of the aluminium timing-case.

This means that the running clearances between the teeth must be greater when hot than when cold. Moreover, the severity of the effect is entirely a matter of the total distance between the centres of all the gears in the train. The increase in backlash between one pair of gears is exactly the same as the combined increase which would occur if three or more smaller gears were arranged along a common centre-line, but less than if they were not arranged along this line, as then the total centre-distance length would be increased.

Teeth cut with $14\frac{1}{2}°$ pressure angle are less sensitive to backlash increase than those with 20° pressure angle, but it must be remembered that obtaining silence is rather like trying to score a "bull" with a rifle—the best you can do is hit it, and an error in any direction will lose points. Similarly, any departure from perfection may lead to noise in gears subjected to irregular torque; if too tight, they whine, and if too loose, they rattle. If they are eccentric or out-of-round, they may do a little of both.

Noise will also result if the tooth-form is incorrect or the shafts are subject to flexure—as, for instance, when the mainshaft pinion is overhung a fair distance from the nearest bearing and alters its position at every firing stroke.

Lack of space precludes the use of wide, large-diameter wheels such as are employed in car engines and consequently hardened gears are essential. Heat-treatment almost invariably causes some amount of distortion or alteration in size. Subsequent grinding of the bore to bring this to an accurate diameter may do nothing to correct the defect—in fact, it may aggravate it unless the bore is ground with the wheel centred on the pitch-circle by means of three rollers located between the teeth.

Some makers prefer to eliminate grinding and leave only one or two thou. to be honed out of the bore after hardening; but, whatever method is used, gears must be checked for concentricity before being passed to stores.

Size variation may be corrected, together with errors of form or concentricity, by tooth grinding, but this is an expensive process. The usual method is to assemble the gears selectively in sets, and/or make the final adjustment by fitting a pinion of the appropriate size.

In the Velocette design the idler gear is carried on a spindle which is adjustable for position, and thus may be set in correct engagement with both mating gears. The teeth are unusual in being very small, their diametral pitch being 48 instead of the more usual figure of 16 or 20, and are also helical. These proportions were adopted in the interests of silence, partly because helical teeth obtain continuous contact and partly because the frequency of any noise generated by the numerous small teeth is so high that it is above the range of audibility of most human beings.

O.H.C. PROBLEMS

When the valves are operated by overhead camshafts, the drive has to be conveyed over a considerable distance. The usual method is to utilize a shaft with bevel gears at each end and if two camshafts are used, to take the drive out to each by a train of spur gears. The bottom bevels are necessarily rather small and inertia of the rest of the mechanism is high, so it is not surprising that bevel-gear failure has been known to occur, especially when the lower one is mounted on the engine mainshaft, which must deflect to some extent under the high stresses from the engine itself.

The NSU system of interposing a spur-gear reduction just before the bevel drive would seem to be preferable. On racing double-o.h.c. parallel twins manufactured by this company, designs which vary in detail have been used, but most of them employ a separate drive to each camshaft, which materially assists efficient barrel and head cooling.

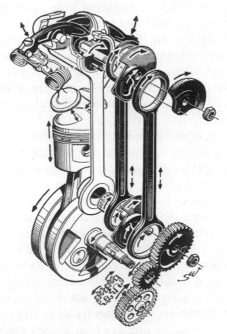

FIG. 11.7. Unique eccentric drive of the NSU "Max" series embodies a spacing member to maintain constant shaft distance.

Their single-cylinder "Max" engines feature an ingenious drive by means of two pairs of eccentrics, each pair being phased at 90° and coupled by links resembling con-rods with two big-ends. The lower eccentric shaft is driven at half engine speed and the problem of over-coming differences in thermal expansion between the links and the cylinder is met by providing a member between the two shafts which maintains them at the same centre-distance as the links, the variation in timing thus caused being negligible (Fig. 11.7).

This form of drive is naturally very silent, a characteristic which it shares with chain-drive, familiar on the 7R A.J.S. and less obviously employed on the touring 125 c.c. Honda. In the latter example, the layout is extremely simple, consisting merely of a small sprocket on the mainshaft, one twice the size on the single overhead camshaft and a tensioner-pulley housed in a tunnel cast on the side of the iron block. The whole arrangement is very neat, but neatness has been purchased somewhat dearly, as the tunnel completely shields the left-hand barrel, which is virtually uncooled on this side.

The only other drive system of any significance is the train of gears favoured mainly by Italian designers for racing models. This is in-herently prone to be noisy—a matter of little moment in this field—and is seen at its best on fours and twins in which the gears are carried in a central housing. On the 1960 250 twin racing double o.h.c. M.V. all the gears are contained in a split housing, two at the top driving the camshafts by large Oldham couplings, while the lowest one engages with the crankshaft pinion. Thus the entire assembly can be removed as a unit, and being situated well away from engine heat, expansion is not a serious matter.

The o.h.c. layout, especially in its double-camshaft form, is the logical selection for pure racing engines, partly because the valve-actuating mechanism is as light as it is possible to make it, and partly because the existence of flexure or lost motion between cam and valve is also reduced to the minimum. The second point, however, will not guarantee that valve-motion bears the designed relationship to crank-pin position at all times, irrespective of speed and load, unless the drive to the shafts is itself free from backlash or torsional flexure.

A really satisfactory overhead camshaft is an expensive thing to produce compared to a push-rod design which, though not so good in theory, is in practice adequate for all everyday needs and even for many forms of competition. Consequently all British touring machines in production today, whether single or twin, employ push-rod operation.

Apart from the question of first cost, it is much simpler to achieve oil-tightness with push-rods because of the relatively small amount of lubricant required as compared to the copious flow demanded by an overhead camshaft. Routine maintenance and decarbonizing, too, are much simpler.

Where a parallel-twin or straight or "square" four is concerned, the position is somewhat different, especially if only a moderate power output is aimed at and parallel valves are adequate for the job. The original Ariel "Square Four" and the post-war Sunbeam twin both provide good examples of compact and inexpensive overhead-camshaft valve-gear.

Rocker Details

The best form for a rocker (as for so many things) is the simplest, consisting of a light, stiff beam with a central bearing, square to the plane of the beam, which is preferably of "I" section to provide the greatest strength with the least weight. This design is very simple to forge and machine and is the natural selection for use with push-rod operated parallel valves, or with a single overhead camshaft, but is not too easy to use in conjunction with valves inclined at wide angles without departing from a design rule which must be rigidly observed if good valve-action is to be obtained. This rule is that the axis of the rocker-bearing must lie in a plane which is square to the axis of the valve, and it is difficult to adhere to this condition if the valves have an included angle of 70° or more, without an extreme amount of splay in the push-rods. Occasionally, designers have tried to get away with straight rockers and inclined valves, the push-rods installed approximately parallel to the cylinder axis, in which position they apply a most undesirable cross-loading on the rocker bearings, a treatment which the bearings will not successfully withstand unless specially designed to do so, as on certain aircraft engines.

An ingenious method of avoiding this side-loading was used on the Francis-Barnett "Stag" engine of the middle thirties, the push-rods being crossed and engaging at their lower ends with normal lever-type cam-followers.

Straight rockers, engaging on collars about half-way up the valve stems instead of on the ends, are used in Vincent engines in conjunction with high camshaft location. This layout was originally adopted partly to keep the valve springs well away from heat and partly to reduce the overall height of the engine to that of the 500 c.c. Python which it replaced but, in conjunction with the use of a high camshaft location the result was that the total weight of each valve and its operating gear

215

was only a little over one ounce heavier than it would have been had the much higher single overhead camshaft been used. The original scheme shown in Fig. 11.8 was modified in 1947 to accommodate enclosed coil-springs but the principle remained the same.

By far the commonest method of mounting the rockers is with the bearing centre-lines arranged horizontally and square to the plane in which the valves are situated. Since the arms at the valve ends of the rockers lie approximately at right angles to the stems, the bearing centres must be higher than the valves by perhaps half an inch or so. Looked at in plan view, each rocker is roughly of Z shape, with both arms square to the central portion; the major stress in the arms is therefore almost pure bending, while that in the central part is almost pure torsion, so that the metal is not subjected to the heavy combined stresses which are conducive to fatigue failure.

The central portion is best made of tubular section, bushed to run on a spindle, or merely drilled through but ground externally to act as a bearing surface. This construction has been standardized on push-rod Velocettes since their introduction, and the bearing areas are so great and the unit pressure therefore so low that the rockers can be run direct on the aluminium which forms the rocker-box cover, as wear is

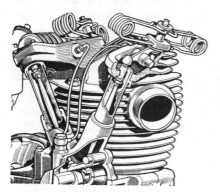

FIG. 11.8. Head of an early Vincent-H.R.D. single, showing straight rockers bearing on valve-collars between upper and lower valve-guides.

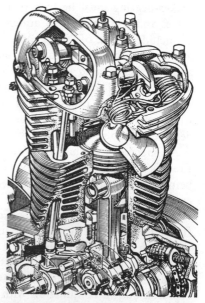

FIG. 11.9. Straightforward o.h.v. layout in a modern engine—the 250 c.c. A.M.C.

practically non-existent. This design necessitates splitting the rocker-bearings along the centre-lines; the lower half of the box is cast integrally with the cylinder head in the all-aluminium engines.

In A.J.S. singles, the rockers are carried in bronze bushes in the cover portion, but are unusual in that each is composed of a hardened and ground spindle to which a pair of arms stamped out of steel plate are splined—a method of construction which lends itself well to quantity production and has been a feature of these engines since it was introduced in 1926 to replace the forged aluminium alloy rockers used for a year or so on the Wolverhampton products (Fig. 11.9).

Speedway J.A.P. rockers are unusual in being carried in roller bearings, the inner tracks of which are formed integrally with the rockers, a construction which, besides being very low in friction, requires practically no lubrication. There is, however, always a danger that rollers, when used in the presence of an oscillating motion which travels through only a few degrees, will indent their tracks locally; this effect can be minimized by using a large number of rollers of very small diameter so that their areas of contact tend to overlap, but most designers prefer to retain plain bearings.

Noisy operation sometimes results from excessive end-float. As end-float is not an easy thing to control in manufacture, springs or double-coil spring washers are frequently employed to take it up. Excessive pressure from these devices can sometimes give rise to an unsuspectedly high frictional drag which can knock one or two hundred r.p.m. off the maximum dictated by the onset of valve-float; therefore, for racing it is best to control the float by some positive method which introduces no friction.

Reducing Noise

Suppression of valve-gear noise has always been something of a problem by reason of the varying amounts of expansion in the cylinder and head, the valves and the push-rods creating significant changes in tappet clearances as between cold and hot conditions. Barrel expansion widens the clearance, while push-rod expansion and valve expansion have the opposite effect. The "cold" clearances must be such that at no time is there any possibility of a valve being propped open as, if so, valve failure or undue wear of the cams or followers is bound to take place.

An austenitic-steel exhaust valve may expand in length as much as thirty or forty thou. under full-throttle conditions, while the expansion rates of the other components concerned varies according to the metals used and the temperatures they attain. For that reason, rather than considerations of weight, some engines use aluminium push-rods in preference to steel, or vice versa.

By a careful selection of materials and also by the provision of quietening ramps on the cams whereby the clearance is taken up very gradually before true valve-lift commences, a very high degree of silence can be obtained. Copious lubrication also assists in this direction by providing some hydraulic cushioning, but horizontal fins which react to valve impact like tuning-forks are a hindrance and are sometimes braced together by webs, thereby helping to achieve silence at the expense of good cooling.

O.h.c. Pros and Cons

Placing the camshaft overhead does away with a considerable proportion of valve-gear weight and there was at one time quite a vogue for the single o.h. camshaft on sports models, even before the advent of the Velocette which so convincingly demonstrated its superiority over push-rod operation for racing.

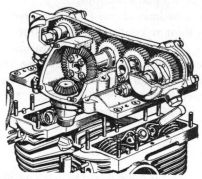

FIG. 11.10. Five-gear drive train to the o.h. camshafts of the 1951 250 c.c. T.T. Velocette.

Many of these early designs paid for lightness with other defects, chiefly noise and lack of oil-tightness. Furthermore, the actual saving in weight, when rockers have to be used anyway, is not quite so spectacular as might be thought when compared to a thoroughly well-designed push-rod layout. In the latter, one is free, within wide limits, to do what one likes in proportioning all the components to reduce their effective weight, whereas with a single o.h. shaft each rocker must perforce be nearly equal in length to half the distance between the valve-ends.

The o.h.c.'s virtual absence of flexure, which is desirable in the interests of accurate valve control, unfortunately increases the stresses created in the rockers by shock loading and they must be made of a strong, deep section to avoid failure from this cause. In the upshot, the weight advantage may be little more than the equivalent of one ounce in ten, as compared with a good push-rod layout.

On some Guzzi singles the length of the rockers was appreciably reduced by arranging them to bear midway along the valve-stems, the rocker ends being forked and bearing on collars in a manner similar to the Vincent scheme. Incidentally, for calculation purposes, the *effective* weight of a rocker can be taken as being one-third of its actual weight, as the heavy central portion moves at a slower speed than the ends.

A small but useful contribution to reducing the effective weight is provided by mounting the rockers on eccentric spindles and thus eliminating screwed clearance adjusters; but the amount of movement must be limited to about 90° in a direction at right-angles to the rocker, otherwise an undesirable variation in valve timing may be introduced, especially if the cams are of small base-circle diameter. Eccentric spindles are sometimes employed with push-rod engines, but generally screwed adjustment, either on the push-rods or the rockers, is preferred.

Satisfactory oil-tightness of an overhead camshaft can only be achieved by total enclosure, either within the actual head casting, as per Velocette, or within a separate casting as on the A.J.S. 7R, a construction which allows the two components to be made from different materials. In this instance, the cambox is in magnesium, which is 40 per cent. lighter than the RR53 aluminium alloy used for the head.

It is, of course, also possible to mount the camshaft and rocker bearings in the head and enclose the lot with a simple cast cover, as on the Grand Prix Ducati and the racing B.M.W. The German twin is peculiar in possessing two camshafts per cylinder, tucked in between the valves, which are actuated by rockers. Presumably, this construction was adopted in order to reduce the rocker weight without increasing the overall width, which would have been unavoidable if the conventional double-o.h.c. arrangement had been employed.

The orthodox plan is to locate each shaft immediately over the valve —or valves, if a twin or in-line four is concerned—merely interposing a light tappet between cam and valve to absorb side-thrust and give a straight push on the valve-stem, a desirable feature for high-speed work. On single-cylinder engines, it is usual to use a train of five gears to distribute the drive from the central bevel or spur gear to the camshafts, clearly an expensive and potentially noisy design, but one which permits each camshaft to be timed individually, either for accuracy or to suit the circumstances (Fig. 11.10).

On some Norton engines, for example, the inlet valve timing can be retarded by 10° for use with a straight exhaust pipe instead of a megaphone on occasions when the superior tractability of the plain system outweighs its reduction in power. Nortons have remained faithful for years to the use of a separate cambox, which leaves the valve-springs and the outer ends of the valves exposed—an arrangement excellent for cooling but detrimental to cleanliness, as leakage of oil past the tappets is difficult to prevent entirely and oil fed to the valve-guides also contributes its quota (Fig. 10.5).

COIL, HAIRPIN, AND NO SPRINGS

English racing engines retain the bulky hairpin springs which were adopted originally to overcome the breakage of coil springs that was a stumbling block to further progress in the early 1930's.

However, improvements in the general design of coils, methods of reducing the surging which was the underlying cause of the trouble, and better material and manufacturing technique, have since made it feasible to run them at very high speeds, as on the Italian four-cylinder engines, where the space available is so restricted that coils are much easier to work into the design. In this application, they have the additional attribute that piston-type cam-followers surrounding the springs can be used, thereby allowing the camshaft to be lowered or the floor of the valve chamber to be raised to obtain better air-flow between it and the head, whichever is deemed more desirable.

O.h. camshaft valve clearances are subject to greater alteration than push-rod clearances under the influence of temperature changes because the self-compensation which can to some degree be provided in the latter is absent in the former. On the other hand, they are less liable to capricious changes at intermediate temperatures and their rate of change through wear is low. Adjustment is usually of the "fixed" variety, made either by the addition of shims or by using tappets of appropriate lengths. This means that adjustment must be made at the time of assembly and cannot afterwards be easily altered, if at all, but the final result is the lightest possible and the risk that loss of tune may occur through the loosening of a screwed adjustment is totally avoided.

From time to time, engines with vertical or near-vertical camshafts have been produced, but none of these appear to have any marked advantages. The most interesting current development is undoubtedly the so-called "desmodromic" valve gear, of which the only successful

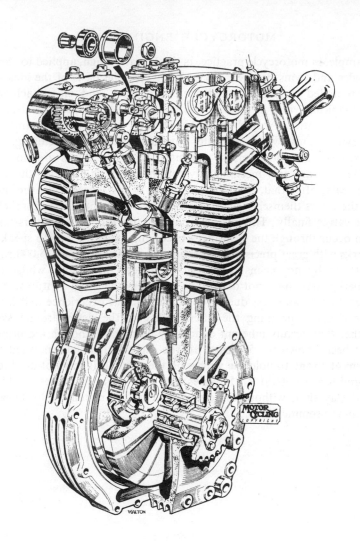

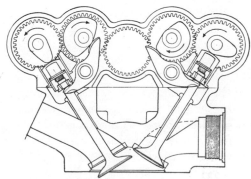

Fig. 11.11. The 500 c.c. Norton desmodromic engine. This valve gear (left), tried experimentally in 1959, used two shafts for each valve. The "closing" rockers are forked and bear on collars. In the Ducati desmodromic valve-gear system the central shaft carrying the "closing" cams is bevel-driven from a vertical drive-shaft.

example, in motorcycle practice, is the Ducati design, applied to various singles and twins between 125 and 350 c.c. The basis of the idea (first propounded early in the century) is to open and close each valve mechanically, and in these Italian products this is achieved by using two conventional camshafts for opening, with a third central shaft carrying cams which operate inverted rockers for closing. The clearances are, however, so arranged that the valves are not quite closed but are only mechanically returned to within a few "thou." off the seats; after that, back-flow of gases at low speeds and the inertia of the valves themselves at any speed above a few hundred r.p.m. closes the valves finally. This method ensures that no violent overstressing can occur through the clearances becoming "negative" so to speak and works with great precision and reliability up to speeds of 15,000 r.p.m., but has by no means rendered the Ducati invincible, whilst other experimenters have not done very well with their first ventures. However, this is doubtless due more to insufficient experience and lack of knowledge concerning the finer points of the desmodromic system rather than to any inherent deficiency therein. Although the principle has been known for 50 years, all the early designs incorporated some form of spring to hold the valves on their seats. It was not until it was found (on the 300SLR Mercedes racing car) that the valves would shut and stay shut, without these springs that the system really began to assume prominence.

CHAPTER 12

The Bottom End

THE reciprocating motion of the piston is converted to rotary motion by means of a crank and connecting-rod mechanism enclosed in the crankcase. A flywheel also is required to smooth out the power impulses (especially with a single-cylinder four-stroke) and to keep the engine running at slow speeds; the larger the number of power impulses and the higher the minimum speed likely to be used, the lighter the flywheel effect may be.

There are, broadly, two systems of disposing these "bottom end" components: (a) the "inside flywheel", in which the wheels form part of, or are bolted to, the crank assembly within the crankcase, and (b) the "outside flywheel", in which the crank is formed from two webs or small discs, with the flywheel outside the case, though usually fully enclosed.

"Inside Flywheel" Systems

In the "inside flywheel" system, the case has to be enlarged to accommodate the wheels, which are usually 7 in. to 8 in. in diameter and, in most single-cylinder designs, are steel forgings, though high-quality cast iron is still in restricted use. The flywheels are united by a crankpin and the mainshafts are usually made from steel bar and retained in the wheels either by press-fitting or by nuts.

Great accuracy is required in manufacture, as the shafts on final assembly should run true to each other within 0·001 in. and there may be upwards of a dozen diameters or faces involved, the slightest error in which will affect the alignment. Fortunately, however, all the machining operations are straightforward, and can be done on regular machine-shop turning and grinding equipment with little difficulty.

Under severe conditions, the crankpin is subject to alternating piston-inertia loads with peak values of 2,000–3,000 lb. and gas-loadings which may well be over two tons in a high-performance single. Though these forces cancel each other to some extent on the power stroke, nevertheless the resultant loads are very heavy.

In order to balance piston inertia loads, as far as possible, and also

223

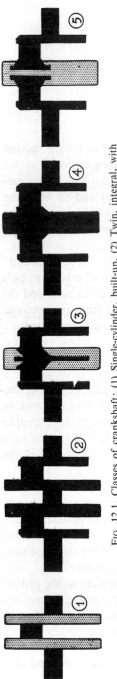

FIG. 12.1. Classes of crankshaft: (1) Single-cylinder, built-up. (2) Twin, integral, with centre bearing (e.g., A.M.C.) (3) Twin, built-up, central flywheel ring bolted-on (B.S.A., Triumph). (4) Twin, integral (Royal Enfield). (5) Twin, built-up, flanged big-end journals bolted to flywheel (Norton "Dominators").

FIG. 12.3. The Norton "Jubilee" crankshaft is a single-piece Meehanite iron casting with integral flywheel, on the flanks of which are supplementary bob-weights.

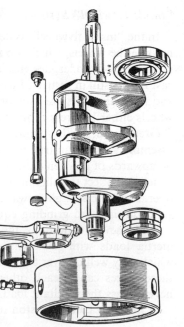

FIG. 12.2. (Left) Crankshaft assembly of the Triumph T21 twin, with bolted-on flywheel ring and built-in sludge trap.

the centrifugal force arising from the big-end itself, the wheels are counterweighted. This may be done either by thickening them on the side opposite to the pin or by forming recesses, or drilling holes, on the same side as the pin. Either way, the effect is to move the centre of gravity of the wheels away from their axes, and the resultant centrifugal forces act substantially in the plane of each wheel.

The result, beside achieving partial balance, is to lessen the inertia loads on the main bearings, and also their bending effect on the crankpin, although this is still so great that the main bearings (usually of ball or roller type) must be kept as close as possible to the cylinder centre-line without making the flywheels so thin that they will constitute another source of flexure.

Clearly the pin itself should be of large diameter—$1\frac{1}{2}$ in. is advisable for a 500 c.c. single—and very firmly anchored in the wheels. There are several methods of anchorage. The pin may have tapered ends pulled in by nuts, or parallel ends pulled up against square shoulders by nuts, or it may simply be made a very tight interference fit in the wheels, which must, in this method, be of high-tensile material.

The usual method in large four-strokes is the "parallel-pin with nuts", which has the advantage that dismantling can be performed with ordinary workshop equipment, but with short strokes and large main-shafts there is always difficulty in obtaining clearance for the box-spanner required to tighten the usual hexagon nut. This has been over-come in "Manx" Nortons by using recessed nuts, with splines instead of flats, and a castellated spanner, while the 7R A.J.S. employs special nuts which, after tightening, are cut off flush with the wheels (these nuts cannot be removed without destroying them).

In single-cylinder Velocettes, the main bearings are closer together than usual because of the extremely narrow primary chain-line, and no nuts are employed. The pin is ground with a very small amount of taper on each end and is forced with 3–4 tons pressure into the wheels until these are hard against the shoulders provided by the central portion of the pin, which forms the track for the caged roller bearing.

The Guzzi "Lodola" employs a somewhat similar construction which, however, is more commonly found on two-strokes, where it is desirable to avoid odd spaces in which "dead" mixture can accumulate.

In conventional designs, the position of the engine-sprocket is determined by the necessity to move the primary chain out far enough to clear the rear chain and to provide space behind the clutch for the inner wall of the primary chaincase—which may result in an un-desirable degree of overhang from the main bearing. To combat this, a second bearing can be added very close to the sprocket, and in rare instances an "outrigger" bearing has been employed—a system which is even more effective, but adds to the problem of machining all the main bearing housings in alignment.

With two bearings on the drive side, the mainshaft is very well supported, but this does nothing to relieve it of torque-loading and may even increase local bending loads due to flexure of the crank-assembly. The fixing of this shaft in the wheel thus becomes very important.

The best method would be to make it integral. While this is sometimes done when the crank-web is small, forging difficulties are encountered when the flywheel is large, and it is more usual to make the shaft a semi-permanent fitting by employing a heavy press fit and locking the shaft in some manner which will prevent its subsequent removal. After that, the crankpin hole is bored and faced true to the shaft to eliminate any errors introduced during the fitting of the shaft: it is at this stage that the greatest care must be taken in machining, to avoid scrapping a valuable component.

On the timing side, there is usually one roller bearing, but on occasion a plain bush is used, oil being fed directly to the bush and thence up drilled holes to the big-end. Alternatively, either oil is fed into the end of the shaft via a quill, or a bronze bush is located in the timing cover to steady the end of the shaft and also to act as retainer for oil which is supplied to the blind end of the bush.

There is not much oil pressure involved when roller big-ends are used, because these offer little resistance to flow, nor do they need pressure feed as do plain bearings. So long as enough oil is supplied to the mainshaft, the centrifugal force generated in the radial oil-way will ensure that it goes out through the big-end.

V-twins

The general construction of V-twins duplicates that of singles, and the rods can be accommodated either on the "fork-and-blade" principle or by mounting them side by side.

On J.A.P. engines, the forked rod is fitted with a sleeve which runs on rollers on the crankpin, while the blade rod oscillates on the outside of the sleeve. This construction permits the cylinders to be in the same plane, and the overall width is less than when the rods are side by side, as in the Vincent. However, the offset of the Vincent barrels provides slightly better airflow over the rear one and is also a help in obtaining clearance between the two heads to permit the rear exhaust port to face forwards. The pin is rather long, but the rods are identical.

226

Parallel-twin Four-strokes

In order to obtain even firing impulses, the crankpins of parallel-twin four-strokes are in line and, naturally, the whole crank assembly is twice as long as in a single. Undesirable flexure would occur owing to this great length unless adequate precautions were taken, which may consist of adding a centre bearing, as in A.J.S. and Matchless products, or the usual practice of making the centre portion extremely rigid either by bolting the flywheel to a heavy integral flange (Triumph), sandwiching it between the flanges of a two-piece shaft (Norton) or making an integral assembly, cast in high-tensile iron (Royal Enfield) (Fig. 12.1).

Split big-ends with their accompanying bolts are necessarily heavier than the plain eyes used with roller big-ends, and high-tensile aluminium forgings are used. This material also forms a good bearing surface and can be run directly on the pins, but it is common to fit renewable bearing shells of thin steel lined with white-metal or, for very ardous work, with indium-coated lead-bronze, sometimes called "tri-metal".

The stresses in the drive-side crank-web are considerable. In particular, the explosion load from the timing-side cylinder is applied several inches away from this web, so subjecting it to a twisting action in addition to the loads imposed merely by the transmission of torque. Consequently, should a failure occur, it will almost always take place through fatigue in this region; it is fortunate that such failures are rare, because they can be followed by the most disastrous consequences.

Outside Flywheel Designs

The presence of inside flywheels naturally makes the crankcase large, which is undesirable in a two-stroke because it reduces the pumping efficiency of the crankcase. Hence, the diameter of the shaft assembly is reduced as much as possible and the required weight is supplied by an outside flywheel, a convenient system because this component can then be utilized as part of a flywheel magneto, or even of a starter-motor.

The crank-webs can either be disc-shaped in order to fill up the maximum amount of space, or be made simply as webs with crescent-shaped balance weights, which is the usual Villiers system and is an assistance in forging the drive-side web and shaft in one piece. Press-fit, nutless crankpins are usual, though not universal, those in the Villiers being hollow and fitted with expander plugs which are driven home after lining-up the assembly.

Since a flywheel magneto is large in diameter and must be run free from oil, it is not feasible to enclose it in the primary chaincase, but instead it is often carried on the "idle" end of the crankshaft and protected simply by a light weather-proof cover. One disadvantage of this scheme is that under very rough conditions involving severe changes in (or even reversal of) the drive load, the inertia of the fly-wheel tends to pull the assembly out of line, and a very secure method of fitting the crankpin is necessary, this being particularly important in moto-cross engines.

In the flat-single Guzzi, which has an outside flywheel, the primary drive is taken through dogs on the face of the flywheel boss to the pinion, which is otherwise a free fit on the shaft. Thus all transmission "snatch" loads due to rapid flywheel-speed fluctuations are absorbed at the source and have no effect at all on the crankshaft assembly.

In small two-strokes, an overhung crank-pin is sometimes used. This system is the simplest possible and avoids all the trouble of building up a composite assembly accurately in line, at the expense of placing very heavy loads on the main-bearing nearest to the crankpin. To reduce this, and also to minimize bending loads in the mainshaft, the big-end and crank-web must be made as narrow as possible consistent with adequate strength.

The twin-cylinder Scott is a good example of this construction (Fig. 12.4). By placing a crankpin at each end of the shaft and the flywheel in the centre, the number of main bearings is reduced to two and the problem of isolating the crank-chambers from each other is very neatly solved—but, of course, the drive also has to be taken from the centre, which is not convenient when a conventional type of gearbox is to be used, but it suited the original two-speed drive admirably.

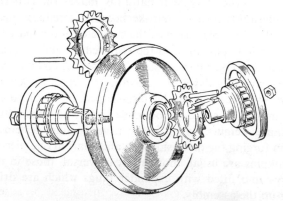

FIG 12.4. Central flywheel of the Scott twin two-stroke is located between the two crank-chambers and the bosses of the overhung cranks are bolted to it. Only two main bearings are necessary. Two sprockets are fitted to give a two-speed primary drive.

The general system with twin two-strokes is, therefore, to put the sprocket at one end of a two-throw assembly which is supported in the centre by a pair of bearings and seals installed in a centre wall. This construction, though sound, is not easy to put into concrete form, and necessitates a "semi-permanent" arrangement, as on the Villiers twin (Fig. 12.5), which cannot easily be dismantled without special equipment, or the use of a sliding-fit crank-web on the drive side (the Excelsior

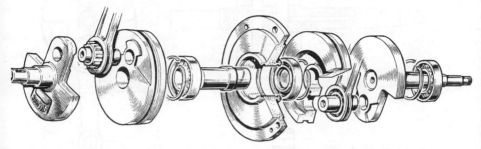

FIG. 12.5. Crankshaft assembly of the Villiers 2T twin two-stroke is supported in the centre by a pair of bearings, with seals, installed in a central wall.

method) which permits access to a draw-bolt holding the two halves of the centre portion together. In the second system, the drive-side shaft must be mounted in two bearings, in order to maintain it in true axial relationship despite the lessened rigidity occasioned by the sliding fit of the adjacent crankpin.

FLAT-TWIN SHAFTS

Flat-twin shafts are always built-up assemblies, the easiest method being to form the pins in one with the centre-web, which can then be less than $\frac{1}{2}$ in. thick. By this method, together with the use of narrow roller-bearing big-ends, the cylinder centre-lines can be kept close together, which is desirable both for balance and for rigidity. The outer webs, formed with balance weights, can be either pressed-on to the pins or retained by nuts. There is, however, a tendency to twist the drive-side pin in relation to the web which is not present in a single-cylinder layout, and for that reason the pins may be keyed to the webs as a precautionary measure (Fig. 12.6).

ROLLER-BEARING BIG ENDS

Roller-bearing big-ends were originally introduced because they can operate quite well at moderate speeds with the most rudimentary lubricating arrangements, and at first merely consisted of a row of

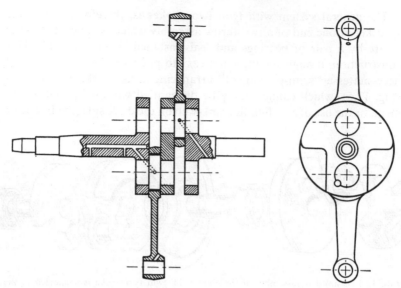

FIG. 12.6. Section and end elevation of the flat-twin LE Velocette crankshaft assembly. Note the keying of crank-pins to webs.

rollers interposed between the crank-pin and big-end eye. However, as engine-speeds rose, this simple "crowded-row" design became inadequate, tending either to seize at high speed or to wear rapidly; both defects were cured by the adoption of the "caged" bearing, together with a copious supply of oil circulated at the rate of 30 gallons an hour in some high-output engines.

Main bearings give very little trouble, though they rotate just as fast as the big-end. But there is a fundamental difference in working conditions between any bearing which rotates around a fixed axis and the big-end, which, besides rotating, is moving in a circular path around the crankshaft axis and is thus subjected to centrifugal forces which are not present in the main bearings under steady conditions.

These forces have the effect of causing the rollers to press outwards (Fig. 12.7) and, if no cage is fitted, the inter-roller pressure is cumulative and the outermost pair rub against each other with a severity which increases as the square of the crankshaft speed. As an example, take the case of a bearing containing 12 rollers, each 0·312 in. in diameter and 0·312 in. long, on a crank-radius of 45 mm.: the maximum inter-roller pressure in round figures is 40 lb. at 5,000 r.p.m., increasing to 57 lb. at 6,000 r.p.m. and 98 at 7,000.

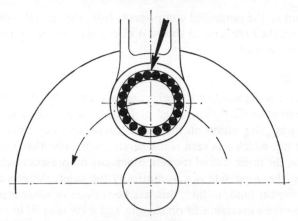

FIG. 12.7. How the rollers in an uncaged rotating assembly tend to crowd at the outer side of the pin (arrowed).

To prevent this action, which tends towards roller wear, if nothing else, slotted cages have been adopted in which each roller is separated from its neighbours by a bar and the load existing between each roller and its restraining surface is reduced to the tangential component of the centrifugal force at any given instant (Fig. 12.8). As each roller passes through the centre-line of the cylinder, it momentarily ceases to bear on the bars at all, its centrifugal force being carried by a pure rolling

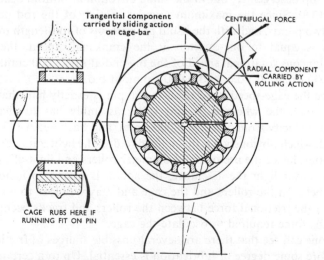

FIG. 12.8. Two views of a caged roller big-end, showing (left) where friction occurs if the cage is a running fit on the crankpin and (right) how the load between each roller and its restraining surface is reduced to the tangential component of the centrifugal force.

action; but all the tangential components from the several rollers acting together on the cage tend to throw it outwards—as, of course, does its own weight as well.

Cage Design

Usually it is the practice to make the cage a running fit on the crank-pin, relieving the bars of the cage or locating it on raised shoulders to avoid any lapping action on the roller-tracks, and examination of any cage and pin which has seen some service will show that wear is only evident on the inner side of the pin. Since any oil present is also thrown outwards, the inner side is automatically the drier, therefore it would be more logical (and, in fact, this has been done in some instances) to make the cage a clearance fit on the pin and a running fit in the bore of the outer race, so that it would constantly benefit from any oil present. For the sake of lightness, the cage is usually made of a strong aluminium alloy, and in order to avoid any possibility of differential thermal expansions taking up all the clearance, even under extreme conditions, it is necessary for the cage to be quite a loose fit inside the sleeve.

There is still another factor to be considered, namely the oscillating action super-imposed upon the main rotation by reason of the angular swing of the connecting rod. The rod can be considered as swinging about the gudgeon-pin, its motion being opposite to that of the crank-pin at top dead centre, but in the same direction at bottom dead centre (Fig. 12.9). Since the maximum angular motion of the rod occurs at these two points, and with the usual proportions of rod-length to crank-radius is equal to one-quarter of the crankshaft speed, the *actual* instantaneous rotational speed of the big-end at say, 8,000 crank r.p.m. is 10,000 r.p.m. at t.d.c. and 6,000 r.p.m. at b.d.c.

Since the cage-speed in relation to the pin is exactly half that of the sleeve, then the whole cage and roller assembly has to change its angular velocity from 5,000 to 3,000 r.p.m. and back again 133 times a second, which obviously it is disinclined to do. The lighter it is, of course, the better, hence the use of small-diameter rollers and light-alloy cages; but, however light the assembly, the action is bound to increase the loads between the rollers and the cage and may well lead to a skidding effect if the frictional force between the rollers and tracks becomes less than the force required to oscillate the cage.

So one can see that there are several possible sources of friction, and therefore some degree of lubrication is essential. Up to a certain point, this need not be very great. T.T.s have been won with engines lubricated only by occasional shots from a hand-pump simply squirting oil into the crankcase, and thence into the big-end (somewhat problematically) through a couple of holes, while even today the Speedway J.A.P., normally not running much above 6,000 r.p.m., performs very well with a flow to the big-end which is only a fraction of that normally provided on a road-racing engine. In the latter, of course, the copious flow provided assists greatly in internal cooling which is not of much importance on the speedway motor run exclusively on alcohol and only for short distances.

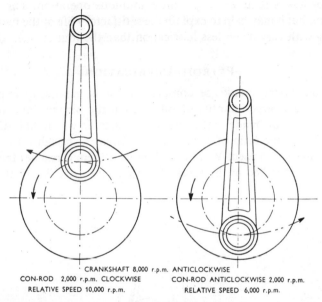

CRANKSHAFT 8,000 r.p.m. ANTICLOCKWISE
CON-ROD 2,000 r.p.m. CLOCKWISE   CON-ROD ANTICLOCKWISE 2,000 r.p.m.
RELATIVE SPEED 10,000 r.p.m.   RELATIVE SPEED 6,000 r.p.m.

FIG. 12.9. The effect of the angular swing of the connecting rod upon the rotational speed of the big-end at constant crankshaft revolutions.

It is a well-established fact that if any caged ball or roller bearing fitted to a high-speed spindle is run full of oil, it will become very hot through the churning action set up in the lubricant. This has lead to the development of other systems, such as that in which a jet of compressed air is used to blow oil in the form of mist into the bearing, so lubricating it and cooling it at the same time; there is little more than a film of oil present on any of the surfaces, and so no extraneous heating from churning.

On the other hand, if enough oil is poured through by a circulating system, heat is carried away with the stream and can be dissipated elsewhere, this being the normal state of affairs with an ordinary dry-sump engine. If the oil-supply is accidentally cut off, the bearing is momentarily still full of oil, which rapidly heats up due to frictional heat plus churning heat. At around 300°C. (depending on its composition) the oil will start to vaporize off, and at 450° the rollers will commence to bond themselves to the aluminium cage, after which complete seizure follows immediately.

The inference is that there is a "pessimum" (opposite of "optimum") quantity of oil which is particularly conducive to seizure, and either more or less is required to permit continuous operation. This is only a theory, but it may help to explain the satisfactory life of the two-stroke bearing with very much less lubrication than the four-stroke.

PETROIL LUBRICATION

When employing crankcase compression, it is manifestly impossible to circulate a large quantity of oil through the big-end, and resort is almost invariably made to the "petroil" system, in which oil is dissolved in the fuel in the ratio of 1:16 for some engines, though ratios as low as 1:40 have been used. What little lubricant there is reaches the rollers through slots milled in the sides of the big-end eye (Fig. 12.10) or via

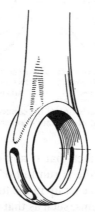

FIG. 12.10. One accepted method of lubricating a two-stroke big-end—through slots which do not interrupt the most heavily loaded areas.

grooves in the faces of the flywheels. The bearing is thus lubricated on the "oil-mist" system, so there is no heat generated by oil-churning, and the surrouding conditions are favourable towards heat-dissipation because the crankcase is continuously ventilated by air which is cooled by evaporation of the fuel contained in it, whereas the air inside a four-stroke may be somewhat in the region of 100°C.

Heat generated in the two-stroke big-end, therefore, has more chance of being dissipated directly through the surface of the big-end to the air. In that connection, although racing rods are usually highly polished, it would be more logical to dull the surface by shot-peening, or even to blacken it with one of the chemically applied finishes commonly used for rust-proofing, in order to increase its rate of heat-dissipation.

Alternative Cage Materials

There has also been a trend recently towards the use of steel for cages, as steel cages can be made just as light as aluminium ones of the same strength by suitable heat-treatment. A refinement which has not, to the writer's knowledge, yet been used would be to silver-plate the cage, as this treatment (used, for instance, on some aero-engine components) is excellent for preventing seizure between two steel surfaces. Titanium which is half the weight of steel for the same strength, would also be worth consideration despite its high cost and difficulty in machining.

THE CRANKCASE

The crankcase has one obvious duty to perform, namely, that of acting as a container to keep oil inside and mud and water outside. Less obvious, though more important, functions are to act as a mechanical connection between the cylinder and the crankshaft bearings, to provide a firm foundation for the cylider block, to accommodate the oil-pump and timing gear and, in some instances, to act as a frame member.

A further function in two-strokes is to act as a pump in transferring mixture from the carburetter to the cylinder. So, in one way and another, a great many points have to be borne in mind at the design stage to obtain a component which is neither too heavy nor too difficult to machine, and yet is not so flimsy that undue flexure will occur under operating loads.

With one or two exceptions (notably the Barr and Stroud single-sleeve-valve units in which the barrels were cast integrally with the upper crankcase halves) crankcases are made in light alloy, either as sand-castings or die-castings, and, except for those of flat twins, are usually split vertically into two components, spigoted or dowelled together.

The foundry work entailed in this construction is quite simple, demanding the minimum number of cores, chills or loose pieces in the pattern equipment, and the castings can be easily and rapidly machined on turret lathes without expensive tooling. After part-machining, it is necessary to assemble the halves before milling and boring the cylinder register, and, of course, great care must be taken to ensure that the main-bearing housings are accurately in line, especially when there are more than two.

In a single-cylinder or V-twin engine, the construction is quite straightforward. The crank-chamber is in one compartment and the timing gear in another, closed by its own cover.

Parallel-twin Problems

Complications begin to creep in with a parallel twin, partly because the camshaft or shafts must be housed within the crank-chamber so that they can operate the drive-side valve gear, which means that they, too, are carried in bearings in each half (unless an overhead camshaft layout is used). Further, the span between the main bearings is so wide that some designers prefer to incorporate a centre bearing, which must be carried in some fashion that permits of easy assembly.

In modern A.M.C. twins, the solution is to carry a split plain bearing in a plate sandwiched between the two case-halves. Their predecessor, the "Porcupine", had a similar scheme, but the crankcase was in one piece. The crankshaft, with the centre-bearing attached but without the rods, was slid in through one end of the one-piece case and, after adding the drive-end cover, the centre bearing was pulled up against the bored inner surface of the case by bolts reaching down from the cylinder face. The rods were assembled after this operation, the big-end nuts being accessible through the cylinder base mouths.

The problem becomes more acute with two-strokes because of the necessity to seal each chamber individually, and achieving this inevitably introduces complications or difficulty in assembly.

In the present Villiers system, a central circular casting containing a roller bearing and double-acting seal is assembled on a spindle to which the adjacent crankwebs are pressed. The disc is spigoted into the case on the split-line to centralize it, and slots are provided in both half-cases to clear the con.-rods which are, of course, non-detachable. The upper ends of these slots are closed by what appears to be, but actually is not, a full-width compression plate. In the Jawa twin a somewhat similar idea is used but the slots are closed by a light metal block.

The difficulty with this method is that the central bearing or seal can only be renewed after pressing off one of the inner crankwebs, which requires special equipment.

In the Excelsior twin two-stroke, a three-part case is employed, split on each cylinder axis. The drive-side crankweb, being only a sliding fit on its crankpin, can be withdrawn with its part of the case, after which the two-piece central portion can be divided and removed. In the Ariel Leader, the centre portion can be separated after removing a tension-bolt via the hollow drive-side shaft, thus enabling either crank assembly to be removed without the need for loose parts or special presses.

Horizontally Split Cases

Another solution, more favoured abroad than in England, is to split the case horizontally instead of vertically, along the axis of the crankshaft. The shaft can then be built up, complete with rods, bearings and seals, and placed in position in one half before bolting the other in place.

From the manufacturing angle, this still means preliminary machining

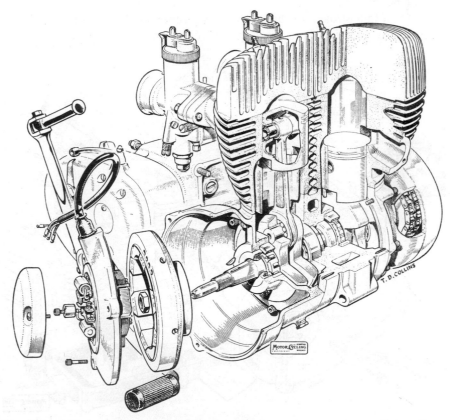

Fig. 12.11. A three-part crankcase, split vertically on the axes of the cylinders, is employed in this 328 c.c. Excelsior twin two-stroke.

in halves, followed by final machining after joining together to form a unit, but it is probably simpler overall than the vertical-split method. If the gearbox is made integral (as in the Suzuki and Rumi) the split can be continued right through and the gearbox shafts arranged with their bearing centres on the line of the split.

Occasionally four-stroke units have been made in this way. In fact it was the only sensible method with a "straight" four, and it presents the possibility of making the sump as a steel pressing which, on removal, would disclose split big-ends and perhaps the gearbox internals as well.

This idea would not be practicable with a two-stroke, since when crankcase compression is utilized it is necessary to reduce "idle" spaces to a minimum. Hence the practice of using disc crankwebs which clear the machined surfaces of the case by only half a millimetre in some engines.

On a four-stroke, it is better to allow a generous clearance to reduce the drag resulting from the large amount of oil present, and at one

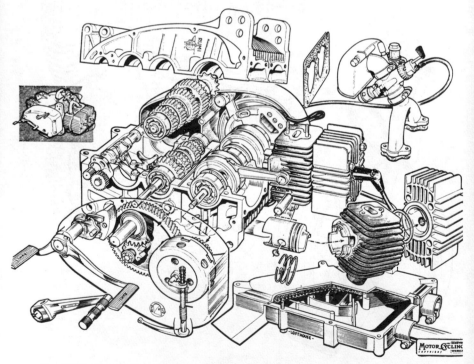

Fig. 12.12. A good example of a horizontally split crankcase-gearbox—the 125 c.c. Rumi twin two-stroke.

point only to provide a scraping edge by which oil adhering to the wheel rims is directed into a small sump, where it can become quiescent before being drawn into the scavenge pump. In the early days of the dry-sump system, trouble with faulty scavenging was encounted due to the pump having to handle a great mass of froth instead of liquid.

Oil as a Coolant

If circulated at a rate of 30 or 40 gallons an hour through external pipes to a dark-coloured tank, oil can be used to remove a lot of heat and can exercise a great effect in keeping the piston cool.

In order to eliminate the separate tank and its plumbing, some designers prefer to cast the tank integrally with the crankcase, still retaining the dry-sump system if there is insufficient room below the case to allow the oil simply to drop in by gravity. This is usually the position with a largish vertical single, but it is possible to use the sump system if the crank assembly is small, as in the B.M.W. twin and M.V. four.

While oil is good at collecting heat, it is very bad at getting rid of it again, because the layer directly in contact with a cool surface increases in viscosity and simply stays there, acting as an insulator and effectively preventing heat being dissipated from the hotter oil in the interior. Ribbing a sump which contains a quantity of oil is not very effective unless there are some internal ribs also to transfer as much heat as possible from the body of the oil, but ribs placed on areas against which hot oil is violently thrown by centrifugal action can be made to radiate a lot of heat.

In this connection, the polishing of crankcases, though pleasing to the eye, may cost almost as much as the whole of the machining and cuts down the heat-radiating ability to a fraction of what it would be if the metal were left "as cast".

Allowing for Stress

The areas of major stress, so far as the engine itself is concerned, are the main-bearing housings and the cylinder-bolt bosses, the metal in between these localities being subjected to tensile loads of varying intensity. There are also stress concentrations in the region of the fixing-bolt bosses, especially if the crankcase forms a part of the frame—or even if, as sometimes happens, it is stiffer than the frame which is supposed to be carrying it, in which event the case may be doing more work than the frame in maintaining alignment.

In a single, the best way to dispose the metal between bearing and cylinder flange is in the most direct line, but this may imply that the wall is practically a flat disc which is likely to "pant" in and out, especially if the flywheel assembly is located laterally between the sides of the case. If there are two bearings on the drive side, they may be insufficiently supported against radial loads, especially those applied by the primary drive, and it is therefore advisable to provide a number of ribs to give additional stiffness without much weight increase.

Unfortunately, ribs, if placed externally, collect dirt and are difficult to clean, so on touring engines they are usually placed internally. If this course is adopted, plenty of metal must be left around the main-bearing outer races, otherwise they will inevitably come loose.

Stud Details

Cylinder-base studs, especially in a high-compression engine, should be screwed into the metal for a distance at least *twice* their diameter, and the bosses should not be over-hung from the parent metal, even if this does assist the machining operations.

The run-out at the end of a thread cut with a self-opening die-head exercises a powerful wedging action if the stud is tightened on this portion, and the boss may split. This can be avoided either by bottoming the stud in the hole, or by the simple expedient of turning a groove at the end of the thread to eliminate the run-out portion. Studs treated in this fashion screw up to the end of the groove and then stop, so their projecting length is not indeterminate, as it is when the run-out is present. "Heaping-up" of the soft aluminium around stud-holes can be avoided by counterboring two threads deep before tapping.

Provided attention is given at all localized high-stress points, any good-quality aluminium alloy will suffice, and the design should be such that it can be readily die-cast without too much intricacy in the permanent moulds.

When lightness is a primary consideration, magnesium alloy can be used, with a saving for equal section thickness of 40 per cent. in weight. For various reasons, such as thickening-up at high-stress areas or the use of steel locking plates for the main bearings, the saving may not be much more than 30 per cent. This is worth while in bulky single-cylinder engines and is common English practice, though the Italians, who are thoroughly weight-conscious in their racing models, are not very keen on magnesium.

One reason for this is magnesium's coefficient of thermal expansion which, at 0·000028 in. per in. per degree C., is much higher than that of a low-silicon aluminium alloy at 0·000022. Even this second figure is an embarrassment, because it means that when cold a bearing of $2\frac{1}{2}$ in. diameter must be fitted 0·003–0·004 in. tight to prevent it coming loose at operating temperature.

At lower temperatures, considerable "hoop" tension is developed in the housing metal, and the additional interference necessary with magnesium alloy increases this tension to an extent which may cause the metal to stretch, after which the bearing is loose, or at least free to creep around at working temperature. For that reason, it is necessary to hold the outer rings in and prevent them from rotating by some form of retainer-plate or a flanged outer race.

The problem is not so acute if a bronze bush is used on the timing side to act as an oil-feed as well as a bearing, because the coefficient of expansion of the yellow metal at 0·000018 is higher than that of steel (0·000012). On the other hand, such bushes should always be pegged or dowelled, because if a bronze bush does start to turn it wears away with great rapidity, though the aluminium, oddly enough, does not suffer nearly so much.

CRANKCASE FIXINGS

Crankcases which are subjected to heavy stressing should always have the bolt-bosses blended well into the casting walls with generous fillets, and extending if possible to the full width available. Cracks are very likely to develop adjacent to the holes if the bosses are narrower than the main walls and thus place the neighbouring metal in a peculiar state of stress which combines shear, bending and tensile loads—a dreadful combination which should be avoided at all costs.

To quote one actual example of failure from this cause, an early version of a popular speedway engine had bolt-bosses only $2\frac{1}{4}$ in. wide attached to a crankcase about $3\frac{1}{2}$ in. wide, and it was not unknown for a piece of aluminium, complete with the two rear bosses and part of the crankcase, to be pulled right out. A cure was effected by bringing the bosses to full crankcase width.

Another concerns the original Vincent-H.R.D. singles which did have full-width bosses, spaced, however, fairly closely together for interchangeability with Rudge engines. After a week's T.T. practice, cracks developed round the lower rear bosses, necessitating some frantic rebuilding and extension of the engine-plates to the extreme bottom corner to utilize another bolt, which previously had only helped to hold the halves together. Spreading the load in this manner entirely eliminated cracking even on the "Rapide" engine which, though a V-twin of twice the power, used similar rear engine plates and bolts.

CHAPTER 13

Two-stroke Power

IT is common to think of a two-stroke as being a type of engine which fires twice as often as a four-stroke and is very much simpler mechanically. This conception is quite correct as far as it goes, but is a drastic over-simplification of the fundamental differences between the types, which are affected much more strongly by two less obvious factors.

One is that the processes of expelling burnt gas from, and admitting fresh mixture to, the working cylinder occur simultaneously, or nearly so, instead of on two separate strokes as in the four-stroke. The admission (commonly referred to as "transfer") ports are open for nearly as long as the exhaust ports, and this immediately introduces the problem of getting all the spent gas out without losing a lot of fresh charge while the scavenging process is taking place.

The second big difference is that the cylinder is not filled directly from the atmosphere, but the mixture must first be drawn and compressed into some other enclosed space. This is usually the crankcase, but may just as well be an additional charging cylinder or some variety of air-pump, such as a Roots or eccentric-vane blower.

Whatever method is used, energy is lost in work expended on pumping and not recovered, or in additional frictional loss; and in the normal arrangement, using a plain piston and crankcase compression, the overall volumetric efficiency is considerably less than in an equivalent four-stroke.

The net result is that it is not possible to obtain the same mean effective pressure on each firing stroke as it is on a four-stroke. Consequently it is also impossible to obtain twice the power at equal speeds—or anything remotely approaching that—unless by some departure from simple crankcase compression.

Various devices have been used to increase the pumping ability of the crankcase—by a double-diameter piston, as on the Dunelt, or by an additional charging piston, as on some D.K.W.s, or by an external air-pump large enough to act as a supercharger. Whilst these methods may increase the power output they must be paid for either in undesirable limitations on design or in increased mechanical complications, also they usually entail an increase in fuel consumption above a figure which is already not very good, judged by four-stroke standards.

Besides these practical objections, F.I.M. racing regulations have debarred the use of any such aids to power-production for several years, just as superchargers are not permitted on four-strokes. All these considerations have had the effect of stopping further development along the complicated lines which were being followed in the 1930s and focusing attention upon variants of the original "three-port" type which, whatever its shortcomings, possesses the crowning merit of extreme simplicity.

The three ports in the rudimentary (i.e., deflector piston) type consist of the inlet port controlling the entry of mixture into the crankcase, the transfer port controlling the admission of mixture into the cylinder, and the exhaust port. Of these, the inlet port takes no real part in the combustion cycle, and we can for the moment put it mentally to one side.

The exhaust port is opened by the top edge of the piston at around 70° before bottom dead centre and the transfer, which is placed directly opposite to the exhaust, is opened 10 or 15° later—this interval, termed the "blow-down" period, being necessary to allow the cylinder pressure to drop from 60 or 70 lb./sq. in. to a figure much nearer to the transfer pressure, which cannot be more than 5 or 6 lb./sq. in. above atmospheric because of the unavoidably large volume of the crankcase.

Immediately after the transfer opens, a stream of fresh mixture pours into the cylinder at the same time as exhaust gas is still going out. To prevent the new charge from travelling across the piston and straight out of the exhaust port, it is necessary to form the piston crown so that it deflects the transfer gas upwards, which not only discourages it from escaping out of the exhaust port, but causes it to displace the burnt gas lurking in the upper end of the cylinder and thereby promotes good scavenging.

In diagrams illustrating this principle, incoming and outgoing gases are often indicated by separate arrows, but, unfortunately, things are not so neat in practice. Much of the new charge gets mixed up with the old and some is inevitably lost, while the mixture eventually left in the cylinder is contaminated to a greater or less extent by spent products of combustion.

Another source of loss lies in the fact that, in a normal engine, the port timing is symmetrical and there is a period of crank-movement, equal to the "blow-down" period, during which compression is taking place with the transfer shut and the exhaust still open, possibly leading to some more charge being lost.

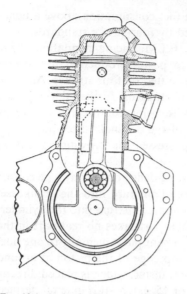

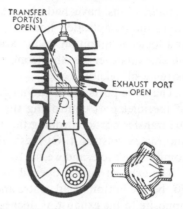

TRANSFER PORT(S) OPEN

EXHAUST PORT OPEN

FIG. 13.1. A classic three-port design—the GTP Velocette, with "squish" combustion chamber.

FIG. 13.2. Simplified diagram of "loop" scavenging with flat-top piston, originally developed in Germany under Schnürle patents and now very widely used.

The deflector-head piston also has other disadvantages which react unfavourably on performance or life. It is heated on one side by the exhaust stream and cooled on the other by the transfer stream; this, in conjunction with its asymmetrical shape, is conducive to distortion. It splits a symmetrical combustion chamber into two portions, and, if the plug is placed adjacent to the top of the deflector, burning becomes a distinct possibility.

An endeavour to overcome these shortcomings was made in the GTP Velocette by forming the combustion-chamber wall to conform closely to the transfer side of the deflector, so concentrating the gas in one space and setting up a squish effect which was beneficial to good combustion; even so, collapsed piston crowns were not unknown (Fig. 13.1).

Today, the sole remaining stronghold of the deflector piston is the American outboard marine-engine field, where the engines have the benefit of water cooling. Although very high powers are obtained (70 b.h.p. from one six-cylinder model of 1,100 c.c., for example) they are achieved only with port timings which give a fuel economy so poor that it would not be tolerated in the motorcycle world.

The "Split-single"

A method of eliminating the deflector head which enjoyed considerable success and is still in limi ed use is the "split-single" layout, in
which a pair of pistons occupy parallel cylinders closed by a common
head. The transfer ports are formed in one cylinder, the exhaust ports in
the other and these can be made of ample area since they can occupy
most of the circumference of each bore.

The mixture has to travel up one bore and down the other before it
can escape through the exhaust ports, which reduces the possibility of
charge loss. Though this distance may seem great in view of the very
short period of time available, in fact it is not further than the bulk of
the mixture has to travel with either a deflector or flat-top single piston.

However, there are undesirable features inherent in the scheme. The
total area exposed to combustion heat is 40 per cent. greater than in an
equivalent single, which reduces the thermal efficiency. Also the
exhaust barrel runs much hotter than the transfer barrel, which is
liable to promote distortion, although the effect can be offset by placing
the hotter barrel towards the front of the block and so equalizing the
temperatures.

There are two ways of coupling a "split-single's" pistons. They may
be caused to move in unison (as in the German T.W.N.) by means of
a forked con-rod (Fig. 13.3); or they can be arranged to move slightly

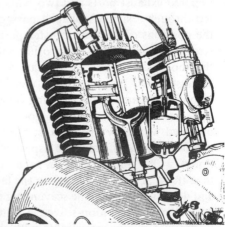

FIG. 13.3. (Left) This 1947 125 c.c. D.K.W. engine had an additional charging piston
mounted below the crankcase. (Right) The T.W.N. "split-single", in which the two
pistons move in unison.

out-of-phase by using a pair of rods on one crank-pin, or a master rod with a second rod pin-jointed to it (as in the Austrian Puch).

In the first layout, the port timing is symmetrical, just as if there were only one piston. In the second the timing is not symmetrical and it is even possible to arrange the transfer ports to close *after* the exhaust ports, while still providing an adequate "blow-down" period, though this would be of no value unless some form of supercharging or augmented crankcase pumping was also employed.

One adverse effect of moving the pistons out-of-phase is that their top dead centres do not coincide and for a short period one is still going up while the other has commenced to go down. The volume of the space between the head and pistons therefore remains substantially constant for a few degrees just when it should be rapidly expanding to take the utmost advantage of the peak pressures, so there are limits to how much phase-difference can be usefully employed. The system shows at its best when water-cooled and supercharged, as in the pre-war D.K.W. racers, though the resulting engine is heavy, bulky and lacking in the simplicity which makes the two-stroke so attractive.

Loop-scavenging

The advent of the "loop-scavenged" engine, developed first under the Schnürle patents in Germany, completely altered the picture by eliminating the deflector piston and also by providing much more efficient scavenging. The earliest flat-top piston engines had two diametrically opposed exhaust ports and two pairs of transfer ports, each pair being fed through a single Y-shaped passage. The arms of the passages and the positions of the four transfer ports were so contrived that the gas-streams impinged upon each other and were directed upwards towards the top of the cylinder, so that, despite the close proximity of the exhaust ports, there was little charge loss because the outgoing and incoming streams were travelling opposite directions.

It was found that equally good, or even better, results could be obtained with only one exhaust port (or a pair of ports divided by a narrow bar which, from the aspect of port timing, comes to the same thing), with a transfer port on each side of it. The entering gas-streams then travel across the piston, up the far side of the barrel, and curl over and down to complete the scavenging process. Some mixing does occur, of course; but the loop-scavenge principle enables two-stroke engines to produce power comparable with that obtained from the best four-stroke practice, with excellent reliability, even if the specific fuel consumption is, perhaps, 15 or 20 per cent greater than that of four-strokes.

Inlet Port Control

Utilizing the lower edge of the piston to control an inlet port and making the crankcase act as a pump to supply mixture to the transfer ports is ideal from the standpoint of simplicity, but is not ideal in other respects.

Due to the inevitably large volume available for mixture in the underside of the piston and in the crankcase itself, the theoretical crankcase compression ratio is only about $1\frac{1}{2}:1$ at low and medium speeds. The pumping efficiency is therefore low and is reduced still further by the short period for which the inlet port can be permitted to open, especially on a touring model, in which excessive blow-back through the inlet port would occur with wide-open throttle at low speeds if the port timing were unduly prolonged.

As the speed rises, the ram effect brought about by the higher gas-velocity in the inlet pipe suppresses the blow-back; but as the speed rises still further, the amount of charge which can be induced through the now inadequate inlet port limits the power output to an extent which cannot be affected by the size or timing of the cylinder ports. It then becomes necessary to increase the effective area of the inlet port by making it as wide as possible and increasing its height, the latter action increasing the power at high speeds, but reducing still further both the pumping efficiency and the tendency to blow-back at low speeds.

Still further potential increase can be gained by lengthening the inlet pipe, thereby increasing the ram effect but also taking advantage of the pressure-wave set up when the fast-moving air-column is suddenly stopped by the closure of the port. This wave oscillates backwards and forwards in the inlet tract, and at those speeds at which it is in resonance with the engine can assist markedly in improving the crankcase filling, though at other speeds its effect may be non-existent or even adverse.

In other words, it is not really possible to make a piston-controlled inlet porting system which is effective at *all* speeds. It must be proportioned according to the kind of characteristics the engine should possess.

There are two alternatives. One is to utilize automatic valves of the reed or diaphragm type, consisting of very light spring-steel blades seating against a flat face. These were used in some pre-war D.K.W.s and have been adopted on the Velocette scooter engine.

They practically eliminate blow-back at any speed and give good breathing, though this is not by any means unrestricted. The reeds require a little pressure-difference before they will open and it is not possible to provide a straight-through passage, as it is with a plain port, but the type in which the reed lies in a position almost parallel to the gas-flow is very effective and offers great possibilities.

The other alternative is to employ a rotary valve, the usual method being to incorporate it in one of the mainshafts. With suitable porting, it can be arranged to give, say, 200° of opening instead of the 120° which is about the maximum that can be used with piston control. This scheme is employed in the British Anzani twin, in which two ports are drilled in the centre main bearing, each feeding one crankcase from a single carburetter. Unless the bearing is extremely large, the effective port area is, however, not very great even though the timing is favourable, because for most of the time the port is not fully open (Fig. 13.4).

This objection is overcome by the disc-valve which is used in the MZ and, no doubt, is part of the reason why the 125 c.c. model can turn out power equivalent to 170 b.h.p. per litre (Fig. 13.5).

The valve itself is of sheet steel, 0·020 in. thick, and rotates in a space only 0·040 in. wide. It is not mounted firmly on the mainshaft, but is driven by splines so that it can centralize itself in the gap or move to one side or the other, so acting like a reed-valve during the closed periods. The periphery is cut away to open the port, which then has a clean, unobstructed entry into the crankcase and, moreover, is fully open for about 140° of its total opening period of 200°. Apart from its vulnerability to foreign matter, it is difficult to see how this valve could be bettered for high-speed work.

Crankcase Pumping Efficiency

Conditions inside the crankcase can be improved by careful disposition of all the components which it contains. For example, if the crankwebs are cut away in the region of the pin to provide mechanical balance, a quantity of mixture will be contained in the spaces which, at b.d.c., are as far as could be from the transfer ports. It is clearly much better to make the cranks in the form of discs, closely fitting the case, and also to use a narrow con-rod, with the big-end recessed if necessary into the discs to reduce the space between them.

Balancing can be effected by drilling the discs and closing the holes with light plugs on the pin side, or by using heavy plugs on the non-pin side, the real object being not so much the increase in compression ratio, as to keep as much gas as possible close to the transfer passages. These should be large in cross-sectional area, smoothly contoured and possess the smoothest possible entry; the last point is sometimes overlooked and the piston is allowed to obstruct the entry very badly just at the moment when the gas-velocity should be at its highest.

Fig. 13.4. A combination of piston-controlled transfer porting and rotary valve (inset) is employed in the 322 c.c. British Anzani twin.

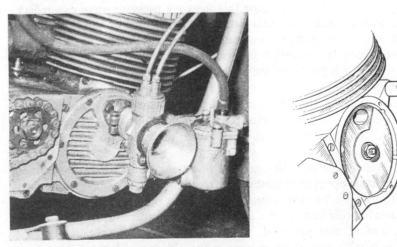

Fig. 13.5. (Left) Carburetter mounting on disc-valved M.Z. (Right) Cover plate removed to show disc-valve and inlet port.

The Kadenacy Effect

It was at one time held that high power could not be obtained at high speed because of the short port opening time available. But actually the reverse is the case—it is precisely because the times *are* so short that full advantage can be taken of pressure-waves in the exhaust system and what is known as the "Kadenacy effect" to get the high outputs previously thought to be impossible.

Kadenacy found, by ingenious experiments with a special engine, that if the exhaust ports were large and opened with sufficient rapidity the imprisoned gas would rush out at such high velocity that it continued rushing out until the port was closed again, by which time the pressure in the cylinder had become sub-atmospheric. It follows that if another valve, which may be a port or may be a poppet-valve, is opened at the right moment, enough fresh mixture may be drawn in to enable the engine to keep running without the aid of crankcase compression. But if crankcase compression is present, this effect obviously assists the entry of mixture from the transfer ports, though at the same time it has a tendency to suck a portion of this mixture out through the exhaust, as there may be a depression of 5 or 6 lb./sq. in. present in this port, immediately after the discharge of the main body of gas.

Exhaust Waves

By using a short, open pipe this negative pressure wave can reflect back as a positive wave that promptly rams some of the lost charge back into the cylinder, with a marked increase in power at the appropriate speeds. It has since been discovered that so far from needing an open pipe, it is better to use an expansion chamber with a restricted outlet, when the desired wave-effects will be intensified. A curious fact is that the outlet area may be less than that which would normally be provided on a touring machine developing about one-quarter of the power; that on the 250 c.c. twin Adler racer, for instance, is only about $\frac{5}{8}$ in. diameter.

Representative port timings for an engine designed on these lines are: exhaust opens (and closes) 80° from b.d.c.; inlet opens (and closes) 68° from b.d.c. The top edges of the exhaust ports should be square to the axis in order to achieve a strong Kadenacy effect in the blow-down period of 12° thus provided.

The trouble with these engines is the old one of lack of flexibility. Maximum power may be in the region of 9,000–10,000 r.p.m., but there is little useful power available at a mere 2,000 r.p.m. less, when the resonant conditions upon which the high power depends cease to exist. Nevertheless, a lot may still be learnt by a modified application of this principle to sports engines.

An interesting recent development aimed at spreading the power over a greater range is the "boost-port" system devised by J. Ehrlich (Fig. 13.6). In one form, two small booster chambers, lying between

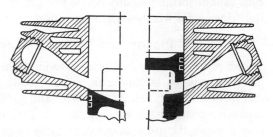

FIG. 13.6. Two half-sections of the Ehrlich "boost port" system. (Right) Booster-chamber being filled via window port before b.d.c. (Left) Chamber discharging into cylinder near b.d.c.

the transfer and exhaust ports, are first filled with fresh mixture through "window" ports cut in the piston below the bottom ring. Further movement of the piston seals off the chambers which then discharge their contents into the cylinder when their openings are uncovered by the piston a few degrees before b.d.c. This is a variant of a system used on the M.Z., in which a third port is located between the two transfers and opposite to the exhaust. This port is the opening of a booster-chamber which is filled via a window-port in the piston, the resulting flow of cool mixture helping considerably to ventilate the interior of the piston in which little gas movement normally occurs.

PORT LOCATION

Accurate location of the port-edges is obviously just as important as the valve-timing in a four-stroke and is normally obtained by machining the cylinder-base to the correct position in relation to the ports, accurate foundrywork being required to ensure that all ports are in correct location to each other. However, this is a method which is open to causing unavoidable discrepancies between one cylinder and another, and when greater precision is essential, the ports should be machined, which is a difficult operation in a one-piece barrel. By using a liner the ports can easily be machined to close limits of accuracy and the transfer passages can be made open-sided in relation to the bore of the aluminium jacket so that their internal surfaces can be given a high finish before the liner is inserted; the jacket is expanded by heat to facilitate this operation. Long bolts running right through from crankcase to head are essential, in order to remove tensile stresses from the barrel which is badly weakened by the presence of the ports, and an austenitic cast-iron liner is advisable, as its high expansion rate will keep it in better contact with the jacket. It will do so, in fact, even if there is a narrow bar provided across the exhaust port in order to prevent ring-interference and breakage. Rings have a bad time passing over wide ports and must in any case be pegged to locate the gaps so that the ends cannot spring into any ports. For greater safety chromium plated steel rings are a worth-while proposition.

Piston and Barrel Materials

As the piston has to work as a valve in addition to its normal duties, the skirt must be as close a fit as possible in the barrel. To maintain this fit at all combinations of barrel and piston temperatures, a low-expansion piston material is essential, and the latest developments have been towards the use of alloys containing 16 per cent. silicon which has a lower expansion rate than "Lo-ex" and is not too difficult to machine. 22 per cent. silicon has also been used but this alloy requires special manufacturing techniques.

When extreme lightness is aimed at, unlinered aluminium barrels with chrome-plated bores may be used, as in the Guzzi 73 and 110 c.c. two-strokes, which have die-cast, longitudinally finned, nearly horizontal barrels. In manufacture, the cylinders are bored, plated and finally just honed to size and wear in service is extremely low, despite the recommended petrol/oil ratio of only 50:1.

Plug Position

The pistons in loop-scavenged engines, though commonly referred to as "flat-topped", are more usually slightly domed, as this shape confers more strength and also gives slightly better gas flow. In touring engines, the combustion space in the head is nearly always machined to a part-spherical shape to provide a ratio around 7 or 8:1, but for racing, where even with 100-octane petrol up to 15:1 may be used, a portion of the head is machined parallel to and just clear of the piston crown by 30 to 40 thou. at t.d.c. and a chamber of much smaller diameter than the bore forms the combustion space. In cylinders of small size, a central plug position is not far wrong, but in fact the best position is quite critical. This has something to do with the paths of the gas-streams during the scavenge period, and the position that gives the best power at maximum r.p.m. is not necessarily best at medium speeds or for a good tick-over. Consequently, some experimenting is always necessary in a new design to find the most suitable position for the work in view.

CHAPTER 14

Ignition

THE process of combustion which produces the power in an I.C. engine is extremely complex—and seems to become more so with the passage of time, as fuel research workers find out more about it by means of ultra-high-speed cameras, engines with quartz cylinder heads and similar expensive apparatus which was not available to the earlier investigators.

At first it was thought that the whole charge went off with a bang immediately after it was fired, hence the use of the word "explosion". Though inaccurate and misleading, this is still the common term, and is convenient to retain because there is no other single word in the language which is at all applicable to the true state of affairs.

If the whole charge did explode simultaneously, enormous and quite unworkable pressures would be generated. This could happen, for instance, with a mixture of acetylene gas and air, and does happen to some extent with a petrol-air mixture when "pinking" or detonation occurs. The last part of the charge then ignites as a whole but this does not usually commit much destruction because only a small volume of combustible is involved.

However, it has long been known that the mixture, instead of exploding, is burnt by the action of a flame which starts at the plug and is carried through the combustion space, partly by its own efforts but more by the action of the turbulence or whirling set up in the charge, either by the location of the inlet-port, the squish action created by the shape of the head, or a combination of both, as described in Chapter 9.

In more recent times it has also been discovered that all sorts of chemical reactions are taking place under the conditions of high temperature and pressure which would not occur in straightforward burning in the open air. These have an effect on the tendency of a fuel to "knock" and also on the life of the engine, as compounds leading to the formation of corrosive acids are formed.

While high-tension spark ignition is the most convenient and precise system yet devised, combustion can be started by other means. In a compression-ignition engine, generally called a "diesel", the heat generated by the compression of pure air is sufficient to ignite a jet of fuel sprayed into the combustion chamber. In some varieties compression ratios of about 17:1 are employed and thermal efficiencies are very good, but even though the fuel injection is spread over a period of up to $20°$, the pressures generated are very high and the general construction of the engine has to be much more robust than a petrol engine need be.

Ignition can be commenced at more normal compression ratios by the action of hot surfaces—intentionally, by the use of a glow-plug, or inadvertently, from the presence of a hot area, such as the exhaust-valve head or a glowing patch of the incombustible deposits left by some of the modern additives to petrol and lubricating oil.

Combustion may also be started by a residual volume of hot exhaust products left over from the previous strokes, as in the "hot-tube" engines, once used for stationary work.

This process can occur with an exhaust valve which has been drilled up from the head end for lightness; the little pocket of gas so formed may remain hot enough to fire the charge at somewhere near the right time. In fact the old "big-port" A.J.S., which possessed this feature, would run without a miss for miles with the plug-wire off, once it was properly warm and the throttle was kept more or less wide open.

An unscavenged area in a two-stroke can also provide a source of ignition. In the marine Vincent two-stroke, which had the exhaust ports at one end of the cylinder and the inlet ports at the other, arranged to give a rapid swirling action to the ingoing mixture, self-ignition arose from the core of hot gas remaining in the centre of the cylinder after the charge had spiralled its way down close to the walls and some of it had escaped out of the exhaust ports.

In the experimental stages, by some fluke the point of auto-ignition corresponded exactly to the correct spark-ignition point and power was identical with or without the plug-wires on, but a reduction in the amount of swirl by altering the port angles suppressed the effect, while giving higher power and better economy through improved scavenging and less charge-loss.

Auto-ignition in fact does not do much harm provided it occurs *after* the correct spark-ignition point. If it occurs earlier, the general engine temperature begins to rise, auto-ignition then becomes earlier still, and the process snowballs until the engine knocks itself to a standstill or suffers mechanical damage unless given a rest, even if only for a few revolutions. This is what may happen when an engine is run at a compression ratio higher than the fuel it is supplied with will accept, as those who were forced to race T.T. machines on "Pool" spirit just after the war will remember only too well.

From the viewpoint of thermal efficiency, it would be best if ignition started at t.d.c. and was completed in one or two degrees; but this would be undesirable, even if it was possible, because the pressure-rise would be so rapid that extremely rough running would result.

It is necessary, therefore, on this count alone, to fire the charge many degrees before t.d.c., so that the pressure can build up fairly gradually to a maximum of three to four times the compression pressure a little after t.d.c., when the piston has started to descend. The high pressure so generated before t.d.c. then constitutes a waste of power and, if the ignition-timing is too far advanced, the useful power developed will be reduced, even though the engine may not give any audible sign of distress by "knocking" or "pinking".

How Much Advance?

The actual amount of advance required is determined by a host of factors, of which the most important are the shape of the combustion

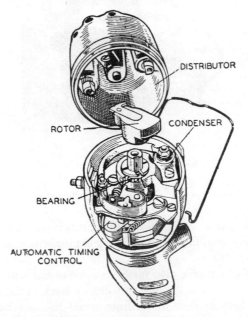

Fig. 14.1. Popular of recent years is automatic ignition advance mechanism adapted to coil equipment. This is an example of the Lucas design employing centrifugally operated bob-weights housed beneath the contact-breaker.

chamber, the compression ratio, and the analysis of the fuel. Others are the amount of pre-heating of the charge (or cooling if alcohol is used), the location of hot areas and the efficiency of scavenging of the products of previous combustion. In general, anything which raises the compression pressure and/or temperature tends towards the need for less advance, anything which has the opposite effect tends towards more advance.

Sometimes these effects overlap or act in opposition. Thus an engine which requires 42° advance at 6·8:1 c.r. on petrol may have to be brought back to 34° when raised to 8:1 c.r. on the same fuel, but will still require 34° when raised to 13:1 and changed over to alcohol. There is no formula for determining the correct figure; previous experience is a good guide, but the final setting can only be obtained by testing.

Some engines are more sensitive to the ignition timing than others. In any case, the higher the power per c.c., the more accurate must the

FIG. 14.2. Side location of the plug was favoured for this early single-cylinder Guzzi—forerunner of an outstandingly successful Italian design.

timing be; a degree or two may not make much difference in a touring engine, but may spell failure to a racing engine which is being pushed to the limit.

The amount of advance also varies to some extent with engine speed. At starting, for instance, the engine will kick back at full advance, and when pulling hard at slow or medium speed less advance is required than at open throttle at high speed, because the mixture has a longer time in which to burn completely.

Consequently, it is necessary to incorporate a method of varying the timing, either by moving the contact-breaker or by moving the whole magneto armature relative to the crankshaft by means of some centrifugal contrivance, such as the Lucas or B.T.H. automatic advance devices, though these need to operate only from zero up to 2,500 or 3,000 r.p.m.

From then on to maximum revs in a normal, well-designed engine, the advance appears to be independent of speed, because the higher this is, the higher the turbulence in the mixture becomes, and the rate of combustion is automatically speeded-up in unison with the increase in r.p.m.—a fact which permits some racing engines to be run with fixed ignition timing.

Manual advance, by means of a handlebar lever was favoured for a long time, and still is by riders who have the ability and a preference for adjusting the ignition themselves rather than let some mechanism do it for them. In a sense, this can give better results, because while both speed and throttle opening exert independent effects upon the liability to knock, a centrifugal advance device can only take notice of speed. Also, when endeavouring to ascertain the correct advance for maximum power, the ability to alter the timing by small increments while running at full bore is invaluable and much quicker than making repeated runs with the timing laboriously altered each time. This aspect is of course only important for racing; for touring, the automatic advance is superior to manual for the average rider, and has the additional merit that the spark intensity is constant whatever the amount of advance. It would be still better with a vacuum control operated by manifold pressure, but this device cannot be applied to a magneto and does not work well with a single cylinder's variable suction when applied to coil ignition.

Starting

Before an engine can run, it must, of course, start. For it to do this, the mixture-strength in the little space occupied by the plug-points— or, more precisely, *between* the plug-points, which may be only 0·018 in. apart—must be within the limits of 16:1 and 12:1 by weight if petrol is the fuel, or about 8:1 if alcohol is used. This applies to the amount of fuel present *in the form of vapour;* droplets, however small, do not count, and it is easy to see that at the low speeds of starting the mixture is hardly likely to be homogeneous, but is more likely to be of varying consistency, with some areas too weak to ignite and some too rich, or merely containing wet fuel in suspension.

As only a portion of petrol will vaporize at ordinary temperature, it is necessary to provide a temporary surplus for cold starting, and modern petrols are blended to suit the prevailing weather conditions so that starting is not much of a problem. If, however, a flooded engine does not start at once, it will be reluctant to do so at all, because the previously unvaporized fractions have been given time to vaporize and the mixture then becomes too rich to maintain combustion, even if the spark does manage to initiate it.

PLUG POSITION

The necessity to provide an ignitable mixture at the plug-points remains paramount at all other speeds, and it may well be that the condition does not exist at some point in the speed range because of the presence of pockets of residual spent gas.

This is particularly likely to occur in two-strokes, which depend upon the direction of the stream of gas from the transfer ports to scavenge the upper end of the cylinder. Even a small dilution of a correct mixture with spent gas may cause either a complete misfire or an unsuspected lag in the commencement of combustion which may have a great effect in reducing power at, say, 9,000 r.p.m., when the time available for the whole process is less than one-thousandth of a second. Sometimes a seemingly trivial change in position of the plug will result in an appreciable gain in power because the points have been moved into an area more favourable for combustion.

The same effect has often been observed in four-stroke engines, in which, generally speaking, the plug is best placed at the apex of the angle made by the offset inlet and exhaust ports, rather than in the space between them.

One difficulty associated with excessively domed pistons, especially in small bores, is that the plug is severely masked by the dome just when combustion is occurring; the bonfire lights up all right, but immediately afterwards the spread of flame is severely hampered by the rising piston-crown and power is lost. An endeavour to cure this may be made by using an amount of advance so great that the combustion is well under way before the piston intrudes itself, but this is only an expedient and may well yield little increase of power because the advance is really too great; in other words, the second error introduced does not completely cancel out the effects of the first. A better idea is to make a local flat or depression in the crown adjacent to the plug, or to use an asymmetrical crown.

Dual Plugs

In view of the frantically small time available, it appears at first sight that a second plug could not fail to be an advantage in obtaining complete and rapid combustion, and would also be better from the viewpoint of reliability. Some years ago, almost all English racing factories swung over to two-plug heads, stuck to them for a couple of years, and then went back to single plugs.

When all the secrecy had cleared away and notes were compared, the general opinion seemed to be that power in the medium-speed range (and consequently the acceleration) was improved, but there was little or no gain at top revs. From the reliability aspect there was no gain at all, because the amount of advance required for two plugs was five or six degrees less than with one. If one failed, the engine still kept going, but at reduced power; the rider then had to choose whether he would lose the race through lack of speed, or lose it through stopping for a plug change which also entailed determining which plug was at fault.

If one discounts the reliability feature in view of modern improvements in plug technique, there may be grounds for resuscitating the scheme in large-bore high-compression engines, where the combustion chamber shape does not lend itself to efficient ignition from one spot, and also in ultra-high-speed engines of small bore, where the time element is so small that halving the distance through which the flame has to travel is likely to pay a dividend.

One snag, of course, is simply the mechanical one of finding room for the second plug so that it can easily be changed. Some designers have had to resort to the 10 mm. range of plugs in order to do this. Whilst these small plugs function quite well, they do not have quite the safety margin possessed by the usual 14 mm. types, owing to the restricted space in which the points and insulator have to be accommodated.

Firing both plugs at the correct instant in relation to each other is also a problem. It may be that optimum results are obtained with simultaneous firing, or that one plug should "lead" the other by one or two degrees because of their positions in the combustion chamber, but the advance will be less than that required with a single plug. If the spark at either plug occurs for any reason a little too soon, the spark at the other will not do anything much and the engine will then be running with single ignition at less than optimum advance, and consequently at reduced power.

One solution, if absolute synchronization is required, is to use a double-ended coil or a magneto, such as the rotary-inductor Lucas, with a divided high-tension coil and two plug leads. However, if a small phase difference is necessary two contact-breakers must be employed, irrespective of whether they operate coils or are built into magnetos, and the problem of setting them accurately except under test-bed conditions becomes acute.

This raises the question of coil v. magneto. Ignition-wise, the difference is that the coil gives its highest voltage at low speeds, and at high speeds eventually reaches a point, measured in sparks per minute, when the secondary voltage becomes too low and misfiring sets in. The magneto, owing to the fact that it generates its own primary current which rises with speed, gives a higher voltage at high speeds, but this does not confer any real advantage over the coil, so long as the latter is being worked within its rated capacity.

Ordinary coils will deliver up to 18,000 sparks per minute, and are on the danger-line on a six-cylinder engine at 6,000 r.p.m. Hence the use of "sports" coils, rated at 21,000 sparks per minute, but it will be seen that even 15,000 r.p.m. on a two-stroke single can be handled quite easily. The situation alters with more than one cylinder; for example, the 3-cylinder D.K.W. racer would have required 33,000 sparks per minute, and would have needed three coils and a heavy battery to cope with the large current consumption. The alternative system used was the ingenious one of using a 6-cylinder magneto running at half engine speed and with the distributor modified to supply only three cylinders. This also surmounted the problem of excessive armature speed, as on a two-stroke it runs at engine speed instead of half-speed as on a single or twin four-stroke.

The Flywheel Magneto

For the same reason, though in an opposite sense, a magneto built into the flywheel is possible on a two-stroke though not on a four-stroke unless one puts up with an idle spark at the plug which, as it occurs when the inlet valve may be open, is a possible source of external combustion of the whole machine. By mounting the magnets in the wheel, the coils can be transferred to a stationary locality and hence relieved of centrifugal stresses. Usually the ignition coils are located together with the lighting coils within the boundaries of the flywheel so that the whole thing forms a self-contained unit, but if desired low-tension current can be brought out to an external coil as in the Spanish Bultaco. Flywheel magnetos were inclined to be rather heavy and bulky when first developed, but the advent of high-retentivity materials such as "Alnico" (which moreover were not affected by heat and so could be cast in position) helped materially towards reduction of weight, as indeed they also did in normal magnetos.

Two-stroke Idling

A defect which has always plagued the two-stroke is erratic idling, caused by the difficulty of igniting a minute quantity of fresh gas when mixed with a cylinderful of burnt gas. One certain method of curing this is to retard the spark until it occurs well after t.d.c., which means that the combustion efficiency is so poor that a much larger amount of throttle and hence of fresh gas is required. This system is used extensively on American multi-cylinder outboard engines, but as the range between maximum power advance and idling advance is about 50°, which is much more than could be catered for in the magneto itself, the whole instrument is made to pivot around its own armature axis, a method which, though efficacious, would be difficult to achieve on a motorcycle. At one time, conventional flywheel magnetos were made so that the timing could be varied by a hand-lever, but nowadays they are invariably made with the timing "fixed", which does not assist in any way towards improved idling. With battery and coil ignition there would be little difficulty in intercoupling the throttle and ignition controls (as is done on the outboards) to bring the idling retard into action only when a slow tick-over was required and not just when the throttle was closed when running down-hill.

TWIN-CYLINDER PROBLEMS

Firing a parallel-twin four-stroke is easy; as a magneto gives two sparks per revolution, all that is needed is a two-lobe breaker cam, a slip-ring and two high-tension leads, though considerable precision in manufacture is required to ensure that the sparks occur exactly at 180°. With a V-twin, it is not possible to use the same basic idea just with the cam-lobes altered in angular position to suit the cylinder angle, because the sparks produced are only at maximum intensity over two narrow angles. If the lobe positions are altered much from 180° one or other of the two sparks would be ineffective; to cure this, the pole-pieces are "staggered", an expedient which produces sparks of nearly equal intensity at one cam-ring position, but at any other position one spark becomes weaker than the other. It may still be good enough to fire the charge, but generally speaking a V-twin magneto is not good with manual advance, especially when starting from cold when one needs the most retard and two of the best possible sparks. For that reason, better starting is obtained with a centrifugal advance mechanism which, of course, only alters the position of the contact-breaker with relation to the crankshaft, but not the contact-breaker in relation to the pole-pieces, as the manual advance does.

Another solution adopted on J.A.P. racing engines is to use two single-cylinder magnetos, separately driven, an arrangement which, though effective, is heavy and costly. Still a third, and probably the best, for all-round work is to resort to normal coil ignition which is not subject to spark inequality and when a battery has to be carried anyway is no heavier than a magneto system.

LIGHTING SYSTEMS

Current for lighting has for long been supplied by 40 or 60 watt 6-volt d.c. generators; at first these were mounted pick-a-back on the magneto body to save an extra drive, and traces of this practice still exist on a few models fitted with the Lucas "Magdyno", which though much smaller than and a vast improvement upon its original form is still big enough to be awkward to house; also, it must have manual advance, as the power needed to drive it would prevent an automatic advance from functioning. Separate generators can be driven by gears, chain or belt: the latter is preferable from the aspect of isolating the armature engine oil and also from destructive high-frequency oscillations, but is used only on Velocette products. Another source of lighting current was the alternating output obtainable from a flywheel magneto simply by including a couple of coils extra to those for the ignition, and taking off the current without the need for a commutator or bushes. The output was, however, low in wattage, and could only be used to charge a battery by adding a rectifier and so the system whilst being tolerated was not very highly esteemed until developed by obtaining a greater output and charging the battery by means of a full-wave rectifier of the modern and much smaller pattern developed by the electrical industry.

The next step was to adopt the a.c. generator on four-stroke engines, and as there were no brushes involved and the presence of oil not objectionable, the obvious thing was to build it into the primary transmission, mounting the rotor containing several magnets on the mainshaft and fixing the stator containing the coils to the crankcase so that the current could be led out to a full-wave rectifier and thence to the battery. This system eliminates any form of drive and absorbs practically no power when not actually charging; also the voltage generated is sufficient to energize the ignition coil even at starting speeds, the engine can be started thereby with a flat battery or even with no battery at all. It is used extensively now on Triumph and A.J.S. machines.

THE ENERGY-TRANSFER SYSTEM

A further development of the a.c. generator is the inclusion of what is termed the "energy-transfer" ignition system. In this, two out of the six coils normally devoted to current for battery charging are wired up in series and connected to the low-tension side of an external ignition coil. Bridged across this circuit is a contact-breaker which is normally closed so that the current flows mainly through the low-

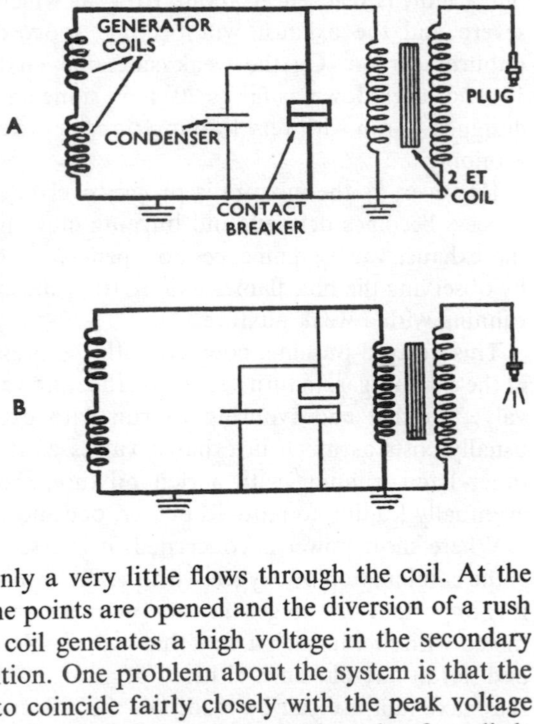

Fig. 14.3. A simplified diagram, showing in heavy line two phases with (A) the contact-breaker closed and energy building-up within the generator coils and (B) induction in the 2ET coil as the points open on the upward-surging energy pulse from the generator coils.

resistance points and only a very little flows through the coil. At the appropriate moment, the points are opened and the diversion of a rush of current through the coil generates a high voltage in the secondary winding to provide ignition. One problem about the system is that the moment of break has to coincide fairly closely with the peak voltage generated in the alternating primary current and this makes for a little difficulty in obtaining a wide advance range, but the arrangement has undoubted merits and has been adopted on 1960 Triumphs.

CHAPTER 15

Carburation

PETROL, in the form of vapour, combines completely with air when in the proportions of 15 parts of air to 1 of petrol—by *weight*, not by volume.

If there is more petrol present, the mixture will still burn effectively, but a limit is reached at about 10:1, at which point misfiring will be severe and the exhaust will become sooty due to the presence of unburnt carbon. On the weak side, the mixture can be reduced to 17:1, or even down as far as 20:1 on some engines which are specially designed to run with very lean mixtures in order to achieve outstanding economy.

However, as the mixture is progressively weakened the combustion process becomes delayed, and burning may still be taking place when the exhaust valve commences to open—a fact which may be verified by observing the blue flames issuing from the exhaust port of an engine running with a weak mixture.

This delayed burning, coupled with the presence of unburnt oxygen in the exhaust gas, in turn causes overheating and burning of the exhaust valve, so that endeavouring to run with excessively weak mixtures usually costs as much in exhaust valves as it saves in petrol. On the other hand, running with a rich mixture, though uneconomical and eventually leading to reduced power, does no actual harm.

Where sheer power is concerned, it is essential to remember that it is the combination of oxygen with the fuel which counts. Consequently, it is important first to get the maximum *weight* of air into the cylinder, mixed with fuel in such a way that every molecule of oxygen is burnt—and not at any old time, either, but at or near top dead centre so that the maximum use can be made on the power stroke of the expansion created by the heat of combustion.

The Fuel Factor

The nature of the fuel, provided it is not an oxygen-carrier like nitro-methane or a high explosive like picric acid, does not actually matter. Any of the regular fuels, ranging from kerosene through ordinary

264

petrol to benzole and the alcohols, ethyl and methyl, will provide almost exactly the same theoretical emission of energy in the form of heat, the actual amount being, on average, equivalent to 46 ft./lb. per cubic in. of mixture at normal temperature and pressure (60°F. and 29·92 in. of mercury).

Alcohol in fact gives slightly less than 46 ft./lb., benzole slightly more; this is no mere matter of opinion, but of remorseless scientific fact. Any doubters can speedily set their minds at rest by studying Sir Harry Ricardo's book, *The Internal Combustion Engine*, Vol. II, Chap. 2. Despite this, alcohol is widely used for racing.

The basic difference between petrol and alcohol is that the former is prone to detonation above a certain compression ratio, whereas the latter is almost knock-free and can be run at ratios of 14:1 or higher, even in a relatively hot-running engine. Advances in petrol technology, marching hand-in-hand with engine development, have steadily reduced the gap until ratios of 11:1 are now usable with petrol even in large-bore half-litre cylinders.

The other theoretical advantage of alcohol is its high latent heat of evaporation (that is to say, the large amount of heat which is required to convert it from a liquid to a vapour) which results in a colder, and therefore heavier, charge of mixture and also provides a perceptible amount of internal cooling. This advantage, though real, does not have such a profound effect on power output in practice as it does in theory, and the better the engine is cooled externally the less important does the internal cooling become.

However, this is not the time to discuss the very wide subject of fuels, but to consider the ways in which they are introduced into the air-stream by the carburetter with the necessary accuracy, under every possible combination of engine speed, throttle opening and air temperature.

Throttling the Air Supply

On any carburetter feeding fewer than four cylinders, the air-flow fluctuates violently from zero to a maximum on every induction stroke. It may even at times reverse in direction and flow outwards due to the air bouncing back off the closed inlet valve, or being actually blown back under conditions of low engine speed, wide throttle opening and a late-closing inlet timing.

This fluctuation has been turned to good account in nearly all motor-cycle carburetters because it permits the use of some form of sliding throttle valve instead of one of the butterfly type. The latter variety, which is standard in car carburetters, rotates about a central axis and is balanced against pressure; it can therefore open or close quite freely even when subjected to very low manifold pressures.

The sliding type, on the other hand, will not close readily against the friction produced by a steady (or nearly steady) pressure unless fitted with an inconveniently strong spring, but it will do so if the pressure fluctuates. Even on a twin-cylinder two-stroke, a single carburetter will close properly, because the port-controlled induction periods do not overlap as they do in a multi-cylinder four-stroke.

The most common form of throttle valve is the annular one, familiar in Amal carburetters, but it can equally well be solid (Villiers) or made from sheet metal as in some Fischer instruments. As will be shown, the sliding throttle exercises a "variable choke" effect—a very valuable feature which is absent from any fixed-choke butterfly type.

BASIC PRINCIPLES

Carburetters work on the principle that if a restriction is placed in a pipe conveying a gas, a depression is created at the narrowest point of the restriction—which preferably has a rounded entering edge and a

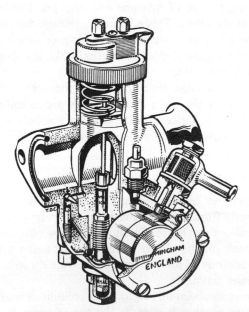

FIG. 15.1. In this Amal "Monobloc" touring carburetter, flow is controlled progressively by pilot jet, throttle slide with tapered needle, and main jet.

conical exit, and is termed a venturi, or choke-tube. If a jet is arranged to project into the neck of the venturi, the reduction in gas pressure will draw petrol through the jet into the air-stream, only a low pressure difference being required if the jet is supplied with fuel from a float-chamber so that the normal level is very close to the top of the jet.

Advantage is also taken of the fact that merely blowing a stream of air across the top of a jet will draw liquid through it. This principle is to be seen in operation in a spray-gun or barber's scent-spray and historians will recollect the "Senspray" carburetter which derived its trade name from the latter source.

Unfortunately, the rate of delivery of fuel from the jet is not directly proportional to the air-speed through the venturi. Instead, the amount of liquid discharged increases more rapidly than the increase in the amount of air passing through.

Therefore any selected combination of venturi and jet can deliver a mixture of correct strength at only one air-speed. At higher speeds the mixture will be too rich and at lower speeds it will be too lean. In any of the butterfly-type carburetters with fixed chokes, correction has to be made for this by the addition of compensating jets, air-bleeds, or a combination of both.

Another method of correction would be to vary the choke area according to speed or throttle opening as in the "constant-vacuum" S.U. fitted to some Triumph twins. It is also achieved to a degree in the Amal and kindred instruments by the action of the throttle valve which, as it closes, automatically decreases the area available for gas-flow in the immediate vicinity of the fuel orifice and thus provides a variable-choke effect.

Further control of mixture strength at small throttle openings is provided by varying the height of the outer edge of the slide in relation to the engine side. Increasing this height, termed the "cutaway", decreases the suction on the jet and weakens the mixture; decreasing the height has the opposite effect.

In the carburetters developed for tracks such as Brooklands used to be and for speedway work, when the throttle is usually either open or shut and is seldom in a midway position, sufficient accuracy can be obtained by the cutaway alone in conjunction with a main jet of the correct size. For road work, where greater flexibility is desired, a tapered needle is attached to the throttle slide and exerts an effect on fuel flow which is most pronounced at around half to three-quarter throttle. In later designs, such as the Amal G.P., an air-bleed has been added to avoid over-richness at very high air-speeds.

At the very low air-speeds, which occur at starting or when idling, virtually no petrol would be drawn through the main jet, so a small auxiliary jet and air-passages are provided to deal with these conditions. These tiny passages are brought into action only when the throttle is almost closed; that is why it is almost impossible to obtain a start with what is termed a "handful of throttle", unless for some reason, such as excessive flooding, the mixture has accidentally become over-rich.

Jet Position

If the jet were to be placed on the same level as the fuel in the float chamber, slight alterations in level—such as might be caused by leaning the machine to one side or by braking or acceleration—would cause the fuel either to flood from the jet or to recede from the outlet, obviously affecting the rate of delivery. To avoid this, the main jet is located somewhere about level with the bottom of the float chamber, so that it is always submerged and acts purely as a metering device.

Above the jet is a space or well which fills up with fuel during periods when the throttle is nearly closed and little fuel is required. This provides a reservoir which can be drawn on instantly when the throttle is slammed open and the air-speed over the spray-tube through which the fuel finally

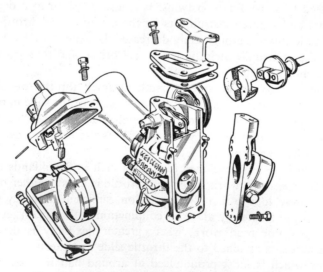

FIG. 15.2. Four of these Keihin carburetters were used on the Honda "250" with their flat slides operated in unison by a cable-drum and universally jointed cross shaft.

emerges into the mixing-chamber is low until the engine increases its speed.

Further to assist vaporization of the fuel, and also to provide a greater measure of automatic control of mixture strength, a small amount of air is bled into the system between the main jet and the spray-tube. In racing instruments the quantity of air so admitted can be varied by the air control in order to modify the mixture strength without interfering with the main air-flow. In touring instruments the air control is used only for starting, not as a mixture-strength corrector, and if closed partly or wholly does restrict the main orifice. In fact, it is often omitted and a simple strangler is fitted for use only when starting conditions demand it.

The Italian Dell'Orto carburetter works on a somewhat similar principle with a circular slide and unobstructed air passage, but several designs employing flat slides have been used from time to time. The Japanese Keihin instrument (Fig. 15.2) has such a feature, but even so it retains the "variable-choke" idea which assists greatly in maintaining a correct mixture strength at all speeds and loads.

Mean Air Velocity

In order to obtain adequate atomization and subsequent vaporization of the fuel by the time the spark occurs, a considerable air velocity is essential and maximum torque is usually obtained at a nominal mean air velocity of 300 ft./sec. through the choke.

The mean air velocity is determined by multiplying the mean piston speed by the factor D^2/d^2 (where D is the cylinder bore and d is the inlet diameter). If D, d, and also the stroke S are quoted in inches, the mean air velocity, V, in feet per second, is given by the expression:

$$V = \frac{S \times 2}{12} \times \frac{\text{r.p.m.}}{60} \times \frac{D^2}{d^2}.$$

From this it will be found that a 500 c.c. engine will have a mean velocity of 300 ft./sec. through a $1\frac{1}{8}$ in. bore carburetter at 3,500 r.p.m. This speed is close to that at which maximum torque is developed in an engine for sports use and indicates a good correlation between theory and practice. Maximum power is usually attained at a much higher speed than maximum torque, because the drop-off in torque due to air restriction is less rapid than the gain in power due to increase of rotational speed.

Racing Requirements

For racing, however, where greater power is demanded even at the expense of low-speed performance, a larger choke size is required. A $1\frac{1}{2}$ in. carburetter on the same engine will have a mean air velocity of 300 ft./sec. at 6,200 r.p.m., so should provide maximum torque at somewhere near that figure, with maximum power perhaps 1,000 r.p.m. higher. These theoretical figures are borne out in the G50 Matchless, which develops $52\frac{1}{2}$ b.h.p. at 7,200 r.p.m. with a $1\frac{1}{2}$ in. G.P.3 Amal. Because neither the piston velocity nor the air velocity is steady, but both fluctuate violently, the so-called "mean velocity" figure has no relation to reality, but is a convenient convention to employ as a basis for calculations. The figure of 300 ft./sec. is considerably higher than that usually quoted in books dealing with multi-cylinder engines, probably because the total time during which the inlet valve is open is much longer than the time of the induction stroke, which lowers the actual velocity in the case of a single or twin, but does not do so in the case of a single-carburetter "four" or "six" in which the inlet-valve opening periods overlap each other.

If an engine with a very large-bore carburetter is held on open throttle while the speed is progressively reduced by climbing a steep hill, obviously the air velocity through the choke will become progressively less until a point is reached where the carburetter cannot deliver a burnable mixture and the engine will stall: though if the throttle is gradually closed the "variable choke" effect exercised by it will enable power to be maintained down to a lower speed. However, the gas velocity in the tract between the throttle and the inlet valve will still be too low to ensure effective vaporization of the fuel, so for engines which require good low-speed pulling powers, small-bore induction pipes and carburetters are needed.

For maintenance of power at high r.p.m. a straight, smooth, circular bore is the ideal. It is partly attained through elimination of the butterfly throttle which, however thin or streamlined it is made, is bound to obstruct the flow to some extent.

In needle-type instruments, the small-diameter needle and the projecting tip of the spray-tube are the only real obstructions, and even the former can be moved out of the stream by attaching it to one side of the throttle-slide, as is done in the remote-needle and G.P. Amals (Fig. 15.3).

The air-passing ability can be still further enhanced by the addition of a long, tapering extension with a curved edge to lead the air smoothly in; such an extension is also of value when very large-bore instruments

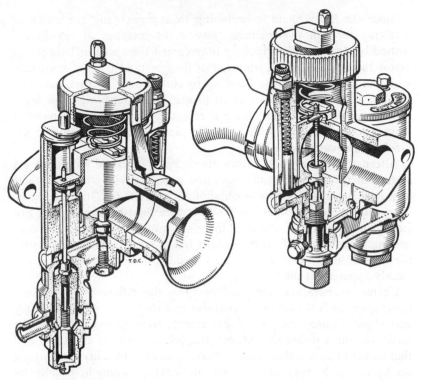

FIG. 15.3. Amal racing carburetters—the R.N. (left) and the T.T. In both, the air control beside the mixing chamber permits mixture variation without obstructing the main air-flow. The R.N.'s remote needle leaves the orifice completely clear.

are used because its presence increases the suction applied to the jet. Also, under certain conditions a considerable amount of fuel may be blown back through the mouth of the carburetter. While this may be entirely lost if the intake is short, a large proportion may be retained and fed back into the engine again if the bell-mouth is long and of perceptible volume, with beneficial effects on fuel consumption, which may be quite as important to a racer in saving a pit-stop as it is to a workaday rider in saving his pennies.

Whilst the theoretical air-fuel ratio for complete combustion of petrol is 15:1 it is impossible to ensure that every particle of fuel is vaporized and consumed at the correct time. Some, inevitably, escapes the fire or is burnt too late in the cycle to be effective. Maximum power, therefore, is developed with a mixture-ratio of 13 or even 12:1, depending upon the characteristics of the engine.

Since the latter figure is beginning to approach the borderline of misfiring through over-richness, any slight increase of enrichment caused by float-chamber flooding may curtail the speed or hold it just below the figure at which vibration of float or float-bowl in resonance with the engine causes the flooding to commence. To overcome this trouble, it is common practice to protect the float-bowl from high-frequency vibration by mounting it remotely on rubber or hanging it from a rubber support, with a flexible pipe to convey fuel to the jet-block on the carburetter body.

Alternatively, the whole carburetter may be insulated by inserting a section of rubber hose in the induction pipe, a device which also acts as a heat break and assists in obtaining a cold charge. It must not be overlooked, however, that the flow between float-bowl and jet is not steady, but pulsating, and it is therefore advisable to keep the connecting pipe from the float-bowl short but of large diameter, otherwise the mixture may weaken-off at high speeds for a reason which is not clearly apparent at the time.

Correct carburation is dependent upon the difference in pressure existing on the fuel in the float-chamber and that at the jet. This is only very slight. Consequently stray air currents blowing across or into the air-intake, or a difference between the pressure at the air-intake and that at the float-chamber such as may be caused by eddy-currents set up by the tank, may easily upset the mixture strength, usually by making it momentarily weaker and causing a hesitation. For that reason, carburetters are best placed in still air; and though facing the intake forward appears to offer a minor increase in power, in practice it is a thing to be avoided, for unless the intake is shielded from any direct blast it is extremely difficult to achieve correct carburation at all times.

The theoretical increase in power due to increased intake pressure is 1·2 per cent. at 100 m.p.h., 2·7 per cent. at 150 and 4·8 per cent at 200, but these increases are of little moment except possibly for world's maximum record attempts, and could even be non-existent or even negative unless some pains were taken to ensure that the pressures existing in the float chamber and at any secondary air entrances were at every instant on a par with the intake pressure.

Angular Mounting

Although generally mounted with the body of the carburetter or "mixing-chamber" located vertically, this is not essential and in fact on most racers the whole instrument is inclined to give a downdraught angle of anything up to 20° in relation to the cylinder axis, which might mean considerably more or less actual inclination of the cylinder itself is inclined. All that matters is that the level of fuel in the float chamber should be correct in relation to the jet, but if the actual inclination exceeds 15° downwards, the carburetter will flood through the pilot-jet when standing and the fuel-tap must accordingly be closed when not on the move.

On some installations, it is convenient to twist the mixing chamber out of the vertical even sometimes to the extent of making it lie horizontally, as in the 350 Guzzi (Fig. 15.4). This position would have the

Fig. 15.4. The 350 c.c. "World Champion" Moto-Guzzi, showing long, straight induction tract and Dell'Orto carburetter with 37 mm. choke and horizontal mixing-chamber.

effect of bringing the main jet just level with the fuel in the float chamber and a small inclination either way would result in it either rising above or falling below the level with a consequent alteration of mixture strength. This can be obviated by arranging a "dropper" from the existing jet-block into which the main jet is screwed in a position where it will be submerged at all times. Horizontal chambers should however be avoided unless the design justifies their use.

Air Cleaners

For road work, or for that matter trials or scrambles where dust and grit abounds, air cleaners are essential for the well-being of the engine and also to prevent lumps of grit from jamming the throttle slide. Contrary to some beliefs, an air cleaner has little effect on power provided the filtering element has ample area and there are no sharp elbows connecting it to the carburetter. Generally, a slightly smaller main jet is required, but if the size reduction is more than 10 per cent. it may be taken as an indication that the cleaner is offering too great a resistance to air-flow and is therefore inadequate. Dust can enter the side air intake of racing carburetters, whereas the Monobloc Amal has no openings outside the confines of the main air inlet, so it is dust-proof when coupled to an air cleaner which is best housed in a large container under the saddle (Fig. 15.5).

Fig. 15.5. Royal Enfield method of mounting air-cleaner unobtrusively below saddle.

Villiers carburetters are unusual in possessing an annular float, concentric with the jet and are thus relatively insensitive to quite large changes of attitude. They are frequently equipped with a gauze-type air cleaner, which though not large works efficiently because of the open weave of the steel-wire mesh. This is kept oily by the blow-back which unavoidably occurs at some load conditions with piston-controlled inlet ports, and dust is collected by adsorption on the oily surfaces rather than being filtered out by passing through fabric as in the ordinary "dry" cleaner. By collecting some of the blow-back, the Villiers cleaner also does something towards improving petrol economy.

274

CHAPTER 16

Balance and Torque Reactions

THE piston-connecting-rod-crankshaft mechanism which forms the basis of most reciprocating engines suffers from the inherent defect that it gives rise to unbalanced forces which may reach very high figures and cause either vibration which is externally noticeable, or internal deflection which may reduce the mechanical efficiency, or bearing-wear which limits the life of these components according to their ability to withstand the loads and speeds imposed.

This chapter is mainly concerned with the problem of vibration—or rather of reducing it to acceptable proportions, since it is an inconvenient but incontestable fact that one cannot balance completely a single-cylinder engine, or, for that matter, any form of twin or four-cylinder engine commonly employed in a motorcycle, unless it is built with two sets of opposed cylinders.

Of the lot, the single and the parallel-twin four-stroke, which mechanically is the same as a single since both pistons move up and down in unison, are the least well balanced. Yet, by skill in internal design and mounting in the frame, even these can be made to run very smoothly, except, possibly, at or above some critical speed at which vibration becomes annoyingly evident. That this is no mean feat will be appreciated from a consideration of the magnitude and complexity of the forces involved and how they are generated.

Basic Principles

Once started on its way up the cylinder, the piston with its related components endeavours to keep on going, its motion being arrested and immediately reversed only by the action of the connecting-rod and the momentum of the crankshaft. In fact, if the latter component could be made absolutely weightless the piston would go up to top dead centre and *stay there*, however fast it might have been travelling on the up-stroke.

The force required to stop and restart the piston is at a maximum just at t.d.c. and if the con-rod were infinitely long, a force of the same value, but opposite in direction, would be required to perform the same function at b.d.c. The piston would then possess what is known as simple harmonic motion, or S.H.M., but this condition never exists because, for reasons some of which are obvious and some are not, the con-rod has to be a lot shorter than infinity and is usually somewhere around four times the crank radius or twice the length of the stroke.

Because of the angularity of the rod to the centre-line at or near mid-stroke, the points at which the piston attains its maximum upward or downward velocity, assuming, as is usual, that the cylinder is central and not offset, occur not at the 90° crank positions but at about 76° before or after t.d.c., the precise positions depending, of course, on the con-rod/crank ratio. This means that the piston has 152° of crank rotation to get from maximum speed down to zero and back to maximum during the upper half of the stroke, and 208° to go through the same sequence during the lower half; the upward inertia force must, therefore, be greater than the downward force.

With simple harmonic motion (which, incidentally, can be obtained in a swash-plate engine of the Michell crankless type as well as by the impracticable scheme of an infinitely long rod) the inertia forces can be represented graphically on a crank-angle or time base, as a symmetrical sine wave of which the maximum values are given by the expression

$$0 \cdot 0000142 W N^2 S$$

where W = weight in lb, N = r.p.m. and S = stroke in inches.

The effect of the necessarily short rod is to modulate this symmetrical curve by superimposing on it an infinite number of other harmonics, forming a Fourier series of increasing frequency and decreasing amplitude. Of these, only the secondary harmonic of twice the frequency and one-quarter the magnitude of the primary need concern us here, as the higher harmonics assume any importance only in engines with six or more cylinders.

This secondary harmonic gives rise to forces which act upwards at *both* t.d.c. and b.d.c., hence accounting for the increase in the actual force at the former point already noted; but it is also present at both 90° crank positions, at which it acts downwards, irrespective of the direction of piston travel. It has therefore within itself the possibility of initiating a secondary vibration at twice engine speed. This may become a reality in a four-cylinder engine where the secondaries from all four pistons act in unison although the primaries may cancel each other out; in a single, it is so small in relation to the primary out-of-balance forces that its effect may almost be disregarded and, anyway, there is nothing one can do to counteract it.

Arithmetically, the effect of a rod with a comparatively short length is to increase the primary force at t.d.c. and reduce it at b.d.c. by the factor R/L, where R is the crank *radius* and L is the rod length (both, of course, measured in the same units); this factor can for our purposes be taken as $\frac{1}{4}$, the slight differences encountered in practice having only a minor effect.

A Practical Example

To take a concrete example, in an engine with 3 in. stroke, a piston weighing 1 lb. complete with rings and pin and running at 6,000 r.p.m., the primary force, using the formula already quoted, works out at $0·0000142 \times 1 \times 6,000 \times 6,000 \times 3 = 1,534$ lb. The effect of the rod is to modify this figure by $\frac{1}{4}$, or 383 lb., so the actual upward force at t.d.c. becomes $1,534 + 383 = 1,917$ lb., and the downward force at b.d.c. becomes $1,534 - 383 = 1,151$ lb.

Since these forces vary in direct proportion to the weight of the piston and to the length of the stroke, and also vary in proportion to the *square* of the speed, the figures given may be taken as basic ones for estimating the forces generated in any other size of engine very quickly. Thus, by increasing the piston stroke from 3 in. or 76·2 mm. to 80 mm., with all other things remaining equal, the maximum load goes up in the ratio of 80:76·2 and thus becomes 1,600 lb. in round figures which are easy to memorize; while at 7,000 r.p.m. it goes up in the ratio of 49:36, or nearly one-third more, and thus becomes 2,200 lb.

The last figure is rather staggering when one realizes that it is about five and a half times the weight of the complete machine and would, if it were to be applied continuously, give it an upward acceleration of

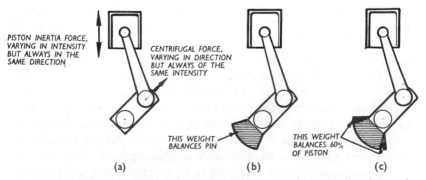

FIG. 16.1. Simplified diagrams of a basic single-cylinder engine: (a) completely unbalanced, (b) with weight added to balance the crankpin and big-end and (c) with further weight to balance the piston partially.

$5\frac{1}{2}g$ and a vertical velocity of over 1,200 m.p.h. in a mere 10 seconds, by which time it would have attained an altitude of nearly a mile and three-quarters!

Fortunately, it is not applied continuously but only momentarily at the end of each stroke, so that an instant after the machine begins to rise under the action of the upward force, it is pulled downwards again by the force existing at the bottom end of the stroke. The net result is a vertical vibration of small amplitude—unless the frequency, which is equal to the rotational speed, happens to coincide with that of the whole machine or some part of it which is free to vibrate. The ends of the handlebars and the tail portion of an overhung rear guard are two common instances of parts which will vibrate in resonance and may develop quite a large amplitude, even though located at some distance from the exciting forces.

These forces are transmitted through the con-rod and crankshaft to the crankcase, and it is sometimes thought that the action of combustion pressures on the piston will counteract the inertia force and thus help to balance the engine, but this view is erroneous. It is true that the gas-pressure may be equal to, or even exceed, the inertia force and will therefore relieve the connecting rod of part or all of the tensile stress, but this is purely an internal effect and the out-of-balance forces are still present. Gas-pressure reactions *can* however make their presence felt in other ways, as noted later (pages 290–292).

Having seen that the piston gives rise to forces which alternate in direction but are unaffected by gas pressure, the question arises as to how their ill-effects can be minimized. The only component which offers any assistance is the crankshaft, which itself is unbalanced by reason of the weight of the crankpin and the big-end of the connecting-rod. This weight can be balanced quite easily by adding counterweights opposite to the pin, or, if disc flywheels are used, by removing metal from them on the same side of the pin until the centre of gravity of the assembly is brought exactly on the mainshaft axis (Fig. 16.1 (b)).

If this result is achieved, the way in which weight is added or subtracted is immaterial so far as balance is concerned, provided that it is carried out equally on each side of the cylinder centre-line. If it is not, an unbalanced couple is set up which tends to make the crank assembly rotate conically instead of on its own axis, though the effect would not be very serious unless all the counterweighting were done on one flywheel, especially if this happened to be an outside one and therefore some distance from the crank-pin (Fig. 16.2 (*B*)).

Balancing the piston is not so easy—in fact it is out of the question, because if an additional counterweight were added so that the centrifugal force it generated during rotation was equal to that generated by the piston at t.d.c., it would achieve balance at that point, but at that point only. It would be too great to balance the lighter inertia force present at b.d.c. and, worse still, at the 90° positions the centrifugal force would be acting horizontally, with no other force present to counteract it at all.

The final result would be merely to convert an engine which was unbalanced in the vertical plane into one which was just as badly unbalanced in the horizontal plane (assuming that the cylinder itself was vertical). While the effect might be, in certain circumstances, to confer greater smoothness of running, it would be by no means a solution to the problem and would do nothing towards lightening the loads imposed on the main bearings.

The best that can be done is to effect one of those compromises with which all forms of engineering are liberally sprinkled, and counterweight the crankshaft by an amount equal to some percentage of the reciprocating weight which inspired guesswork and previous experience indicate to be adequate, then to alter it in the light of experimental results until the desired degree of smoothness is obtained (Fig. 16.1 (c)).

This may seem to be a light-hearted way of describing a lamentably haphazard procedure. Nevertheless, there is no magic formula to enable one to do anything else and, despite that lack, excellent results can be obtained in quite a short time by knowledgeable people, especially when working on familiar ground so far as the frame and the method of installing the power-unit are concerned.

Frame and installation affect the issue partly because of the aforesaid resonant effects, partly because the method of mounting the engine has a bearing on its ability to vibrate in relation to the frame, and partly because the selected balance-weight percentage, commonly termed the "balance factor", alters not only the amount of unbalanced force unavoidably remaining, but also the plane in which it reaches its maximum value and which lies somewhere between the cylinder axis and the 90° crank positions.

Usually, a balance factor of 60–65 per cent. will be found to be correct, but it may vary widely; the factor for the MOV Velocette was as high as 85 per cent., while some engines have been down to 40 per cent. The reciprocating weight to which this factor applies consists of the complete piston plus the top half of the connecting-rod, as measured with the rod horizontal and with the big-end supported in some frictionless manner. The lower portion of the rod is considered as being purely rotating, and can therefore be perfectly balanced.

Because the eventual smoothness obtained depends so much upon the frame, a balance factor which suits one installation may not suit another, using the same engine—a fact which used to plague proprietary engine manufacturers, some of whose customers insisted upon some specified percentage which others would not accept.

An instance of this was found in the original Vincent-H.R.D. singles. These engines ran very smoothly in the standard spring frame with a factor of 66 per cent., but the speedway versions, of which a very few were made, vibrated badly in a cobwebby dirt-track frame until the factor was reduced to 61 per cent., this not-very-large reduction making all the difference between a machine which was passably smooth and one which shook itself out of your hands.

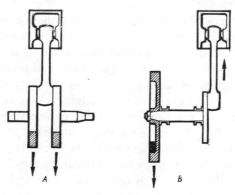

Fig. 16.2. Counterweighting must be equally disposed in relation to the cylinder, as at *A*. An extreme case of offset counterweighting is shown at *B*.

The 66 per cent. factor was still employed on the post-war "Comet", with an inclined engine forming part of the frame structure. This model was notably smoother than the diamond-framed edition and, in fact, was free from any definite vibration periods of the kind which are occasionally found and are so difficult to eliminate. Whether this virtue was due to the type of mounting or the angle of inclination is, however, difficult to assess and impossible to prove, because in this case the construction was such that you could not have the one feature without the other. It was, however, possible to employ without ill-effects pistons varying by as much as two ounces in order to obtain some desired compression ratio, whereas some models of different construction are very sensitive to piston weights.

When a periodic vibration is very persistent and altering the engine balance only chases it up and down the speed range, the best solution is to arrange matters so that it occurs at a speed as far removed from normal usage as possible. On a touring model, vibration at the highest engine speeds will rarely annoy most riders, and when it does set in at least it constitutes a warning against over-driving, while on a racing model any resonant period below 4,000 or 5,000 r.p.m. will never be noticed, except momentarily when getting away from the start.

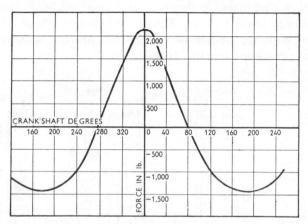

FIG. 16.3. Out-of-balance forces in a single-cylinder engine at varying degrees of crank-shaft angle from t.d.c.

Sometimes it is simpler to eradicate undesirable resonant vibrations by attending to the offending component rather than by altering the balance of the engine. This does not necessarily mean simply stiffening it up, though that is the procedure which is most likely to produce results. Softening the component or its attachments may be just as effective, as witness the occasional use of rubber-mounted handlebars.

Resonance can also occur in the crankshaft assembly, sometimes with destructive results, and this condition must be specially guarded against in engines with more than one cylinder.

MULTI-CYLINDER BALANCE

In the final analysis, any multi-cylinder engine amounts to a collection of singles which offers an opportunity of solving, in whole or in part, the problem of obtaining perfect mechanical balance by arranging the cylinders in such a fashion that the forces generated by one or more pistons are at any instant opposed by forces of equal magnitude but opposite in direction. The latter need not necessarily be generated by reciprocating motion, but may arise from a pair of geared contra-rotating components.

It is impossible to obtain balance when there is only one reciprocating component and one rotating component, for the former creates forces which are always in the same direction but vary in value, whereas the latter generates a centrifugal force which is constant in value but varying in direction.

It is clear that mere duplication of the pistons is no help at all if both crankpins are in line, as they must be on a parallel-twin four-stroke to obtain even firing intervals. Despite the shorter stroke or smaller pistons, or both, the amount of unbalance is just the same as that of a single of equal capacity (Fig. 16.4 (a), (b)).

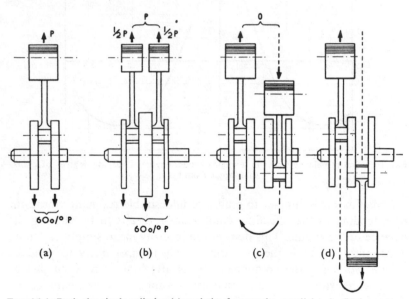

FIG. 16.4. Both the single-cylinder (a) and the four-stroke parallel twin (b) have poor balance. Primary inertia forces cancel each other in the two-stroke parallel twin (c) and the horizontal twin (d), but the former has a large rocking couple and the latter a small one.

To cite a simple example, imagine two 350 c.c. engines, one a single of 68 × 96 mm., the other a twin of 68 × 48 mm., both using the same pistons. The total reciprocating weight of the twin is double that of the single, and this exactly offsets the effect of halving the stroke, so at equal crankshaft speeds the forces to be dealt with have precisely the same value.

The twin has, however, a longer crankshaft which, if of the usual two-bearing type, must be designed with great care to avoid the possibility of destructive internal vibration—a precaution less necessary with the more expensive three-bearing arrangement. The precise balance-factor to employ depends upon circumstances, but it averages about 66 per cent. of the total weight (i.e., the weight of both pistons and the upper ends of both rods). The counterweighting must be symmetrical with relation to the centre of the engine, but can be distributed between the two end webs and the central flywheel in a way which will impose the minimum bending loads on the shaft.

The cranks of a parallel-twin two-stroke are phased at 180° instead of in line, in order to obtain even firing intervals (Fig. 16.4 (c)). At first sight it might be thought that, as one piston is going up while the other is going down, the conditions are propitious for obtaining perfect balance.

Unfortunately this is not wholly true. The primary inertia forces from one piston do in fact cancel out the primary forces from the other; but, as the cylinders are necessarily widely spaced in order to provide room for a centre bearing and gas-seals, the two opposing forces combine to form a couple, or turning effect, which tends to rock the engine from side to side. A rough idea of this action can be gained by holding a fixed-wheel pedal cycle up in the air with one hand and smartly twitching the pedals; when released, these will oscillate the machine from side to side due to the rocking couple they exert.

This effect can be eliminated, so far as the crank-pins and related parts are concerned, by straightforward counterweighting. But, whatever is done in the way of balancing the pistons, there will always be a rocking couple present, which will be at a maximum in the vertical plane with near-zero balance factor, and at a maximum in the horizontal plane with 100 per cent. factor. At any intermediate figure, there will be a tendency to give the crankshaft a kind of conical motion, with its axis describing a figure shaped like a diabolo.

If the engine is reasonably compact, these effects are not serious provided the engine-mounting is designed to cope with them, as it is, to take one excellent example, in the Scott; but even without going to such lengths a duplex cradle frame is desirable when the crankshaft lies athwart the machine. If the crankshaft is in line, as in the old Francis-Barnett "Pullman", the rocking couples would be predominantly in the vertical plane, i.e., the plane of greatest stiffness of the frame and thus be scarcely noticeable.

Irrespective of whether the two pistons move in unison or alternately, the secondary harmonic of the primary inertia force acts upwards at t.d.c. and b.d.c., but downwards at the mid-positions. As each secondary force is one-quarter of the primary, and both act together, the net result is a secondary out-of-balance force equal to one-half the primary from one cylinder only, but occurring with a frequency of twice engine speed. Thus the secondary out-of-balance of a 500 c.c. twin at 3,000 r.p.m. is exactly equal in frequency to the primary from a single-cylinder "250" running at 6,000 r.p.m., but has only one-eighth its value, so is not particularly noticeable (if at all) at normal road speeds.

The Horizontal Twin

In the horizontally opposed twin, the two-throw crankshaft can easily be balanced in itself, and no additional counterweighting is required, because the motion of one piston is duplicated exactly by the other, but in an opposite sense (Fig. 16.4 (d)). Thus *all* forces arising from the complex piston-acceleration graph cancel each other out within the crankshaft-and-piston assembly, so achieving near-perfect balance and relieving the main bearings of a lot of inertia load as well.

But for one thing, the balance *would* be perfect. This fly in the ointment is the small rocking couple due to the fact that one cylinder must be offset in relation to the other by the thickness of the centre web plus the width of one big-end. As this distance can be reduced to less than an inch by using narrow roller-bearing big-ends and a thin circular web, the couple is virtually imperceptible, especially in the duplex-frame shaft-drive machines which nowadays utilize this type of prime mover.

The Geared Twin

Many years ago, Dr. Lanchester propounded the theory that a reciprocating weight could be balanced by two weights rotating in opposite directions, and this system was used for some time in the "Valveless" car, which had two crankshafts geared together and operating pistons which moved in unison.

The idea was resuscitated by Velocettes, 20 years ago, in a pair of experimental machines. The crankshafts of these parallel twins lay fore-and-aft and were coupled by gears of approximately 5 in. pitch diameter (Fig. 16.6).

With the shafts rotating in opposite directions, it becomes possible to counterweight each shaft by 100 per cent. of the reciprocating weight, because at the mid-points the unwanted horizontal force which makes this amount of counterweighting impracticable with a single is exactly balanced by a similar force from the other shaft. Consequently, the running is extremely smooth, although the effect is achieved at the expense of increasing the average main-bearing loading somewhat.

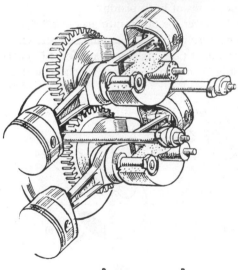

FIG. 16.5. Two rare (but well-balanced) birds. Sketch on the left shows the basic layout of the Brough Superior "Golden Dream", with four h.o. pistons coupled to two single-throw geared crankshafts. Above is the power unit of the 1935 three-cylinder Scott "1,000".

FIG. 16.6. (Below) On the geared twin 100 per cent. counterweighting gives perfect primary balance; (a) centrifugal force from one weight cancels that from the other when no primary inertia force is present (b). Secondary forces not shown.

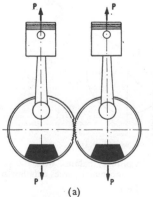
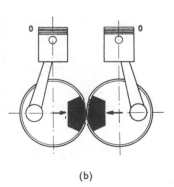

(a)   (b)

A secondary out-of-balance force is present, just as in any other parallel twin. Though it is only of minor importance, it could be eliminated entirely by using another of Dr. Lanchester's ideas, and driving a further pair of small wheels at *twice* engine speed, each being counterweighted to supply a combined force sufficient to balance the secondary vibration.

The V-twin

The V-twin is an interesting form of engine to balance. In the 90° form, perfect primary balancing is obtained by counterweighting to 100 per cent. of *one* piston plus the small-end (Fig. 16.7). The unwanted centrifugal force from this weight at the 90° positions from No. 1 cylinder exactly cancels out the primary inertia force emanating from No. 2 and this applies to all positions of both pistons.

The secondary forces must, however, be taken into account, because they can be large enough to be serious in a big engine. As shown in Fig. 16.7 (c), when No. 1 piston is at t.d.c. its secondary force (*S*) acts upwards but the force *S* arising from No. 2 piston which is near its

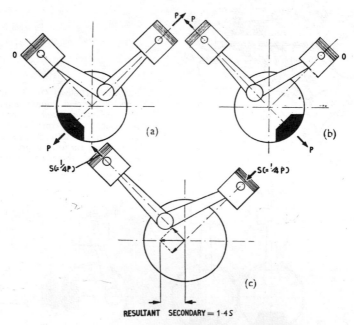

RESULTANT SECONDARY = 1·4 S

Fig. 16.7. The 90° V-twin also has perfect primary balance with 100 per cent. counterweighting (a–b) and the resultant of the secondary forces acts horizontally (c).

midstroke acts downwards. These two forces combine together to give a resultant equal to 1·4S, acting horizontally. 90° later, both forces S will have reversed in direction and the resultant will have meanwhile diminished to zero and increased again to the same value, but exactly in the opposite direction. In fact, what we now have is an unbalanced secondary vibration occurring at twice engine speed in a horizontal plane, the maximum value being 1·4S or 0·35P.

In addition to this, a 90° twin is not an attractive proposition because of its very uneven firing impulses and its large block bulk in big capacities. Consequently, it is usual to reduce the included angle to 50° or 45°.

The pre-war Vincent "Rapide" struck a slightly different note with 47°—an odd sort of angle which was adopted, as so many things are in commercial engineering, because it was expedient to do so, rather than for any theoretical reason. For one thing, it was found that the prototype crankcase could be machined at little cost by reversing the expensive and accurate jig used to bore the single-cylinder's timing-gear holes; and for another, the valve gear would just, but only just, clear the tubes of a lengthened frame which happened to be on hand.

Not that the exact angle matters much; at anywhere around 50° the balance is about midway between that of a single, which can be half balanced, and that of a 90° twin, which can be fully balanced. In practice, a factor of 35 per cent. of the *total* reciprocating weight is found to give a satisfactorily smooth performance, even in sizes up to and over one litre, when mounted in the conventional position.

A secondary vibration is still present, but has both a vertical and a horizontal component, the latter being less than if the cylinder were at 90°, and has practically no effect when the engine is mounted in the conventional position. When the cylinders are placed across the frame, however, the horizontal component acts at right angles to the machine and moreover is applied to the lower front section which is least able to resist the application of a lateral vibrating force. At 4,000 r.p.m. the maximum value of the force generated in a one-litre twin would be of the order of 250 lb., and the effects of this may account for the number of times this layout has been tried and then abandoned, although there are a couple of examples, both with small engines, in current production; one is shown in Fig. 10.20.

Although it has nothing to do with balance, the fact that in a medium-angle V-twin one piston is moving nearly at its maximum velocity when the other is passing through a dead-centre point, means that the amount of energy stored in both pistons by virtue of their velocities is roughly constant, whereas in any engine where all the pistons reach their extremes of travel simultaneously the stored energy goes from zero to a maximum and back to zero on each stroke. The former therefore needs less flywheel weight because the pistons and rods can be counted as contributing to the total flywheel effect—a characteristic shared by the three- and six-cylinder engines.

The Three-cylinder Engine

The three-cylinder engine is a rather neglected type. This is somewhat surprising, because it possesses perfect balance without the disadvantage of an awkward shape, its worst shortcoming being in the presence of a rocking couple, similar to, though less intense than, that of a 180° twin of equal capacity.

Rocking couples exist in any in-line engine unless the crankshaft has "looking-glass symmetry", i.e., one half of it looks exactly the same as the other half if reflected in a mirror held at the centre. For that reason, there is a rocking couple in a straight three, but not in a straight four with the two end pistons moving 180° out of phase to the centre two —which, of course, is the standard arrangement (Fig. 16.8).

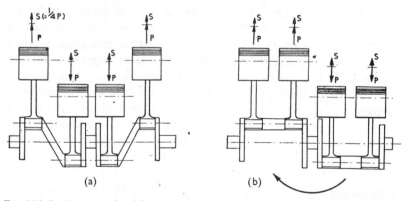

(a)   (b)

FIG. 16.8. In the conventional four (a), primaries are balanced and secondaries add up to the primary of one cylinder (P); due to "mirror symmetry", there is no rocking couple. A four with a two-throw crankshaft (b) has the same balance pattern, but a large rocking couple.

THE FOUR-CYLINDER GROUP

A straight four is in perfect primary balance, but as the secondaries from all four pistons act in unison, the total out-of-balance force from this source is considerable, being equal to the primary force from one piston alone. Fortunately, the fact that it occurs at twice engine speed makes its frequency so high that it is well above the natural frequency of most other parts which might vibrate in resonance. Nevertheless, size for size a four is not quite so smooth as a six which is in practically perfect balance and is free from rocking couples.

The "square-four" arrangement, with geared shafts, is equivalent to a straight four bent in the middle, and for balance it is no better and no worse than that type (Fig. 16.9).

The situation is different with the geared four-cylinder engine of the Brough Superior "Golden Dream" (Fig. 16.5). Here, each shaft has a single pin, to which two opposed rods are attached so that all four pistons reciprocate as a block. Mechanically, therefore, the layout is

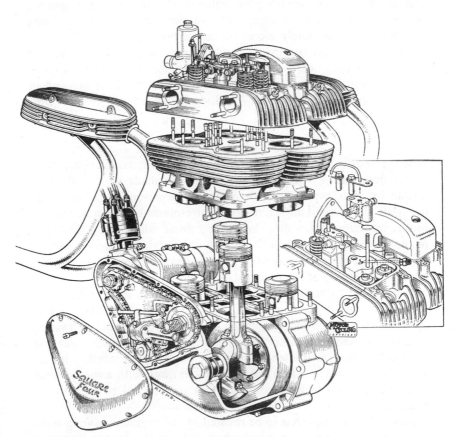

FIG. 16.9. Compactness plus conventional four-cylinder balance: the Ariel "Square Four" engine.

similar to that of the Velocette geared twin, with another pair of pistons added, and the primary balance will be perfect if both shafts are counterweighted to an amount equal to two pistons and rods. The secondary forces also cancel out, because when the pistons on one side are at t.d.c. both their secondaries act outwards and exactly oppose those arising from the other pair which are now at b.d.c. At mid-stroke both pairs of secondaries act inwards and the engine is therefore in perfect balance although this is achieved at the expense of additional loading on the main bearings at the 90° positions due to the heavy counterweighting required.

So one can appreciate that where vibrationless running is concerned, "You pays your money and you takes your choice." Any method of improving on the inherently poor balance of a single is accompanied by an increase in cost or complexity, or both, and even then results may not be outstandingly successful unless the installation of the unit is correct for its type. However, it must be appreciated that the balancing problem has been dealt with only in a very sketchy manner. Anyone who is interested in the complicated mathematics involved will find an excellent chapter on it in A. W. Judge's *Automobile and Aircraft Engines*.

TORQUE REACTIONS

When assessing the merits and demerits of the basic engine types briefly described in Chapter 8, reference was made to the effects of torque reaction, especially with regard to power units in which the flywheels lie at right-angles to the centre-plane of the machine. As torque reactions in any direction have a great influence on the "feel" of the whole machine when the engine is revolving, and vary in their intensity and direction according to the overall design, they must be taken into account at the design stage.

When Isaac Newton propounded the law that to every action there is an equal and opposite reaction, he stated one of the major truths upon which all engineering is based. It applies to torques or twisting moments as well as to direct forces. The simplest instance, in our own particular sphere, is the tendency of the engine (in a model with all-chain drive) to rotate *backwards* in its mountings, with a torque equal to that developed at the crankshaft and transmitted to the primary chain.

This reaction torque has to be resisted by the engine mounting-bolts. It will be seen that if the crankcase were held merely by one transverse bolt fore and aft in a weak rectangular frame with little corner rigidity, the whole thing would distort at every firing stroke and spring back again during idle strokes. If the natural frequency of vibration of the assembly ever coincided with the rate of firing, the induced vibrations might build up to very uncomfortable proportions.

While nobody would be silly enough to build a frame as badly as this, the same *kind* of effect must exist, however well the design is executed. Hence it is advisable to space the engine-bolts widely apart, preferably using two at the front and two at the rear to spread the loads over as large an area as possible and also to give stiffness against "lozenging".

Head-steadies

Some makers, however, prefer to employ stays attached to the cylinder head and running to some suitable anchorage on the frame. These can sometimes be a mixed blessing; they may hold the engine firmly enough, but at the cost of transmitting vibrations of small amplitude but intense effect to areas where the rider is uncomfortably aware of their existence.

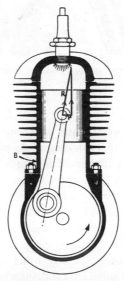

FIG. 16.10. Gas pressure on piston creates a compression load *R* in connecting-rod. Angularity of rod creates a horizontal component *r* which tends to cause fracture at *B*.

The effect of a head-steady on the internal stresses in the engine depends to a degree upon the circumstances. In an engine with the crankcase held quite rigidly in torsion, the rearward thrust of the piston against the cylinder tends to push this component backwards in relation to the crankcase—and, in fact, on occasion has accomplished this feat by fracturing the wall just above the base-flange. If one now imagines the engine to be fitted with a head-steady and the crankcase anchorage considerably reduced in stiffness, the effect will be to *reverse* the direction in which the barrel tends to rotate on the crankcase. In other words, *without* a head-steady the front cylinder bolts have a tensile stress to carry in addition to that due directly to explosion pressure, while *with* a steady and a flexible crankcase mounting the additional tensile stress is applied to the rear bolts.

Fig. 16.11. Head steadies on the James "Flying Cadet" (left) and the Royal Enfield "Crusader".

Mean Torque

The nature of the power torque reaction varies according to the number of cylinders and the working cycle of the engine. As a rough approximation, the mean torque of a sports engine of contemporary design is 56 lb.-ft. per litre of swept volume.

"Mean torque" is the twisting moment which the engine would exert if it had an infinite number of cylinders and the power were delivered in a smooth stream. It is numerically equal, on the ft./lb./sec. system, to the power output at 5,250 r.p.m., so if the latter figure is 28 b.h.p. the torque is 28 lb.-ft. Obviously at any other speed the torque can be found by multiplying the power by 5,250 and dividing by the speed in question.

In practice, the torque is not steady but fluctuates above and below the mean figure by an amount which varies mainly with the number of explosions per revolution. Thus the single-cylinder four-stroke, firing once every two revolutions, has a very irregular torque, with the maximum reaching anything between 4 and 10 times the mean, while in the smoothest practicable types—the four-cylinder four-stroke and twin-cylinder two-stroke, with power impulses occurring twice per revolution—the peaks are only about twice the mean value.

It is difficult to be dogmatic about the ratios of maximum to mean, because the exact figure also depends upon the flywheel weight, the compression ratio, the effectiveness of the engine-shaft shock absorber (if any) and some other minor factors; all of which would give even an electronic computer a headache, or maybe valve-bounce, in endeavouring to assess their combined results with any degree of accuracy. In any case, the rough running associated with irregular torque is seriously apparent only at low engine speeds in top gear, higher speeds or a change to a lower ratio making it less noticeable—unless, as has been noted, the frequency of fluctuation happens to correspond with that of some other part of the machine which may then vibrate in resonance, even though it is a long way from the source of excitation.

Inertia Torque Reactions

Torque reactions still exist even when the transmission is in neutral, because by their very nature the flywheels resist being accelerated violently and a rearward thrust of the piston against the cylinder is created at each firing stroke. The shudder which is evident in some models if the throttle is opened quickly is due to this effect rather than to the imperfect balance inherent in any single (or four-stroke parallel-twin) engine. In fact, vibrations due to the latter cause are dependent solely on the speed of rotation, whereas any vibrations which vary with throttle opening while the speed remains reasonably constant are due primarily to torque reactions and secondarily to the resonant frequency of some portion of the frame.

Inertia torque reactions when the flywheels are located parallel to the centre-plane do not disturb the machine as a whole, because they act in the plane of support. If, however, the flywheels are at right-angles to this plane, as in horizontally opposed twins and in-line fours with fore-and-aft crankshafts, the reaction tends to push the model to one side against the direction of rotation of the flywheels, but only when the latter are being rapidly accelerated.

This effect is quite noticeable in neutral when the throttle of a large transverse twin is "blipped", but becomes less so when travelling in gear because the rate at which the wheels can be accelerated rotationally is then automatically limited by the rate at which the whole machine can be accelerated linearly. The higher the gear and the lower the power-to-weight ratio, the less evident does this adverse feature become.

When the throttle is closed with the engine running at high speed, there is a tendency, if only a single transverse flywheel assembly is used, for the model to bank over in the same direction as this wheel rotates. The effect, though present, is not very noticeable when the road wheels are on the ground, but if they are in the air it could be great enough to have a pronounced influence on landing. This is so because, when not supported on its tyres, the machine is free to rotate about the crankshaft axis, and it has less polar moment of inertia (or flywheel effect) of its own in relation to this line than it has in relation to the line of contact with the ground.

Therefore, if the rider of a flat twin crosses a humped bridge very fast, and in a panic snaps the throttle shut when the engine screams up as the wheels aviate, the machine is bound to bank over to some extent in unison with the flywheel. If there is a curve immediately following the touch-down, it may well be that the bank acquired during flight is the wrong way to that required to take the bend, and considerable riding skill may be necessary to avoid unpleasant consequences. The smaller the flywheel in relation to the total mass of the machine, the less the effect will be, but the only way to eliminate it entirely is by adopting the geared-crankshaft principle, with flywheels of equal weight.

GEARBOX REACTIONS

Since the input torque to the gearbox is always less than the output torque in any of the indirect ratios, the difference appears as a tendency to rotate the whole gearbox backwards about the mainshaft (which may be a contributory factor to down-tube breakage in some frames).

There is also a tendency to rotate the box about a vertical axis due to the primary and secondary chains being at different distances from the centre-line of the frame; but as the primary chain, with the lesser pull, is usually farther out than the final chain, which has the greater pull, this effect is not very great in a conventional layout with both chains on one side. It would be of serious proportions, however, in a cross-over box mounted separately from the engine. In the Scott, which has its primary drive located near the centre-line and therefore about $3\frac{1}{2}$ in. away from the rear chain, an additional outboard bearing is mounted on the frame to maintain the box positively in alignment.

Unit Construction

When the gearbox and crankcase are either constructed as a true unit, using common castings, or as two assemblies rigidly bolted together, all the primary transmission forces become internal to the unit, and it no longer becomes advisable to keep both chains on one side to avoid this undesirable twisting action. In fact there seems little justification for retaining this system, as the cross-over drive confers advantages in the way of simplifying oil-retention in the primary-drive casing.

Another advantage of unit-construction is that the engine bolts are spaced on a very broad base, thus reducing torque-reaction loads in the mountings and generally providing a construction with more potential rigidity. However, this is no justification for employing a frame so lacking in stiffness that under lateral deforming forces the power unit is doing most of the work of holding the thing straight—unless the castings and bolt-bosses are strong enough, or have been specifically designed for this purpose.

GEAR DRIVES

A power unit with fore-and-aft crankshaft, but with integral bevel gearing and chain-drive to the rear wheel, is exactly the same as any other engine so far as its power torque reactions affect the frame; but when shaft-drive is used the unit tends to rotate in the opposite way to the shaft, while the bevel casing tends to rotate in the same direction as the shaft. This imposes a twisting effect on any portion of the frame lying between the unit and the bevel-box (Fig. 5.4).

Hence it is advisable either to mount the rear forks on the unit or to brace them thereto as directly as possible (the Velocette "Valiant" is an example of the second arrangement). Any deflection can then occur only in the forks themselves and ample provision can be made for resisting the torque within the forks; unless this is done, the wheel will twist out of the centre plane, either under power or when the gears are used on the overrun to provide engine braking. The tail will then veer to one side or the other to quite a marked extent, partly because the rear tyre contact-point is out of alignment with the front, and partly because the wheel is inclined and consequently endeavours to run in a circle.

On top of all these internal torque effects and reactions, there is the overall tendency for the front wheel to lift under power whatever the form of drive may be. This is most evident during a violent standing start. The lifting of the front wheel is accentuated by the fact that the line of thrust is at ground level whereas the centre of gravity of the whole machine is about 30 in. above this line; but, even at steady-speed conditions, with full power applied this effect still results in a considerable transfer of weight from the front to the rear wheel.

CHAPTER 17

Gearboxes and Transmission

IN some ways, a petrol engine is about as bad a choice as could be made for propelling a road vehicle. It cannot start itself, it must be rotating at a reasonable speed before it can develop any usable power, and if overloaded sufficiently it will stall.

To overcome these shortcomings, it must be provided with a transmission system which will enable the drive to be disconnected or taken up smoothly at will by some sort of clutch, and which will also provide some means whereby the engine speed can be varied in relation to the driving wheels to suit varying road conditions.

There has been a prodigious number of solutions to this problem, including simple two-speed engine-shaft gears, epicyclic multi-speed gears together with a friction clutch built into the rear hub, and almost infinitely variable drives with V-belts running over expanding pulleys—to mention only a few. But in the end the system which has won the day is the countershaft box mounted between engine and rear wheel and containing any number of ratios from two to four on touring motorcycles and from four to six on racing models; in fact even a seven-speeder has recently made its appearance.

As most racing is done on fairly level surfaces and with the machine as lightly loaded as possible, it may seem odd that more ratios are employed than is usual with touring machines which are expected to climb steep gradients or traverse mud or sand when heavily laden. The underlying reason, however, is quite simple.

In a tourer the gearbox primarily acts as a torque-converter, and the provision of a bottom gear with, say, a 3:1 speed reduction in the box, multiplies the torque of the engine at any given speed by 3. The pull exerted at the rear wheel is thus increased by a similar amount and simultaneously the engine is able to turn over at a speed high enough to be developing a reasonable torque. The two effects taken together enable the machine to climb a hill, even at slow speed, in a way which would be quite impossible in a higher gear.

It is worth noting here that the clutch is in no sense a torque-converter. When it is being slipped it is really acting as an energy-absorber.

296

The only reason why slipping the clutch will sometimes enable a machine to be extricated from a bad situation is, that it allows engine speed to rise well above the stalling point to a speed at which the motor is capable of developing perhaps three or four times the horsepower, power being proportional to torque multiplied by speed. Then, even though half the power developed is wasted as heat through friction in the slipping clutch, the net result is more pull applied at the rear wheel—and also, of course, a burnt-out clutch if the process is continued for any length of time.

Choosing the Ratios

The highest gear is normally chosen to suit the weight and bulk of the machine, not necessarily to give the highest maximum speed, but rather to give a comfortable cruising speed with the engine turning over at around 4,000 r.p.m., or somewhat less in the case of large-capacity power units.

This gear is so much higher than any useful bottom gear could be that the gap between the two is too great either to suit the torque curve of the engine or to permit easy changing, so it is necessary to insert at least a middle gear to bridge the gap and to provide a ratio which is useful on normal hills.

For many years, three speeds were considered ample—and, provided the engine has a torque curve which does not droop badly at low engine speeds, that number is still sufficient for a "bread-and-butter" mount especially where weight and bulk are items to be considered.

The snag with only three ratios is that there is bound to be a fairish gap between top and second and often, when hill-climbing, one has to choose between slogging up at a slow rate in top gear or going at an almost equally slow rate with the engine screaming round in second.

This situation can be surmounted by including a third gear between top and second. Then, if the two upper ratios are fairly close—somewhere in the region of 1·25:1—it is possible to over-gear a little in top to keep the cruising revolutions down, and rely upon third for moderate up-grades or for routine acceleration to get past a slower vehicle.

Given four nicely chosen ratios, the low-speed pulling power of the engine ceases to be very important and it becomes possible to use longer valve timings and higher compression ratios, thus providing more top-end power with little or no sacrifice in fuel economy.

In road-racing, the box still acts as a torque-converter to improve acceleration at low speeds, but the power-to-weight ratio is very high and there is no point in having the lower ratios so low that wheel-spin will set in long before the throttle is fully open.

(As a matter of strict terminology, a *ratio* of, say, 10:1 is higher than one of 4:1, although the *gearing* is lower. However, it has come to be colloquially acceptable to refer to a low gear as a low ratio.)

Also, the solo road racer rarely has to make a clutch start from a standstill, so its low-speed performance is not a very vital factor. On the other hand, as more and more power is wrung out of engines by raising their normal speed into five figures, the low-speed end of the power curve virtually vanishes and it becomes necessary to keep the engine turning over at nearly its maximum speed all the time by making full use of a gearbox with several very close ratios.

If, for instance, an engine has a usable power-band between 8,800 and 10,000 r.p.m., the widest gap between any two ratios should not be greater than 12 per cent. and preferably rather less, otherwise, when an up-change is made, the revs. will drop below the minimum unless they are taken up above the permissible figure before the change, a practice which is not to be recommended. It is simple enough to over-rev. an engine inadvertently at such a moment, without the designer going out of his way to make matters worse.

On almost any circuit there is some corner which cannot be negotiated above a fairly modest speed, or a tricky up-hill stretch which demands a lowish bottom gear to avoid excessive, even if temporary, clutch-slipping. It then becomes necessary to fill in the gap between the top gear required to give the highest maximum speed and this essential bottom gear, with enough ratios to suit the characteristics of the engine.

With five or six ratios, it becomes possible to arrange matters so that the highest is used only on down-hill sections or with a strong following wind, thus taking full advantage of the favourable conditions whilst holding the engine revs. at or below the permitted maximum. This is obviously both faster and safer than gearing exactly for level-road, still-air conditions and trusting to the rider to "roll it back" when the revs. go too high, especially as he may be rather loath to do so if it means losing the lead into the next corner.

GENERAL DESIGN

While it is one thing to say how many ratios are needed, it is quite another to translate the needs into concrete form—in the least expensive manner consistent with long life on touring models, but with the emphasis on lightness consistent with adequate strength for racing, where cost is a secondary consideration.

With a separate box and all-chain drive, it is desirable, and nowadays almost standard practice, to locate both chains on the same side, with their sprockets co-axial. A simple two-speed box then consists of a clutchshaft, extending right across to the far side and carrying one loose pinion, a co-axial sleeve carrying another gear inside the box and the final sprocket outside, with another shaft, the layshaft, lying parallel to the clutch-shaft and carrying two gears splined, keyed or even made integral with it (Fig. 17.1 (a)).

By cutting dog-teeth in the sides of the gears on the clutch-shaft, splining this component and mounting thereon a double-faced dog-clutch operated by a shifter fork, a direct drive top gear is obtained by engaging the sleeve-dogs, and bottom by engaging the clutch-shaft pinion. By mounting the shafts on ball-bearings and cutting down the

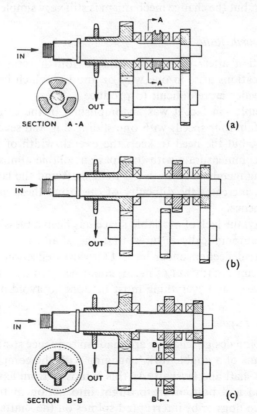

FIG. 17.1. Three basic gearbox layouts. (a) Simple two-speed with dog engagement. (b) Three-speed, with dogs for first and top and "crash" change for second. (c) Three-speed all-constant-mesh, with dog engagement for first and top and short splines for second.

299

"neutral" clearance between the dogs, to reduce the shaft-lengths as much as possible, the box can be made very narrow, quiet-running, easy to change and with a transmission efficiency of 94 per cent. or better in bottom gear.

This design can be altered to a three-speed version simply by adding external teeth to the dog-clutch and another gear to the layshaft, so that their respective teeth are slid endways into mesh to obtain a middle ratio by what is called a "crash" change (Fig. 17.1 (b)), which demands much more finesse in handling the controls than does the dog-tooth change. This type of box, though popular for a while, was rapidly superseded by several variations in which the second gear wheels also were constantly in mesh, so providing a "constant-mesh" box which could be changed up or down with ease. This box is naturally wider than the two-speeder, but the change mechanism is still very simple (Fig. 17.1 (c)).

Adding a Fourth Ratio

The position alters drastically when a fourth ratio is introduced, and complications arise in one way or another which inevitably make the four-speeder more difficult to produce.

It is possible—in fact it was accomplished in the extinct "Jardine" box—to obtain four speeds with one sliding dog and several concentric components, but the need to keep the overall width of the box down to a figure commensurate with the space available almost enforces the use of sliding members on both the mainshaft and the layshaft—which immediately increases the difficulty of operating these members in the correct sequence.

In one way, the lack of available space has been a blessing in disguise, because it automatically ensures that the shafts are short and thus reduces their deflection under load. Outward deflection, which causes the teeth to run slightly out of mesh, could be a fruitful source of noise and tooth-wear, and everything must be done to avoid it.

Shifter Fork Layout

In the Albion design, changes are made in sequence straight across the box, by means of a double fork, engaging with the components sliding on the main shaft and layshaft. As this is moved from left to right, top, third, second and bottom are brought into action in turn, either by means of face-dogs or by interrupted splines on the shafts. The idea has recently been extended to incorporate a fifth gear, still with the same relatively simple shifting mechanism.

For various reasons, it is more usual to fit two separate shifter forks operated independently. For one thing, it permits the third-gear pinions, which are the most-used of all the indirect gear wheels, to be located close to the bearings in the gearbox end-cover, a position in which they are the least likely to suffer the ill-effects of shaft deflection (Fig. 17.2).

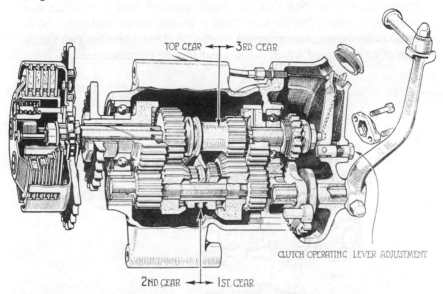

FIG. 17.2. The Burman four-speed box, with bottom- and second-gear dogs on the layshaft and top- and third-gear dogs on the mainshaft.

Bottom and second gears, which are not used so much and in which silence is no so vital, are located in the centre. They are changed by dogs on the layshaft, while top and third are changed by dogs on the mainshaft, but for a third to second change, or vice versa, one dog must be moved into the neutral position and held there while the other is moved to engage the gear desired.

This compound movement is simple enough to obtain if something like the gate or ball change used on a car gearbox could be employed. While this is not impossible—and, in fact, some machines have had this feature—it simply is not a very convenient system on a motorcycle with hand-change, and is quite out of the question when a foot-change is employed.

One of the first really successful four-speed boxes which could be operated by a single rod and a lever working in a quadrant was the

Rudge-Whitworth, in which the shifter forks were actuated by pegs running in two slots formed in a curved plate. This plate was simply mounted on a spindle with an external lever, and only about 90° of movement was required to change right through from top to bottom.

On the other hand, it was a "progressive" change; it was not possible, as with any form of gate, to select any one gear without going through intermediate ones. Not that this really matters, and in practice it is probably a good thing because there is no chance of inadvertently, or through ignorance, endeavouring to effect a change involving an alteration of engine-speed which is too great for the circumstances.

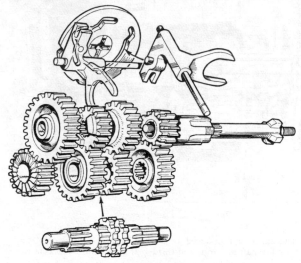

Fig. 17.3. Velocette gear set with circular cam-plate. Note cut-back of alternate teeth on top gear.

Most modern gearchange systems employ either a flat plate with what the patent attorneys describe as "arcuate slots therein" (Fig. 17.3), or a drum with wavy slots milled in the periphery. In the former design, first adopted in the Sturmey-Archer box, the forks slide on a bar (or two bars), but in the latter they can be carried by the drum, on which they are a sliding fit, or on bars or pivots.

Many successful examples of both types have been built, and it is hard to say which is intrinsically the better. Much depends upon the general design of the box and the facilities available for its manufacture.

One difficulty with a circular cam-plate is that it has to be several inches in diameter and of reasonable thickness—$\frac{3}{16}$ in. or so. It therefore possesses a fair amount of inertia which, when a quick change is made, tends to make the plate overrun the correct position, so that it brings the gears into the next neutral position instead of engaging the next gear; with its much smaller diameter, a cam-drum possesses far less inertia and is almost immune from this trouble.

A cam-plate which moves through only a small angle and obtains the necessary length of fork movement by leverage is an increasingly popular alternative to the circular plate (Fig. 17.4). It is especially

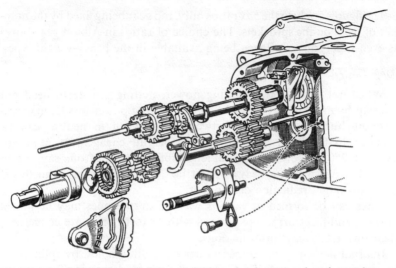

Fig. 17.4. Internals of Triumph "Tiger Cub" box, showing sector-shaped cam-plate and circular bottom gear dogs engaging in elongated slots.

suitable for unit or semi-unit designs in which it is not particularly easy to couple a rotary plate to the ratchet mechanism embodied in the foot-change.

Besides making gearchanging so easy that synchro-mesh devices are unnecessary, the constant-mesh principle with dog engagement is a help in accommodating the widest possible teeth in the available space, and also in reducing the distance which any dog has to travel.

For all ordinary use and most forms of competition, four speeds are sufficient, but the actual ratios depend upon the engine characteristics and the class of work in view. Some models lend themselves to adaptation to various sorts of competition, and the boxes are designed so that different gears can easily be fitted to alter the internal ratios—a procedure which is inevitably simpler with a conventional box than with a cross-over drive.

As one instance of such variations, the following tables shows the gear-sets available for the B.S.A. "Gold Star", and is representative of the ratios which have been found suitable for the work listed.

	Top	3rd	2nd	1st
Road racing	1	1·1	1·33	1·75
Standard	1	1·21	1·76	2·58
Scrambles	1	1·32	1·75	2·34

The figures apply to the *box* ratios only, top gear being fixed by the number of teeth on the sprockets. The choice of ratios in Albion gear-boxes is even wider, up to a dozen being available in the heavy-weight types.

Dog Design

When not actually transmitting power, mating gear-teeth need not overlap by more than $\frac{1}{4}$ in. or so, thus reducing power-loss from excessive oil-churning. Clearance between dogs when in neutral can be reduced to 0·060 in. and movement for full engagement need not exceed 0·250 in., so that the total length of movement from, say, top to third, is 0·625 in. on a heavy-weight box, and can be less than this if space or weight reduction demands it.

Dogs can be formed in various ways. External ones may be milled into the end-faces or, where pinions with 18 teeth or so are concerned, their own teeth may form the dogs.

Internal dogs may be formed either by drilling holes, by splining or by gear-shaping. It is preferable to make the load-carrying faces on all members of equivalent shape to reduce impact wear; but if there are a number of dogs, so that the load on each is relatively light, it does not matter much if the contacting faces are not quite of the same geometrical form.

Backlash between the dogs is detrimental at low speeds, tending towards transmission-snatch in top or third gear, especially with a single-cylinder engine, but it is desirable in the interests of rapid gear-changing because the greater the backlash the more time is available for the dogs to enter.

When using gear-teeth as dogs, it is possible to allow only 3° or 4° of backlash without making the mating dogs too frail, but a compromise can be effected by cutting back every alternate tooth on both members for about a quarter of their length of engagement.

This allows about 20° backlash at the commencement of engagement, after which the dogs can slide right home and then be almost free of backlash. This system is only applied to top and third gear.

However, if the change is missed, or the "proud" dogs become rounded, there is a chance that the dogs will in effect just bounce over the top of each other and it will be difficult to complete the change at all. For fast work, therefore, it is better to cut away each alternate tooth completely, though obviously there must be an even number of teeth originally, a fact which places some limitation on the design. In the lower ratios, backlash is not detrimental when running slowly and it is best to allow plenty, especially in bottom gear, to facilitate engagement from neutral with the model stationary.

Face-dogs are sometimes undercut at an angle of 2° or so in order to prevent them working out of engagement. This scheme adds to manufacturing difficulty and, if overdone, may make disengagement difficult when the clutch does not free perfectly.

In any case, it cannot be applied to dogs formed by gear-shaping, which are not very prone to slipping-out until badly worn and rounded.

With both drives on the same side, the loads on the main bearing are partially balanced, and there is no relative motion between the clutch shaft and sleeve-gear when in top, while even in bottom the relative speeds are at worst in the region of 1,500 r.p.m. It is usual to employ a long bronze bush to centralize the clutch-shaft, but in some racing boxes needle-roller bearings are fitted. For the layshaft, either bronze bushes or ball or roller bearings are used, the choice depending on the space available and the lengths to which one is prepared to go to reduce friction.

The Velocette box reverses conventional practice in that the clutch-sprocket lies *inside* the final drive, this situation being actually an inheritance from the original two-stroke layout. Its retention is justified on the score that overhang of the engine sprocket is reduced to the barest minimum, and also because it permits the final drive ratio to be altered very quickly and easily. The clutch throw-out mechanism is unusual, and is sometimes maladjusted by those who fail to follow the stipulated sequence of operations; that, however, is no fault of the design.

Sometimes, the overhang of the clutch sprocket dictated by the combination of a proprietary conventional box and a wide primary chain-line is very excessive. In fact, there seems to be little point in retaining this type of box when semi-unit construction is adopted, except that it enables existing components to be employed.

Cross-over Boxes

With a cross-over box, there is no partial balancing of the loads due to chain-pull on the bearing adjacent to the sprocket, and robust ball-bearings are needed on both sides, but when the primary and final chain-lines have been settled to suit the engine and rear-wheel layout, the sprocket overhang on both sides can be reduced to a minimum, which is a very desirable thing (Fig. 17.5). Unfortunately, the presence of a chain on the same side as the kick-starter and foot-change complicates the design considerably on touring models; this condition does not occur on pure racing models, and most of the unit-construction Continental racers for many years have had cross-over boxes.

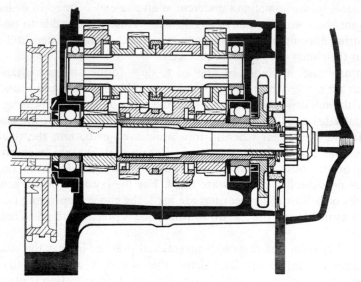

FIG. 17.5. Section through Vincent box, showing very small sprocket overhang obtained with cross-over arrangement. Clutch omitted for clarity.

FIVE SPEEDS

While it is true that five ratios could be obtained from four pairs of wheels by compounding them, the scheme is not very practicable and places limitations on the steps between ratios which may not be acceptable. The usual practice is to add another pair of gears with another shifter fork and a third slot in the cam-plate, in which event fifth gear can be either direct or geared-up to give an overdrive effect.

This raises the question of efficiency. In direct drive, the only power-loss is that due to sliding friction and oil-churning in the box, both being small because none of the rubbing surfaces is carrying load at the time. In indirect ratios, power is transmitted through two sets of gear-teeth and the overall efficiency in a well-designed unit could be about 95 per cent., but might easily be less.

Though the loss of 5 per cent. is not of much moment in touring, in racing it is serious, especially as it is always one of the lower ratios which is in use whenever maximum power is wanted; top gear is strictly for the easy bits. Therefore it is logical to resort to an all-indirect box, which should possess around 98 per cent. efficiency in all ratios, and this is the general trend today, especially for five- or six-speeders with reductions of less than 10 per cent. between each ratio.

To minimize parasitic drag, all the "free" gears are sometimes mounted on caged roller bearings, but, even when the gear and dog widths are reduced to the barely safe minimum, the length of the shafts in relation to their diameters begins to become excessive for high powers. However, the scheme works well with moderate powers and high revolution rates, where the actual torque being transmitted is not unduly high, and is common practice in Continental racers.

All-indirect boxes are not very suitable for touring use, because it is difficult to obtain the required difference between the lowest and highest ratios when only one pair of gears is involved in each reduction.

Tooth Proportions

As a general rule where spur gears are concerned, the total number of teeth in any pair on parallel shafts always comes to the same number, this being numerically equal to twice the centre-distance multiplied by the diametral pitch (D.P.) of the gear teeth. The D.P. is a nominal figure, not an actual measurement, and is equal to the number of teeth divided by the pitch diameter; common figures are 10, 12 or 14, according to the torque capacity required, the smaller number denoting the coarser (and stronger) teeth.

"Stub" Teeth

Sometimes, "stub" teeth are employed, being designated by a two-figure symbol such as 10/12. This particular pitch is used, for example, in the Vincent box and denotes that the teeth are spaced at 10 D.P. but only as deep as those of 12 D.P. This system gives a stronger tooth for the same outside diameter, but at the expense of a little greater "separating force" tending to bend the shafts. As to the actual numbers of teeth, 18 is preferably the smallest size, though pinions with only 14 teeth can be used, if designed so that the tooth flanks are not undercut.

Sometimes, in endeavouring to obtain a particular ratio, one is faced with the fact that a reduction of, say, 18:30 gives too low a figure, yet 19:29 is too high. The way out of this is to cut 18 teeth on a 19-tooth blank and use this pinion in conjunction with a 29-tooth gear, thus obtaining a ratio midway between the other two and, incidentally, a much stronger pinion.

This system cannot be applied to gears cut with a form-cutter in a milling machine, but only to those generated by gear-shaping, and it offers a convenient way of changing a ratio in small steps simply by changing one pinion instead of a pair. In the Vincent box, the second-gear layshaft pinion was changed from 24 to 23 to lower the ratio a little, without modifying the rather complex double-gear with which it meshed or the diameter of the pinion blank.

Gear and Shaft Materials

The steel used for gears can be either a direct-hardening variety, such as $1\frac{1}{2}$ per cent. nickel-chrome oil-hardening steel, or a case-hardening steel with high core-strength, equal to EN 36, a 3 per cent. nickel steel which gives very good results and is not subject to much distortion during hardening if the blanks are stress-relieved or annealed before gear-cutting.

Some makers use a direct-hardening steel, such as KE 805, and heat the parts before final quenching in a carburizing salt bath for about 20 minutes, so forming a thin but very hard skin on the teeth which resists wear yet is unlikely to flake off or "spall", as thicker cases sometimes do, especially when the core is deficient in hardness.

Where the shafts are concerned, strength in bending is the main attribute, and this is a function of the diameter and length, not of the hardness of the steel. Surface hardness is, however, needed for the bearing surfaces, and often good quality case-hardening mild steel will be sufficient for strength whilst providing a dead-hard surface. For more arduous work, 3 per cent. nickel C.H. steel may be necessary, and it is desirable for any shaft formed with small projecting dogs or interrupted splines, which are subjected to shock loading.

Gearbox Mounting

Early gearboxes were mounted on a simple bracket, with provision for adjustment by bolts in slotted holes, but this system was replaced by pivot mounting, in which there is a wide, substantial pivot-lug below (or above) the box and a slotted lug clamped to engine-plates or a frame lug above (or below). The pivot layout provides a much firmer anchorage with a reduction in value of the local stresses developed at the attachment points, and is universally used today by makers who retain the separate engine and gearbox system.

That so many do choose to retain the "separate" system is not due merely to conservatism. One very cogent point in its favour is that an extensive range of models can be produced by using a single basic frame and ringing the changes on a number of different engines and gearboxes. Should one model prove to be in heavy demand whilst some of the others sell slowly, it is easy to concentrate production on the

Fig. 17.6. Typical of its period, the 1922 A.J.S. three-speed gearbox, held by two bolts in slots in the bracket between engine and chain-stays.

popular choice without becoming seriously overstocked with redundant components. Mid-season variations—such as the introduction of a twin-cylinder engine into a range of singles—can also be made without too great an outlay on new tooling.

From the user's point of view, and especially that of the competition rider who does his own maintenance, removal of the motor for overhaul is relatively quick, and a "blow up" in either this component or the gearbox does not affect the other. The separate gearbox can be provided with a large range of adjustment permitting a selection of engine-sprockets to be used for altering the primary ratio without resort to an undesirable cranked link in the chain.

Simple in principle as it is, the "separate" layout demands care in detail design. For one thing, it is essential that the sprockets are maintained in alignment at all times. In the past this point has some-times been given scant attention, engine-plates and lugs being inade-quate in size, whilst in endeavouring to utilize proprietary engines and gearboxes which did not match well in the first place, some makers sank to the level of mounting the engine sprocket with far too much overhang from the nearest bearing. However, such engineering misdemeanours, which lead to a reduction of transmission efficiency and greater bending loads in the frame and engine mountings, are fortunately rare.

CHAIN DRIVE

Sprocket overhang is particularly damaging if a duplex or triplex chain is employed, because when deflection occurs the load is thrown on to one set of rollers instead of being distributed equally. Breakage of the links on the over-loaded side then becomes almost a certainty, although it may be some time before the chain fails completely.

With the wide rear chain line required to give adequate clearance beside the large-section tyres used nowadays, the primary chain, if on the same side as the final drive, is bound to lie several inches from the centre-line. This is especially true when a cast-aluminium chaincase is fitted, since space must be provided between the two chains to accommodate the thickness of the inner wall.

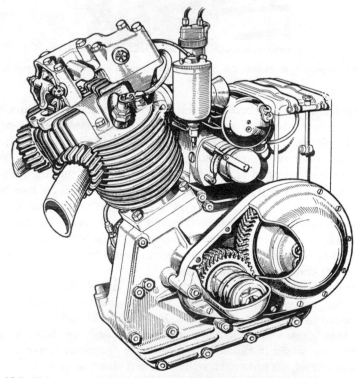

FIG. 17.7. Unit construction with gear primary drive: I—ancient. The engine of the 1938 New Imperial, driving through two double-helical gear wheels, had to run "backwards".

310

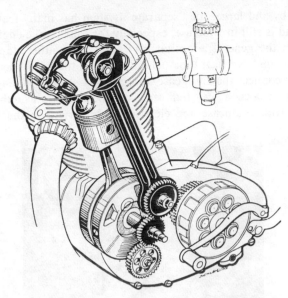

Fig. 17.8. Unit construction with gear primary drive: II—modern. In the NSU "Max" series, "forward" engine rotation is secured by the interpolation of a third pinion, which also drives the eccentrically operated valve-gear.

To reduce sprocket overhang, it is usual with single-cylinder engines to provide either one very wide bearing or else a pair of bearings on the drive side. In the the latter case, it is advisable to make the inner race a roller bearing, as it is subjected to very heavy loads, whereas a ball-bearing of approximately the same diameter and width can be used for the outer race, which can also serve to locate the flywheel assembly laterally. This is treated more fully in Chapter 12.

With the additional width occasioned by the extra cylinder, the crankshaft main bearings of a parallel twin are so wide apart that there is no need to use two on the sprocket side to reduce overhang.

Whatever the general design of the engine, fitting an "outrigger" bearing in a housing surrounding the sprocket would, of course, give support on both sides of the sprocket and deflection would be ruled out completely. This device has been used on some racing engines, notably the T.T. J.A.P.s in 1934 and the V-four A.J.S., in which the bearing housing also contained the coolant-pump impeller; but the idea, though excellent in itself, has never been greatly favoured, possibly because of the manfacturing difficulties involved in attaining perfect alignment of the multiplicity of bearings involved.

311

Taken by and large, the "separate" system has many features in its favour and is still in wide use, especially for four-stroke engines. However, with the general adoption of frames with either duplex down-tubes or a single vertical tube behind the box, the usual method today is to inter-connect the crankcase and gearbox shells with engine plates and bolts in such a way that they can be built up as sub-assembly, complete with chaincase and electrical accessories, on the bench and

FIG. 17.9. Mainshaft deflection was eliminated by fitting an "outrigger" bearing on the 1936 Senior T.T. New Imperial.

then placed in the frame as if they were a unit. In some cases, the entire sequence has to be reversed in order to get either the engine or the gearbox out—in other words, neither can be detached without first removing the whole sub-assembly from the frame.

Semi-unit Construction

From the engineering point of view, and discounting any advantage which the "separate" system possesses in the way of expediency in manufacture or accessibility in service, it is preferable to eliminate all stress-carrying joints between the engine and gearbox and design the crankcase and gearbox shell as a unit, split at right-angles to the major stresses into the minimum number of parts necessary to permit the flywheel assembly and the gears to be installed.

This conception has the effect of making all primary transmission stresses internal to the unit which, being very stiff laterally owing to its inherent width, will deflect by only an infinitesimal amount even under shock loading such as occurs when a rapid change-down is made on the overrun. Also as outlined in the section dealing with torque reactions, greater smoothness of running is almost certain to accrue and local loads present at the points of attachment to the frame are considerably reduced in intensity.

Since the centre distance between the engine-shaft and clutch-shaft is fixed and unalterable, it becomes possible to employ spur gearing for the primary drive—a method which has always had more appeal to Continental designers than to their opposite numbers in England who, as a rule, prefer to retain the roller chain for this duty.

But chain-adjustment sets a problem. As the gearbox cannot be moved, it becomes necessary either to get along with no adjustment at all, or to devise some other method, such as a flexible spring blade or a hardened slipper applied to the slack side of the chain. Either way, it is imperative to enclose the drive in an oil-bath case, which itself can be made to add considerably to the stiffness of the whole assembly.

When the chain-loading is light and the sprockets can be arranged close together, as in small two-strokes with diminutive crankshafts and outside flywheels, a non-adjustable drive will run satisfactorily for a very long mileage if the chain is "pre-stretched" before fitting (i.e., is driven over slave sprockets for long enough to run-in the bearing surfaces of the pins and bushes of which it is composed). This system, which is very simple and light, has long been used on Villiers, B.S.A. and kindred units.

Slipper Tensioners

For duty of a more arduous nature, especially on four-strokes with internal flywheels whose size forces the sprocket centres to be wider than on a two-stroke, some form of tensioner is necessary. It must maintain its effectiveness when the direction of drive is reversed, which rules out the self-adjusting spring-loaded Weller type, since on the overrun this would simply go flat and let the upper run of the chain become slack, so that "snatch" in the transmission would be uncomfortably evident at low speeds.

Satisfactory tensioning can be provided by positively altering the curvature of a blade of hardened spring steel by means of an adjusting screw in compression, or by a tension rod. Undue wear, however, will occur unless the chain is of the right type. It should be duplex or triplex, of $\frac{3}{8}$-in. pitch, and with links which are straight-sided instead of "figure

8" shape, in order to obtain a large and therefore lightly loaded area of contact between chain and tensioner.

Blades which are given an increasing amount of curvature by endwise compression take up a roughly parabolic shape over which the chain runs very smoothly, but their life is not unlimited as the metal cannot be very thick. Consequently some designers prefer to employ a solid hardened steel slipper, suitably curved and moved about a fixed pivot

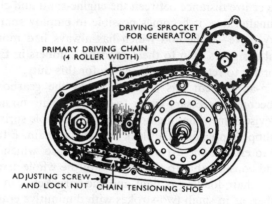

FIG. 17.10. The "Indian" primary drive using a quadruple chain and slipper tensioner. One row of teeth on clutch-sprocket is removed to provide the generator drive.

by means of an adjusting screw. In either case the range of adjustment is necessarily so limited that it is difficult to accommodate sprockets of different sizes, therefore ratios can be changed only by alterations to the final drive.

The efficiency of a chain-drive under these ideal conditions is very high—98 per cent. has been claimed—and, even with no particular accuracy in sprocket cutting, it is almost dead silent.

GEAR DRIVE

Gear drive is a little less efficient and the teeth must be generated with great accuracy if quiet running is to be obtained. Even with extreme care in cutting and hardening, noisy gears may occasionally be made; this is not a serious problem in racing machines but it is so in touring models where a high-pitched whine can be very irritating.

The fewer the number of wheels, the less the noise is likely to be. Units have been made with just a pair of gears, the engine in consequence running "backwards"— an arrangement which does not help autostability of the whole machine, because the gyroscopic precession generated when the model is put into a turn will act in the opposite direction to the rider's effort to apply bank. At least, that will occur when a gearbox with direct drive in top gear is employed; but if all the ratios in the box are indirect—as in the M.Z., for instance—a second reversal of rotation occurs and the engine rotates "forward", so that a single pair of primary gears is suitable.

In fact at the 10–15,000 r.p.m. which the modern short-stroke racing engine attains, gear drive is becoming imperative. Gears are not subject to the high centrifugal loads which a chain generates within itself as it goes round the sprocket. In extreme cases, these loads eventually lead to the chain committing mechanical hara-kiri, although this state does not yet exist in touring engines with oil-bath chain-cases.

Another disadvantage of a two-gear drive is bulk. Since the wheels must be large enough to inter-mesh, the overall length is greater than that of a chain and two sprockets giving the same reduction ratio. This may not be a serious matter; in any case, by using an idler gear in the middle the overall size of the drive (and especially of the clutch-gear) can be reduced, and the engine rotation becomes correct in conjunction with a conventional gearbox (Fig. 17.8).

Since all the primary transmission loads are carried internally to the assembly, there is no longer any need to keep both drives on the same side. In fact it is more logical to use the "cross-over" system, thereby reducing clutch overhang to a minimum and eliminating one potential source of oil-leaks. This method is prone to curtail the amount of room available for the gears—for example, those in the Vincent (Fig. 17.5), though designed to transmit 100 b.h.p., had to be fitted into a space only $4\frac{1}{2}$ in. wide, but in practice that proved to be sufficient.

The cross-over drive also introduces some complication into the layout of the foot-change mechanism. A designer may consider that on this account, and also to utilize as many existing parts as possible, it is better to retain both drives on the same side and leave the arrangement of the final drive, rear wheel and brake mechanism as before.

Basic Unit Layouts

One method of laying-out a unit is to split the main casting vertically so that the flywheel can be assembled in the usual way and the gears inserted through an opening in one wall, which is subsequently closed by an end-plate. Relatively simple, smoothly contoured castings can then be used to enclose the primary drive and the timing gear, the finished product having a clean appearance in keeping with modern styling trends.

An interesting variation of this idea is to be found in the Triumph "Tiger Cub", in which the vertical joint is moved off the centre-line so that the cylinder rests on an unbroken face and the gearbox section has no split. The crankcase is closed by a component which is in effect, a large cover plate carrying the main bearing and extended back to enclose the clutch and primary chain, which is on the same side as the final drive.

The drive-side cover houses the a.c. generator stator and the timing-gear cover is extended backwards to enclose the change mechanism. The whole arrangement provides a neat, light and rigid construction with the additional advantage that the engine can be dismantled without disturbing the gears—which is not usually the case with unit construction and can be cited as an objection, especially for competition work.

The A.J.S. "Porcupine" provided another example of a main casting with no vertical split, but whereas the Triumph design lends itself to die-casting, the "Porcupine" crankcase could only be made with the help of sand cores, a matter of little moment for racing machines but quite unacceptable for production models today.

Continental designers, who are consistently in favour of unit construction, have translated the idea into reality in a variety of ways. The 250 c.c. Guzzi racer, for example, used an outside flywheel which reduced the block bulk of the main casting, and a little further economy of space and weight was effected by eliminating the wall between the crankcase and the gearbox, the wheels being lubricated by oil thrown from the big-end.

This arrangement has been criticized on the grounds that the engine is likely to be damaged by particles of steel thrown off the gear teeth and dogs, but the results in practice seem to indicate that this objection is not so serious as it might appear. Certainly, precautions against such damage should be taken by fitting a magnetic drain-plug and an efficient oil filter and if so no trouble should result.

With a transverse four-cylinder engine, excessive width would be created if the drive were taken off one end of the shaft. On the Rondine, the ancestor of both the Gilera and M.V. racers, this situation was avoided by taking the drive from the centre of the shaft and transmitting it by gears in a central casting to the box, a secondary train being provided to actuate the twin overhead camshafts.

Engineering-wise, it is difficult to find any fault with this arrangement; all the loads are internal, the gears are supported on both sides and cannot be deflected out of line, and the possibility of destructive torsional oscillation in the crankshaft is reduced almost to vanishing point. From the rider's viewpoint, the widest part of the unit is well

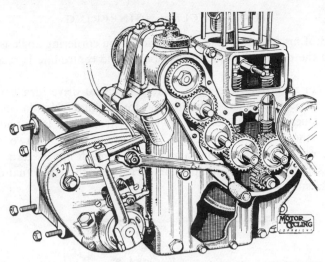

Fig. 17.11. Typical of English "semi-unit" construction is the Royal Enfield "Bullet", in which the flat front face of the bolted-on gearbox mates with a similar surface on the rear of the crankcase.

Fig. 17.12. An early example of "horizontally split" unit construction was the 250 c.c. P. & M. "Panthette" transverse V-twin.

forward of his feet and, despite this width, the cornering angle is good because the depth of the crankcase below the centre-line is relatively slight.

It is not surprising, therefore, that the central drive idea has been applied to other engines, including the four-cylinder Honda, the twin 125 c.c. Ducati and 250 c.c. M.Z. twin two-stroke. The layout adopted both for the Ducati and the M.Z. consists, in effect, of two single-cylinder engines bolted to the centre section; each has its own crankshaft assembly splined to the primary drive gear though actual details are different.

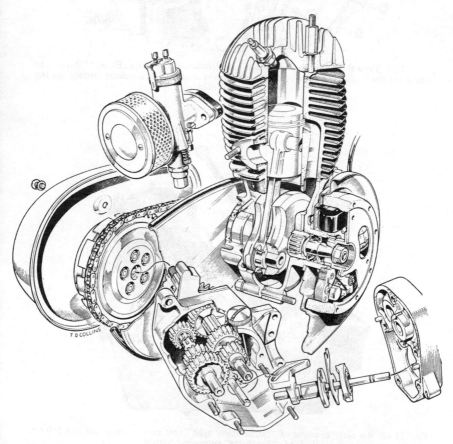

Fig. 17.13. Ingenious variation on the "semi-unit" theme is the 150 c.c. A.M.C. two-stroke, the crankcase of which may be mounted in any one of three positions relative to the gearbox and primary chaincase, corresponding to upright, inclined or horizontal cylinder layout.

There would appear to be quite attractive possibilities in combining this layout with A. A. Scott's ingenious idea of a central drive taken from a built-up crankshaft with two overhung crankpins. With only two main bearings, there would be no difficulty in obtaining accurate alignment and the whole assembly could be as rigid as, or even more rigid than, a conventional built-up crank assembly.

There has been a tendency in recent years for English designers to adopt what might be termed "semi-unit" construction. In this system, a flat face is machined on the back of an otherwise conventional crankcase and bolted thereto is a gearbox which has a mating surface machined on its front face. The rear half of the chaincase may be cast integrally with the drive-side half of the crankcase, as in the B.S.A. twins, or it may be a separate bolted-on component (Fig. 17.11).

In this construction, there are no shear loads applied to the joint, and the assembly is very rigid. From the production and spare-part viewpoint, all the gearbox internals can be identical with those of some existing "separate" gearbox. During a major overhaul, the box can be detached in its entirety and remain undisturbed while work proceeds on the engine, thus reducing the time required for the job.

Although at first sight it does not appear to do so, the 125 c.c. M.Z. utilizes this built-up principle, but in conjunction with an all-indirect gearbox and cross-over drive, which results in a neater and stiffer unit than would be obtained with both drives on one side.

With shaft-drive—or for that matter, with chain-drive in conjunction with a fore-and-aft crankshaft and integral bevel reduction gears—unit construction is a natural choice, but again there are alternative forms. The joints required to permit assembly may be all in vertical planes, as exemplified by the B.M.W. and Douglas (ante-dated by many years by the A.B.C.), but it is also possible to split a combined crankcase-and-gearbox casting horizontally, as in the American Henderson in-line four and the transverse-V-twin P. and M. "Panthette" (Fig. 17.12).

It will be seen that there are so many ways in which the engine and gearbox can be coupled together that making a positive choice is not an easy matter—unless there is some overriding circumstance which dictates the selection, such as the employment of a proprietary engine which cannot be made in unit with the gearbox. On the score of absolute merit, no one system can claim to be outstandingly superior, given the same standard of design in every case, because examples of each have at times shown themselves to be equal to, or better than, their rivals.

Generally, however, for machines produced in quantity but with an eye to future development at a moderate outlay on additional tooling, it is probable that the semi-unit, or built-up system scores most heavily on all-round value. Given cunning design, this can provide an excellent combination of ease of manufacture, light weight, rapid assembly, the good mechanical life conferred by inherent rigidity and full enclosure of the working parts, and a reasonable degree of simplicity in carrying out routine overhauls.

Bibliography

JOE CRAIG. Progress in motorcycle engines, with some notes on combustion. *Proc. Institution of Auto. Engineers.* Vol. 39 (1944-45).

P. M. HELDT. *High Speed Combustion Engines* (16th Edn.). Iliffe and Sons (1956).

P. E. IRVING. Rear suspension of motorcycles. *Proc. Institution of Auto. Engineers.* Vol. 39 (1944-45).

A. W. JUDGE. *Automobile and Aircraft Engines* (4th Edn.). Pitman (1947).

P. V. LAMARQUE. The design of cooling fins for motorcycle engines. *Proc. Institution of Auto. Engineers.* Vol. 37 (1942-43).

SIR HARRY R. RICARDO *The High-Speed Internal Combustion Engine* (4th Edn.). Blackie (1953).

E. TURNER. Post-war motorcycle development. *Proc. Institution of Auto. Engineers.* Vol. 37 (1942-43).

R. A. WILSON-JONES. Steering and stability of single-track vehicles. *Proc. Auto. Div., I. Mech.E.* (1951–52), page 191.

Index

322

DECIMAL EQUIVALENTS

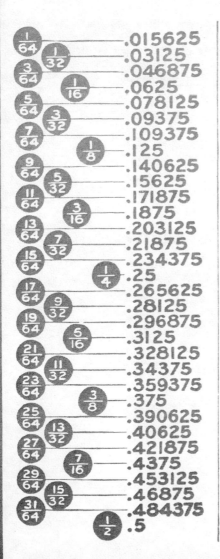
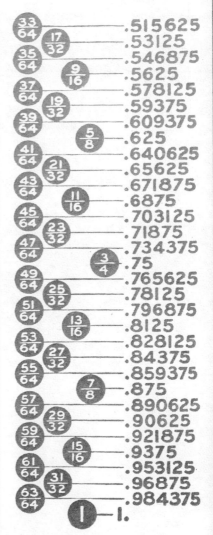

1/64		.015625
	1/32	.03125
3/64		.046875
	1/16	.0625
5/64		.078125
	3/32	.09375
7/64		.109375
	1/8	.125
9/64		.140625
	5/32	.15625
11/64		.171875
	3/16	.1875
13/64		.203125
	7/32	.21875
15/64		.234375
	1/4	.25
17/64		.265625
	9/32	.28125
19/64		.296875
	5/16	.3125
21/64		.328125
	11/32	.34375
23/64		.359375
	3/8	.375
25/64		.390625
	13/32	.40625
27/64		.421875
	7/16	.4375
29/64		.453125
	15/32	.46875
31/64		.484375
	1/2	.5

33/64		.515625
	17/32	.53125
35/64		.546875
	9/16	.5625
37/64		.578125
	19/32	.59375
39/64		.609375
	5/8	.625
41/64		.640625
	21/32	.65625
43/64		.671875
	11/16	.6875
45/64		.703125
	23/32	.71875
47/64		.734375
	3/4	.75
49/64		.765625
	25/32	.78125
51/64		.796875
	13/16	.8125
53/64		.828125
	27/32	.84375
55/64		.859375
	7/8	.875
57/64		.890625
	29/32	.90625
59/64		.921875
	15/16	.9375
61/64		.953125
	31/32	.96875
63/64		.984375
	1	1.